alenai

More praise for
The Natural Advantage

"*The Natural Advantage* is a brilliant synthesis of bio-mimicry and psychology to create a living tool that can transform people, the planet, and organizations. It is thoroughly practical while providing a powerful array of new possibilities for our relationship with each other and the environment."

—Paul G. Hawken, author of *Natural Capitalism: Creating the Next Industrial Revolution*

"Alan Heeks has done a marvelous job in first mapping out the basic principles of organic farming and then demonstrating how each of those principles bears directly on the business of running a successful organization. *The Natural Advantage* is both practical in its day-to-day application to management practices and rich in its philosophical implications."

—Jonathon Porritt, Forum for the Future

"[*The Natural Advantage* is] a personal testimony from a man who has thought a lot about the wonders of life. . . . Many of us are searching for a new story of meaning . . . that could help us to culturally link our work and our society with the life-sustaining world around us. Alan Heeks does that. His book is here to help us create a story of meaning."

—Karl-Henrik Robert, Swedish cancer specialist and founder of The Natural Step

Harvard M.B.A. Alan Heeks is an entrepreneur and consultant with a passion for sustainability in the full sense: personal, business, and environmental. Cofounder of a UK top-100 company and noted performance expert with a diverse client list, he is also the founder of the Wessex Foundation, a nonprofit learning center and 132-acre organic farm in Dorset, England.

AN ORGANIC WAY TO
GROW YOUR BUSINESS

THE
NATURAL
ADVANTAGE

7 PRINCIPLES FOR HIGH PERFORMANCE

ALAN HEEKS

RODALE

RODALE

WE INSPIRE AND ENABLE PEOPLE TO IMPROVE
THEIR LIVES AND THE WORLD AROUND THEM

First published in 2000 by Nicholas Brealey
Publishing, London; some text was added
for the U.S. edition.

Printed in the United States of America on
acid-free (∞), recycled paper ♻

Rodale Organic Living Books

Editorial Director: Christopher Hirsheimer
Executive Creative Director: Christin Gangi
Executive Editor: Kathleen DeVanna Fish
Art Director: Patricia Field
Content Assembly Manager:
    Robert V. Anderson Jr.
Studio Manager: Leslie M. Keefe
Copy Manager: Nancy N. Bailey

We're always happy to hear from you.
For questions or comments con-
cerning the editorial content of this
book, please write to:

Rodale Book Readers' Service
33 East Minor Street
Emmaus, PA 18098

Look for other Rodale books
wherever books are sold. Or call
us at (800) 848-4735.

For more information about Rodale
Organic Living magazines and books,
visit us at

www.organicstyle.com

Editors: Chris Potash and Thomas Akeman
Back Cover and Interior Book Designer:
    Dale Mack
Front Cover Designer: Christin Gangi
Cover and Interior Illustrator: Kevin Sprouls
Photographers: Barry Gomer (198 *bottom*,
    201 *bottom*), Alan Heeks (199 *bottom*),
    Guy Newman/Apex Photo Agency (198
    top), Justin Sutcliff (199 *top*, 200 *top*
    and *bottom*, 201 *top*)
Photography Editor: Lyn Horst
Photography Assistant: Jackie L. Ney
Layout Designer: Bethany Bodder
Researcher: Diana Erney
Copy Editor: Jennifer Hornsby
Product Specialist: Jodi Schaffer
Indexer: Nan Badgett
Editorial Assistance: Susan L. Nickol
Projects Coordinator: Kerrie A. Cadden

**Library of Congress Cataloging-
in-Publication Data**

Heeks, Alan.
    The natural advantage : an organic way
to grow your business : 7 principles for
high performance / Alan Heeks.
        p.   cm.
    Includes bibliographical references and
index.
    ISBN 0–87596–935–6
    1. New business enterprises—Manage-
ment.   2. Organic farming.   I. Title.
HD62.5 .H42 2001
658.4'063—dc21   2001003453

**Distributed in the book trade by
St. Martin's Press**

2 4 6 8 10 9 7 5 3 1
hardcover

To Magdalen Farm, Dorset,
England, and to the vision
of meeting human needs
by natural principles

CONTENTS

ILLUSTRATIONS

TABLES

ACKNOWLEDGMENTS

The experience of writing this book has been enjoyable and renewing. Most of the book was written in six months, and growing such a demanding crop in a short time taught me a lot about human sustainability at work. It also proved that a high challenge can lead to high output without depletion, if the approach and the support are right. I appreciate the ways I have supported myself and the tremendous help I have received from many other people.

The backing from my colleagues at Working Vision has been superb, especially that from my secretaries Lyn Barker and Sallie Mason and my colleagues, including Barry Seward-Thompson, Wynn Rees, and Alexandra Ross. It has also been great to have such professional and enthusiastic support from Kathleen DeVanna Fish and the team at Rodale, including Chris Gangi, Chris Potash, Thom Akeman, and Cindy Ratzlaff.

I have valued both general and specific support from family and friends, especially my brother Richard, my daughters Ella and Fran, my parents, and my friends, including Henry Fryer, Emma Dunford Wood, Nayyer Hussain, and Rachel Cullen. I have also drawn on a high level of professional support to sustain my ground condition while writing the book. This includes coaching from Anna Rushton, counseling and healing from Jan Angelo, aromatherapy from Vicki Poole, and herbal remedies from Dedj Leibrandt.

During my career I have had a succession of excellent mentors who have raised my self-belief and encouraged me to go for my vision. They began with Roger Lonsdale, my tutor at Balliol College, Oxford, when I was an undergraduate, and continued with Graeme Burge at Procter and Gamble. Peter Jansen was an outstanding mentor as well as boss for seven key years of my career, while I was a managing director at Redland and Caradon. He died in 1997, and I hope that my descriptions in this book pay a deserved tribute to his gifts. I am also deeply grateful for the help I have received from my current mentor, Neil Douglas-Klotz, both directly and through his books, *Prayers of the Cosmos* and *Desert Wisdom*.

This book owes much to my workshop and consultancy clients and also to many friends and contacts in organic farming. I am especially grateful to Peter Foster and Christina Ballinger at Magdalen Farm for their contributions and for the wisdom and good humor they bring to their work. Many thanks also to Francis Blake, Mark Measures, Will Best, John Healey, and the previous farmers at Magdalen, Richard van Bentum and Lya Koornneef, and John and Anna Woodward.

I would also like to acknowledge the help I have had from my contacts in the United States, including Scott Silverman, Deben Tobias, Susan Harding, Barbara Keck, and Pierre Ferrari. Also thanks to Tertius Halsey, who seeded the idea of my writing a book back in 1995. Finally, I would like to express my deep thanks to the many people who have helped with the creation of Magdalen Farm Centre and the Wessex Foundation since 1990, especially my ex-wife Ruth, Sir George Trevelyan, and fellow trustees Giles Chitty, Janice Dolley, and John Harrison.

FOREWORD

In his book *Ishmael*, author Daniel Quinn likens civilization to one of our early attempts to fly. A man drives his flying machine off a high cliff, and he is pedaling away, and the wings are flapping, the wind is in his face, and he thinks he's flying. In fact, he is in free fall—he just doesn't realize it because the ground is so far away. Why is his would-be plane not airworthy? Because it wasn't built according to the laws of aerodynamics, and it is subject, like everything else, to the law of gravity.

Quinn says that our civilization is in free fall, too, for the same reason: It wasn't built according to natural laws. We may think we can just pedal harder and everything will be okay, but we will surely crash unless we redesign our craft—our civilization—according to the laws of aerodynamics for civilizations that would fly.

In the metaphor, the cliff represents the seemingly unlimited resources we started with as a species. No wonder it took a while for the ground to come into sight. Fortunately, there are people with vision who have seen the ground rushing up toward us—people who are thinking differently, especially about business and industry.

Alan Heeks is one of these people. His seven organic principles are a map to natural growth for business. In *The Natural Advantage*, Alan shows how business can be transformed from the inside out, beginning with the individual. His inspiration? What our best thinkers and doers are more and more often turning to: nature.

Nature is a teacher with 3.8 billion years of experience in organizing the most complex systems imaginable with such elegance as to produce zero waste. Alan, a highly successful business executive, has discovered a richly instructive metaphor in nature: the organic farm. In *The Natural Advantage*, he explores that metaphor in a delightful and positive way that gives us deeper insight into that greatest mystery of all—ourselves.

But nature as teacher is not to be confused with nature as model. Nature is the real thing. It works. Our present industrial system, arising out of the Industrial Revolution, is an artifice—a pure figment of our imagination, given substance out of itself largely at nature's expense. Author-businessman Paul Hawken maintains in his book *The Ecology of Commerce* that business and industry are the largest, wealthiest, most pervasive, most powerful, and most influential institutions on Earth and do the most damage to the natural world upon which all creatures, including *Homo sapiens*, utterly depend. It follows that, of all Earth's institutions, business and industry most need to rethink themselves and assume the leadership role in conserving, sustaining, and restoring the natural world. As Alan explains, the people who work in these organizations are themselves natural resources, and human beings need to develop sustainably just as much as the planet does.

The new industrial system, the one that will conserve, sustain, and restore the natural world, must be a new, enriched model, patterned after the real thing. Alan Heeks's metaphorical organic farm is the real thing, and he has given us a powerful leg up on the kind of emulation that will help bring about the revolution that will design a new industrial system. Solving the mystery of ourselves is basic to the thought and the design behind the revolution that will save us from ourselves—and nature with us.

—Ray Anderson, chairman, Interface Inc.,
a $1.3 billion multinational,
publicly traded corporation that aims
to become the world's first truly
sustainable business

THE
NATURAL
ADVANTAGE

FORWARD TO NATURE

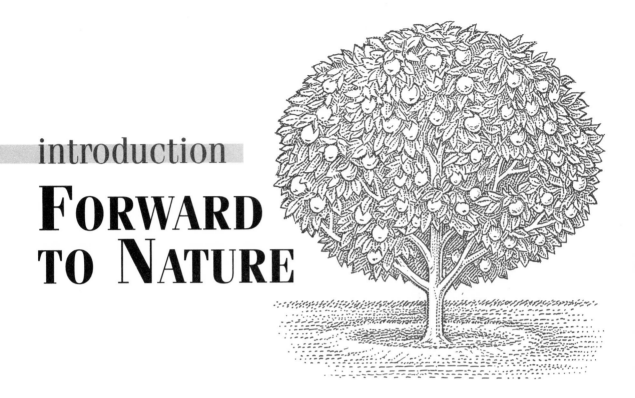

DOES YOUR WORK RENEW YOU, OR WEAR YOU OUT? Are you depleting yourself in the drive to produce? Can you handle the rising pressures we all face: less time, more demands, less control, more change? If these questions concern you, this book offers practical answers.

I want to show you how to get great results without wearing out. In fact, if you sow the seeds of organic success in your life as described in *The Natural Advantage*, you will be able to handle more pressure and more changes more easily, and you can do all of this while renewing your-self. This book will teach you abut human sustainability: refreshing your potential while getting what you want.

Imagine you're holding an apple in each hand. One apple costs 50 percent more than the other. Which is the better buy? If you're like I used to be, you'll pick the cheaper one. After all, success comes from squeezing costs and driving profits, doesn't it? Well, I've learned different. Not only have I discovered that the more expensive apple could be the much better buy, but also I have learned that this Natural Advantage model provides me with a better way to run my life and my business.

The secret lies in organic farming. Back in 1989, I was a high-flying businessman. I went to work in expensive suits and a company Jaguar. I thought organic farmers were just aging hippies who grew expensive food by lazing around, letting nature take its course.

Now I'm an organic farmer. Creating an organic farm has been both tough and satisfying, and it has taught me a whole new approach. Organic success is quite different from my old push-push style. Back then, I got results by driving and depleting myself. Now I know how to work with natural power and natural processes to get great results while renewing my potential.

Renewing Yourself Organically

We all use models to guide the way we work. In business, two favorite metaphors are sports and battle. But what kind of winning do they teach us? Look behind the scenes. You'll find many stars whose victory was not sustainable, whose winning season was followed by exhaustion, sickness, and confusion.

This book shows you how organic farming and gardening are a better model. Organic growth will enrich your life and work, just as it enriches any natural resource—cultivating nature, instead of driving over it. And the beauty of cultivating human nature is that you can achieve superior results.

Although the main focus of this book is work, the organic approach will renew all aspects of your life. I know from my workshop and coaching clients that personal growth issues show through in work issues, and changing the way you work is a great path of self-development. So as you read this book, see how its principles and processes can apply to all aspects of your life.

People Need Maintenance

A recent national study by the Families and Work Institute showed that most Americans work longer hours per week than they did 20 years ago, but most of them *want* to work a lot less. The International Labor Organization states that we are in a worsening crisis because of the way we work. Stress now costs American businesses $30 billion per year. One in ten American workers suffers from clinical depression because of their work. Corporations are finding it ever harder to hire and keep good people because the best people don't want to work in a system that wears them out.

So why are we in this mess? Because the principles we live and work by are mechanical, not natural. These principles emerged more than two centuries ago with the coming of the Industrial Revolution and Newtonian science. The attitude that now dominates in regards to the world's resources is this: Take...Use...Discard.

In the eighteenth century, the scale of the earth's resources relative to human population was so great that they seemed limitless. Waste and pollution were hardly an issue. In the nineteenth and early twentieth centuries, the same mechanistic principles were applied to people. The whole idea of the mass production systems created by big corporations was to exploit cheap, unskilled labor—to treat people like machines. What's ironic is that these outdated principles still shape our society, even though labor is expensive and the problems of depleting and polluting natural resources are all too clear.

Think about all the machines you use every day: computers, heating systems, air-conditioners, and cars. They seem pretty efficient and reliable, which is great, but it misleads us. Because we are surrounded by these machines, we treat people like machines. We expect total predictability. We stop talking and listening to one another.

We think people are just another plug-and-play device, no maintenance required.

But people need maintenance, not only physical but emotional and spiritual maintenance. We all need support, recognition, nurturing, and a sense of purpose, alongside our desire to produce and achieve. To meet these needs means shifting society and work cultures from mechanical to natural principles.

Natural Principles, not Mechanical Ones

It's already obvious that the natural environment won't support continued economic growth without radical changes in our use of resources. The way we work and live now depletes and pollutes natural physical resources instead of renewing them. The same can be said of natural human resources; every company says its people are its greatest resource, but modern corporate production exhausts and pollutes human resources much as it does natural resources.

The economic pressure for more output won't go away. Compare the demands your work puts on you now with the demands of 10 years ago. Imagine the pressures and uncertainties rising even more in the future; can your way of working handle this? The solution is to learn about natural systems' productivity—to work with human nature instead of overriding it and driving ourselves like machines.

To meet future growth without burning out, we have to transform energy produc-

> **The natural environment won't support continued economic growth without radical changes in our use of resources.**

tivity. The value added per unit of human energy input needs to rise dramatically, or we will exhaust ourselves. Organic farming and gardening show how this is possible: free natural energy, waste, and a few non-renewable inputs can be combined in a highly productive and *sustainable* system. *The Natural Advantage* shows you how to draw the parallel in your life and work with nature to increase your productivity.

Working with Nature

Rather than going "back to nature," what we need is to go forward to nature. This is not a retreatist, downshifting approach, since few of us would want to return to Eden without our house and car. The Natural Advantage model comes from working with nature, actively cultivating and shaping it to achieve our productive intent.

We have barely begun to explore how natural systems can be used as a model to

THE NATURAL CYCLE

Food

Oxygen

Nutrition

Carbon dioxide

Waste

Minerals

The natural cycle of life provides us with a basic blueprint for sustainability. Plants use energy from the sun combined with water, carbon dioxide from the air, and minerals from the earth. Oxygen is produced for use by animals and man, and plant waste returns to the soil as input for future growth.

help people at work, although a few writers such as Stephen Covey, Peter Senge, and Arie de Geus have started this process. The tendency when we turn to ecology is to think of wild natural habitats, such as rain forests. However, cultivated natural systems such as organic farms and gardens are much more relevant models. A farmer manages natural resources sustainably to create economic value, and this has direct parallels in organizations and for individuals at work.

Outside In or Inside Out?

Mechanistic thinking often leads to outside-in solutions, in which you start with the apparent problem and the desired outcome, then find a technique to fix it. The result is rarely sustainable, since short-term success falls prey to cumulative problems. An organic, systemic approach works from the inside to the outside—from principles to practice, from underlying causes to sustained results. To the organic grower, both roots and fruits are important, but the roots are the priority. It is by nourishing the roots, maintaining the ground conditions for growth, that we renew the orchard and can expect the fruit to keep coming year after year.

Working with nature may sound gentle and easy, but often it isn't. Some forces in a natural system, such as the weather, can be cruelly destructive or highly unpredictable. There is savage competition as well as exquisite collaboration. The art lies in *managing* your natural resources, using the positive forces of nature to build resilience and achieve a fruitful outcome most of the time.

When I became involved in creating an organic farm in 1990, I was both horrified and fascinated. I had managed some fairly tough businesses, but this was much worse. It felt like I was driving a car without a steering wheel. In organic growing, it is so clear that you have no control, that you can't force things. Instead you have human persistence, ingenuity, and your sense of how to shape natural systems. You learn to read and use the unpredictable forces around you—the weather, pests, weeds, customers, and competitors. Organic farming points to the future way of working for all of us: leading and managing with influence, not control, and in situations that are increasingly complex and uncertain.

Against Conventional

Intensive or factory farming, where the problems are already apparent, offers alarming insights into the parallel problems of conventional ways of working. Consider the comparison in the table "Problems with Conventional Ways of Working," on page 8.

Organic farming has benefited from the catastrophic crises in conventional farming. Sales of organic food more than doubled in the United States in the 1990s, with prices 20 to 25 percent higher than they are for conventional items. Sales are limited by how fast the supply can be increased. This is a happy story because by definition organic farmers make their profits sustainably.

> **I hear more and more people and organizations talking about sustainability.**

PROBLEMS WITH CONVENTIONAL WAYS OF WORKING

PROBLEM	On the conventional farm	In the conventional workplace
Natural fertility and resources are depleted.	Land and livestock	People
Output depends on external factors.	Artificial fertilizers	Deadlines, controls, performance pressures
Problems are created that have to be suppressed.	Pests, weeds, and plant diseases are treated with pesticides and herbicides.	Poor performance met by increased focus on results; stress seen as weakness
Resources are further depleted and polluted.	Additive residues pollute ground and groundwater; fertility is reduced.	Stress accumulates; vitality, motivation, and resilience are reduced.
Output quality is reduced.	Product meets nominal standards, but taste and nutrition are poor.	Output meets nominal standards, but real quality and satisfaction are poor.
Risk of severe problems is increased.	Salmonella, BSE, pollution crises	Stress-related illnesses, failure to adapt to change

The seven principles of organic growth, which are summarized starting on page 12, show how to address the problems of conventional working outlined above. While the application of these principles is different for people at work than for growers, the organic farm or garden provides a powerful, tangible analogy to learn from.

The consumer revolt against genetically modified foods is clear evidence that many people now recognize the dangers of the linear, mechanistic model in farming. With time, many of them may see the parallel with the workplace. I hear more and more people and organizations talking about sustainability. If we are to survive, the continued tension between economic growth and environmental crisis will force us a long way toward environmental sustainability within the next two decades. Revolutionary changes in energy and resource use are already apparent. As we start to live sustainably with our environment, more and more of us will question the human sustainability of work.

The principles of sustainability are the same in every field, whether these principles are applied to individuals, organizations, or the environment. It is ironic that the environmentalist agenda, and public concern about it, is what is driving most businesses to consider sustainability for the sake of marketing and public relations.

Over the next few years, the issues of human and business/economic sustainability will become just as pressing. Organic farming shows us how to address these issues, too.

Sustainability—The Elusive Goal

Whether you work in a large organization, on your own, or somewhere in between, the principles of sustainability are relevant to you. Whatever your work, you are probably finding that its demands and the level of change and uncertainty in your work are more than you can easily handle. You can go forward to meet these pressures constructively. We all have a natural capacity to grow sustainably and adaptably in our work. *The Natural Advantage* describes both the principles and the practicalities of cultivating this capacity.

The desire for sustainability is widespread, but understanding what it really means is elusive. I use this simple definition: Sustainability is *meeting present needs without reducing future potential*. In whatever context this definition is applied, it probably raises many questions, but they are fruitful ones. Which needs must be met, and whose are they? Can all needs be met equally? How are needs different from wants or desires? What level of future potential are we trying to preserve, and for how long? Do we want the future to be better than the present or not much worse? And on what criteria? These are

massively complex but important questions. The Natural Advantage approach explores these questions with regard to the natural environment and material standards of living. Try relating these questions to your work and its sustainability for you personally.

The principles of sustainability apply at all scales—a farm, a region, the global ecosystem—and in all spheres—an individual, a team, an organization. As you understand and apply these principles in one area, you gain the potential to apply them in others.

One of the common misunderstandings I sense around sustainability is that it is a static state, a desirable but nebulous absence of nasty things. A sustainable condition is full of change, tension, and turbulence. The crucial difference between the culture of most workplaces, which seeks to control uncertainty and suppress conflict, and the culture of a sustainable workplace is that these challenging qualities are handled constructively and dynamically. There is flow as well as tension, synergy as well as conflict.

The move toward sustainability is not one frightening giant leap; it's more a matter

9

of progressing cyclically. With each repetition of the cycle, you move closer to true sustainability. The conversion period on a farm that is moving from forced, conventional methods to organic methods is often a tough time. It involves confusion as old dependencies are dropped and new methods are learned, partly by trial and error. Output may fall for a while, until the farm's natural vitality has had time to develop. You may face similar challenges in your own move to the organic way, and these issues are covered in detail in Chapter 8. Going organic requires commitment, but the payback is excellent. It offers the prospect of deeper satisfaction, growing output value, and a way of working that renews you and meets change robustly.

As with many innovations, the move toward human sustainability at work is likely to be pioneered by individuals, small groups, and a handful of leading-edge businesses. Change in this area grows from the efforts of individuals, so this is the main application explored in this book. However, the Natural Advantage is also a blueprint for organizations, of both human and business sustainability. For example, this model could be applied to cultivating markets, developing them organically to create continuing sales, not exhausting their potential.

Origins of the Natural Advantage

My interest in how people can fulfill themselves in an economic system began on the first day of my professional career, when I joined Procter and Gamble's marketing group in 1969. I was a free spirit fresh from studying English at Oxford, believing that work would be creative, worthwhile, and fun. So P&G was a shock: It was a cold, mechanistic company that researched and analyzed everything, even the size of the nozzle on an Ivory Liquid bottle. It was a big factory farm, running like clockwork, wound up and efficient. There was no room for heart or soul in this culture, no genuine feelings, inspiration, or sense of service. I played the game successfully but left in 1973, determined to find a better way to work.

I went on to complete an M.B.A. at Harvard Business School. This was the business equivalent of joining the Marines. It gave me strength and speed in handling complex new situations, as well as an impressive label. I was also able to explore how work could be made fit for human consumption. This area was called job enrichment in the mid-1970s, and some of the pioneering research was by Harvard professors such as Paul R. Lawrence and Jay W. Lorsch.

After Harvard, I decided that working for a high-powered management consultant such as McKinsey would not sustain me, despite the fat salary. I took a job at one of the lowest pay levels in the Harvard class of '76, determined to try out my ideas as a line manager in a company that actually made things. I went to Merseyside, a depressed area of northwest England, as marketing manager of Hygena, a large producer of kitchen furniture—with big losses. From there I moved through two jobs to become president of a subsidiary of Redland, one of Britain's largest building materials groups.

Caradon

The high point of my management career was with Caradon from 1985 to 1989. I was a cofounder of this major building materials group and president of the largest subsidiary, Twyfords Bathrooms, which employed 1,500 people. I am proud of the transformation I achieved in Twyfords' morale, profits, and market position. Starting a business with $12 million of equity and $90 million in loans and concentrating on roots as well as fruits is quite an achievement. (The Caradon story is described in Chapter 2.)

By 1989, I had myself a great track record and a pile of capital. I had surpassed my career and money goals. But I was not completely satisfied. Why? I had learned a lot about how to achieve business results along with human fulfillment, but I didn't have all the answers. I didn't yet have a systematic approach. My way of working was still colored by the push-push, mechanistic culture of work. I could see my own blind spots, and I didn't like them. To achieve results, I still drove myself and the people around me pretty

Organic growing offers a powerful model for human sustainability at work.

hard, and I believed there had to be a better way. This was the seed of the Magdalen Farm adventure.

Magdalen Farm

Caradon had an extraordinarily successful stock offering in 1987, and for the first time in my life, I had a significant amount of money. But my elation soon turned to fretfulness. Why had such wealth come into my life? What was I meant to do with it? I was sure there was some higher purpose, but all my efforts could not reveal it. After three months, I realized I was less happy than before the stock sales, so I got on with life and work as before, trusting that the answer would appear in its own time.

In May 1989 a vision emerged: I envisioned an organic farm where people could learn how to align with natural principles and find sustainable fulfillment. I established an educational charity, the Wessex Foundation, as the framework, giving $1.5 million of my Caradon capital to fund it. In May 1990, the other foundation trustees and I agreed to buy Magdalen Farm, a beautiful 130-acre farm in southwest England, on the border of Dorset and Somerset. Since 1990 it has been transformed from a run-down conventional farm to a pioneering organic farm and residential education center.

The Wessex Foundation's focus is to promote learning about sustainability at all levels, including personal, social, business, and environmental sustainability. In 10 years the foundation has achieved a great deal, but we are not yet fully sustainable in any of these areas. The project has been instructive, satisfying, and difficult. The idea of creating an organic farm as a living basis for learning and sustainability has proved to be even more powerful than I had imagined. We don't have all the answers about working sustainably, but we are certainly learning.

From a starting point of complete ignorance, I learned about the practicalities of organic growing: finding and supporting the managers, creating the business plans, and bringing the farm through the conversion phase and difficult early years. Magdalen has been an intense education for me, both personally and in the nature of management and leadership. Meanwhile, my consulting and training work for organizations continued to develop, but for several years I saw no direct connection. This changed in 1997, when I learned the principles of environmental sustainability through The Natural Step process described on page 191. Suddenly I saw how Magdalen Farm embodied these principles, and I realized that organic growing offers a powerful model for human sustainability at work.

2-MINUTE*CHECKUP*

YOUR WORK IN THE BALANCE

You can do this exercise quickly or give yourself more time to explore in depth. It's designed to give you an impression of the level of sustainability in your current way of working.

Imagine your hands positioned like the pans of an old-fashioned pair of balance scales. In your right hand, gather your impressions of how your work energizes and supports you, such as through creativity, learning, and the support of colleagues. Now, in your left hand, gather impressions of how your work drains you and puts demands on you, such as through long hours, criticism, or never getting finished. Now imagine weighing these two against each other. Are the rewards or the demands greater for you?

Developing this model has been the focus of my work since then. I have led workshops at Magdalen and elsewhere that have confirmed that people see the analogy clearly and that it helps move them toward sustainability.

The Natural Advantage—
7 Principles of Organic Growth

The Natural Advantage model offers a process map for sustainable production. The first three principles, described in Chapters 1 through 3, deal with organic roots: creating the base conditions from which growth arises naturally, without being forced. The next two principles, covered in Chapters 4 and 5, are about organic growth:

how to use sustainable inputs to achieve sustainable outputs. The last two principles, explored in Chapters 6 and 7, are about organic fruits: describing the characteristics of sustainable output and how these evolve from organic inputs and processes.

The icons at the beginning of each chapter help illustrate the principles of organic growth. The tree on page 19, for example, has roots that provide the main inputs and the stable foundation for the whole structure of production; the trunk represents growth processes, the central link between the roots and the fruits. The apple on page 141 is a good example of organic fruit: We can quickly tell the difference between real organic quality, an apple with satisfying taste, and a tasteless one forcibly pushed to meet some nominal output standard. The acorn, the waterfall, and the other images likewise illustrate aspects of the seven principles.

As you might have expected, the principles introduced in *The Natural Advantage* are interlinked and interdependent: Each requires and reinforces the others. The concept is also cyclical: The diversity and quality of outputs contribute to the roots and trunk of the process.

As you read this book, you will notice that it talks about the organic farmer as much as it discusses the farm. It is the combination of both farmer and farm that creates a cultivated natural system. This has a parallel for you and your work. You could say that the farmer represents your awareness, your active intelligence, and your intent. The farm represents the other resources you bring to your work, such as intuition, practical skills, physical stamina,

and feelings. These all combine to form one living, productive organism, just as the farm and farmer operate together.

The seven principles are as follows:

1 Ground Condition

To organic growers, soil quality is the basis of sustainable output. These growers continually aim to improve the reserves and resilience of their soil while increasing its production. By contrast, conventional farming progressively depletes and pollutes the soil so that the output depends on ever-increasing amounts of external stimulants (fertilizers) and suppressants (pesticides).

This offers us ways to understand, improve, and sustain our own ground condition, our reserves, and our resilience. By cultivating our sources of fertility, our output at work grows naturally and sustainably.

2 Natural Energy

The main energy sources for organic growing are sunlight, water, earth, air, and organic waste—all of which are natural, abundant, low-cost, and nonpolluting. Pushing output by control systems, deadlines, or supervisors is similar to using fossil fuels; the process builds up residues that reduce natural resilience and fertility.

Recall times at work when you felt deeply appreciated or highly inspired—remember how energized you felt, how the work flowed more easily. There are simple ways to stimulate and harness these energies that don't have polluting side effects.

3 Composting Waste

The beauty of any natural cycle is that there is no waste: Every output becomes the input to the next stage of the cycle.

The waste in your work includes discarded energy and discarded value—subtle setbacks, conflicting data, or negative feelings, such as anxiety. Waste is usually messy; it takes new skills to collect and recycle it, but this can be done readily. Negativity can then become a source of fresh understanding and constructive energy.

Composting is a classic example of natural synergy: you get more out than you put in, and it provides a model of how to harness human energy waste in the workplace.

4 Organic Synergy

Organic growers achieve results with less control and amid more uncertainty than people in any other job I know. They are great examples of how to achieve synergy through creative tension, by using uncertainty, and through finding the gift in the problem.

By cocreativity, combining our active intent and push with the skills of receptiveness and adaptability, we can create a natural process of dynamic growth that harnesses change to create output.

This cocreative approach is central to achieving results in conditions of change and uncertainty. Elements of cocreativity include tolerance for ambiguity, synergy, assertiveness, and a combination of intuition and logic.

5 Riding the Cycles

The organic approach does not let nature take its course—it works *with* nature. Organic growers use natural cycles, such as crop rotation and seasonal changes, for their own purposes.

To apply this concept to your working situation, picture yourself renewing your own energy by moving from a demanding task to an easy one or from a structured way of working to a fluid one. Or picture your work as part of a full cycle of seeding, growing, harvesting, and rest.

6 Resilience through Diversity

Even small organic farms have a diverse range of products or enterprises. This variety creates resilience; if one crop fails, or if demand drops, the overall business can sustain the blow. The various crops support one another and create synergy. Diversity is key to reducing weed and pest problems. So are wild margins, uncultivated land supporting the birds and insects that keep pests in check.

There are similar benefits at work. We can increase diversity in the way we work as well as in the range of tasks, and the wild margins for individuals and organizations make us more creative and adaptable to change.

7 Real Quality

When you eat a piece of fruit, how do you judge its quality? Real quality is about taste, nutrition, and a feeling of satisfaction. Organic produce may sometimes look irregular, but it delivers genuine quality. Forced farming is geared to deliver only nominal quality in all areas—size, appearance, consistency, and quantity.

An important feature of real quality is a deep, flexible, two-way relationship between producer and customer. The rapport and trust in such relationships are part of the satisfaction that the product delivers, and both parties are able to accept more change and uncertainty because of their relationship.

Many work situations push for nominal quality, but it's real quality that gives sustained satisfaction for the organization and its customers. Understanding the emotional value in your output, building direct and dynamic customer relationships, helping the organization to appreciate all of this: These are ways of sustaining high performance.

How to Use This Book

Before you apply the seven principles of organic growth to your work, I suggest you read through the entire book once. It's important to understand each of the principles as well as the whole model before applying it to your life. For example, in developing your ground condition and your natural energy sources, it helps to have a picture of the diversity and quality of fruit you want to cultivate in your work.

Once you have read the whole book, I suggest that you then apply the principles in the order in which they are presented: Start with roots and inputs, move on to growth processes, and finish with fruits and outputs. Each chapter contains advice and relevant methods for applying the principles, illustrated with real-life examples that are drawn from my own experience, from participants in my workshops, and from business consulting clients, although some names and details have been changed to protect confidentiality.

Exercise: Sustainability Assessment

This exercise will help you make an initial assessment of the level of sustainability of your current way of working. For each question, give yourself an intuitive rating from 0 to 10, circling the appropriate number under each of the seven organic principles that make up the Natural Advantage. Add up your scores across all categories. If your total score is more than 60, your work is probably depleting you significantly. Read on to learn the natural way to improve sustainability.

GROUND CONDITION

In relation to your work, how do you rate your resources, your energy reserves?

| 0 Abundant | | | | | | | | Severely depleted 10 | | |

Physical resources

| 0 | 1 | 2 | 3 | 4 | 5 | 6 | 7 | 8 | 9 | 10 |

Emotional resources

| 0 | 1 | 2 | 3 | 4 | 5 | 6 | 7 | 8 | 9 | 10 |

Mental resources

| 0 | 1 | 2 | 3 | 4 | 5 | 6 | 7 | 8 | 9 | 10 |

Inspirational resources

| 0 | 1 | 2 | 3 | 4 | 5 | 6 | 7 | 8 | 9 | 10 |

TOTAL _____

NATURAL ENERGY

Are the energy sources motivating your work mostly forced, stressful, and polluting, or are they mostly natural, clean, and organic (e.g., enthusiasm)?

| 0 Mostly natural | | | | | | | | Highly stressful 10 | | |
| 0 | 1 | 2 | 3 | 4 | 5 | 6 | 7 | 8 | 9 | 10 |

COMPOSTING WASTE

Do "waste issues" in your work (e.g., anxiety, setbacks, conflict) accumulate and pollute your energy, or do you recycle them as a source of future growth?

| 0 Totally recycled | | | | | | | | Severe buildup 10 | | |
| 0 | 1 | 2 | 3 | 4 | 5 | 6 | 7 | 8 | 9 | 10 |

ORGANIC SYNERGY

Do your ways of working mostly involve push and stress? Are they less flexible than the demands on you? Can you combine active push with receptive flow and find the synergy in tension and uncertainty?

0 Highly flexible, synergistic						Fixed approaches, low adaptability 10				
0	1	2	3	4	5	6	7	8	9	10

RIDING THE CYCLES

Is your work mostly linear, is output constant? Do you use cycles (e.g., push/rest, produce/review)?

0 Fully cyclical							Constant push 10			
0	1	2	3	4	5	6	7	8	9	10

RESILIENCE THROUGH DIVERSITY

Is your work monotonous and repetitive? Do you have enough diversity to give yourself renewal and resilience?

0 Diverse and renewing								Monotonous 10		
0	1	2	3	4	5	6	7	8	9	10

REAL QUALITY

Are the results of your work truly satisfying in quality for you and your clients?

0 Satisfying sense of real quality for all parties								Mostly nominal output, not fulfilling 10		
0	1	2	3	4	5	6	7	8	9	10

YOUR SUSTAINABILITY TOTAL _____

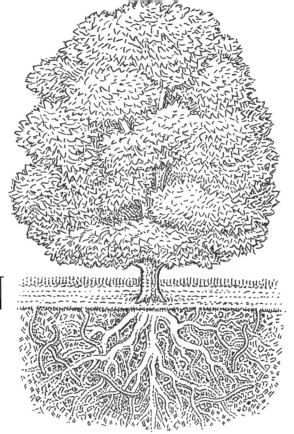

chapter 1

GROUND CONDITION

FOR THE ORGANIC GROWER, the earth is what you start with. Ground condition, or soil quality, remains the barometer of the state of your productive system. Organic growers know that soil is the powerhouse of their business. It may be the crops that earn the money, but the ground condition is the asset that creates them and supports future production. The earth is both a vital input and a vital process in producing the desired output. Ground that's in good condition actually manufactures fertility—from the life within it, from waste, and from the nutrients in the earth, air, and water.

The basic principle of ground condition is that you can only achieve sustainable results by cultivating the underlying fertility, the resources from which output grows naturally. This principle applies equally to crops and to people. The earth is a living organism that, when treated organically, can renew its own potential and keep producing. A human being is a living organism, too, and we can cultivate our productivity by the same principles. This contrasts with the approach in most work cultures and on conventional farms, where output depends on external pressures, and ground condition is depleted, not renewed. Truly, the way the ground operates naturally as a productive ecosystem has specific lessons we can apply in the human world.

Learning from Nature

The concept of the four elements—earth, water, air, and fire—forming the basis of all living matter is an ancient one. (The four elements are explored in more depth in Chapter 2.) Whether we're considering a person or a garden, it is these elements that interact to create fertile ground condition.

Earth. The soil is the growth medium; it provides the physical setting in which all the elements that are required for fertility combine. In people, the earth element relates to our physical body and physical energy.

Water. Water is essential to the whole process of growth. Water carries nutrients from the earth through the root system to provide the material for the plant's expansion. In human nature, water represents the emotional, feeling element. Too much or too little water stifles productivity. If we suppress all feelings in relation to our work, we are likely to be arid—uncreative and unable to relate fully and productively with others. Conversely, if we let ourselves be swamped by emotion, we are like waterlogged soil, and the crops will rot. On the farm or in the garden, physical soil structure, air circulation, and warmth enable water to play its role, and this balanced system has analogies in the human field.

Air. Air is vital as an enabler and a fuel for growth. Ground in good condition is about 25 percent air, and thanks to this air, heat and water can circulate and interact productively with the earth. The nitrogen in air also makes it an important source of fertility. Soil and plants breathe and need air to sustain life, just as we do. In human nature, air equates to inspiration, spiritual energy—the word *inspiration* literally means breathing in.

Fire. The sun's heat is essential to maintain ground condition and generate plant growth. The fire element in the human system is mental energy. It's fast-moving and fast-changing, and it can kindle and fuel growth, but it can dry up growth if taken to excess. For both people and gardens, the fire element needs to be managed carefully; it has to be balanced with the other elements and matched with crops that can use it well.

The Soil Ecosystem

The earth element in the soil has two main components: mineral matter and organic matter (see the diagram below). Although organic matter, humus, makes up only a small amount of the soil, it is central to the soil's productivity. Humus promotes biological activity throughout the earth and enables conversion of inert minerals into nutrients that are usable by the plant. It is also a key to soil structure, enabling the different elements to combine productively. I see the human equivalent of humus as vitality, or what the Chinese call *chi*, life energy. A person with high vitality has naturally high resilience and productivity, just like fertile ground.

The earth, water, and air elements combine with the fourth element, fire (heat), to form the soil ecosystem: a living organism that is both productive and self-renewing. It is inspiring to realize that the earth truly is a living system. Every square yard of organic earth teems with a variety of life that interacts to make the soil a productive, resilient organism. The U.S. Department of Agriculture, in its definition of organic farming, says that "the concept of the soil as a living system that develops the activities of beneficial organisms is central to this definition." In *Organic Farming and Growing*, Francis Blake says, "the number of micro-organisms (principally bacteria and fungi) in one small teaspoonful of soil is greater than the total number of people who have ever lived on this earth."

There are clear parallels between the earth and the human being as living organisms of extraordinary and effective complexity. To understand and control this complexity completely is impossible and unnecessary because if you cultivate your ground condition on the principles of sustainability, you won't need to manage all the details.

To apply this analogy to human productivity, we don't need to go into the details of how this ecosystem works. For our

SOIL STRUCTURE

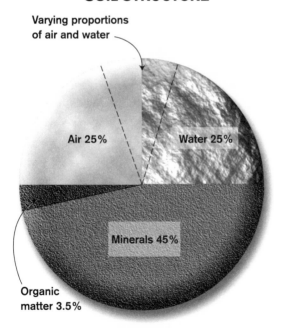

Varying proportions of air and water

Air 25%

Water 25%

Minerals 45%

Organic matter 3.5%

Topsoil consists of minerals, organic matter, air, and water. While the exact proportions of air and water within soil may vary considerably, the surprisingly large volume these two elements represent reflects their importance as constituents of healthy soil.

purposes, it's relevant to know the main features of good ground condition and how to cultivate them. These features include having healthy soil structure, building fertility, and knowing how to manage different soil types, which equate to different temperaments in human nature.

Man and Machine

What image comes to mind when you think of a *system*? For many people, it's a machine: a computer, a refrigerator, an oil refinery. These are essentially mechanical systems, in which a specific input will consistently yield a predictable output. We've been blessed with many of these systems, and they give us predictable results with ever-higher reliability (see the table "Differences between Natural and Mechanical Systems," below.) But they mislead us about the way natural systems operate.

When you picture a natural system, perhaps you see an ecosystem such as a rain forest or a weather system, in which elements are causally connected but the outcomes are unpredictable and chaotic. Of course, a human being is a natural system, even though many of us treat ourselves like machines and our culture promotes this idea.

You may have a clear picture of some of the inputs—such as food, water, and shelter—you need for your own system. What about inputs directly relating to your work and to you as a productive system? Because we associate productive work with mechanical systems, we often expect ourselves to produce without inputs and maintenance. We don't have to make our own electricity, so why do we need to fuel our work? This is the issue that Stephen Covey describes as P/PC balance: the need to consider both production and production capacity.

Ecologists identify ecosystems according to three broad categories: developed,

DIFFERENCES BETWEEN NATURAL AND MECHANICAL SYSTEMS

Natural System	Mechanical System
Inputs are many and are hard to define, measure, or control.	Inputs are readily defined and are usually measured and controlled.
What happens inside the system is hard to specify and predict; it has a life of its own.	What happens inside the system may be technically complex, but it is known and predictable.
Outputs include states or qualities of being, as well as products or actions. Outputs are many and are hard to control.	Outputs are mostly tangible and measurable. Inputs and processes are regulated to achieve specific desired outputs.

GROUND CONDITION

ORGANIC SOIL   FORCED FARM SOIL

High organic content: more fertility, moisture retention, resilience

Low organic content: dependence on external applications of artificial fertilizer to fuel growth

Good structure enables water, air, and heat to circulate

Compacted soil is difficult for air, water, and heat to enter

Greater depth of soil means more reserves; deeper, stronger roots; resilience to weather extremes such as drought

Shallow soil means shallow roots, more dependence on external inputs

Soil is a living organism that renews its fertility and recycles organic waste

Soil is polluted by pesticide and fertilizer residues

Organically managed soil is a living system that can sustain and renew itself while also supporting healthy plant development. Soil managed with conventional farming methods depends on additions of fertilizer and other chemical products to support plant growth.

natural, and cultivated. *Developed systems* are essentially man-made, such as towns or suburban areas. *Natural systems* are primarily wild, not intensively managed by people, and include marshlands and ancient forests. *Cultivated systems* are natural habitats shaped and managed by people for an economically productive purpose, such as farming. Cultivated natural systems are the ones that offer the best model for people at work.

Work is not just letting nature take its course, leaving it wild; nor is it centered on man-made resources. Work is centered on people; it involves taking nature as the basis and working with it to achieve your aims. Cultivating ground condition is the foundation of this approach.

Cultivating Ground Condition

Steve Worowski looked like a withered stick when I first met him—not what you'd expect from a 31-year-old with an M.B.A. I was the newly appointed sales and marketing director. Steve, as marketing manager, was my potential number two.

Dick Belton, my boss, had already warned me: "Steve's got promise, but he's your biggest problem. The guy's demotivated, and I don't want it spreading." I liked Steve, but he was hard to reach. It was in his body language: His chair was pushed hard against the back wall of his cluttered office, defensively facing the door, his head was at an angle, his shoulders were turned in, and he rarely looked at anyone directly. His whole body seemed twisted, dry, airless, stiff.

Our company was part of a much larger group that had a reputation as a progressive, well-managed organization, but in reality, it was more backward. I had joined with an impatient desire to soon be a vice president. All of my military-hero circuits lit up at the sight of Steve. I thought of El Alamein, the turning point in the North African campaigns of the World War II. If I could break through with Steve, I'd be in Tripoli within a week: I'd double my own effectiveness in one move. So I attempted to bounce him into action, smacking into him with the intensity of my will, painting the big picture, setting tough deadlines for him to meet, aiming to fire up his management reflexes. All of these attempts fell on barren ground; nothing took root.

I tried to spark him up with shared enthusiasm, dangling the carrot of our joint triumph and his prospects of succeeding me upon my early promotion. He listened without response, as if this were some alien language, not the shared mythology of a fellow M.B.A. So I switched my approach to the stick, telling him that I wanted to get things moving fast, and I'd have to question his position if he couldn't respond. He seemed indifferent, as if he really wouldn't care if I fired him. Dick, my boss, was even more impatient than I was. Within a fortnight he was jabbing at me for signs of progress. It was embarrassing; what kind of a whiz kid was I if I couldn't turn around someone with Steve's talent?

Clearly, I was going wrong with Steve. I was treating him like a mechanical system. I tried to use him like a machine, a tool, a vehicle to move me toward my output goals. It was only when my simplistic input-output mindset failed that I was forced to see Steve as a person and to cultivate him as a natural system.

You Don't Just Add Water

My intuition told me that this was a deep problem, that it was almost insulting Steve to try the quick-fix methods I had begun with. I sensed he had a genius for implementation that would complement my passion for big ideas, so I persisted. He was like a formerly fertile soil after years of drought. You can't just add water to this type of soil; you have to recondition the whole ground structure.

An organic farmer would never grow wheat on one field for four years in a row. He would know that the crop yield would

2-MINUTE *CHECKUP*

GROUND CONDITION QUICK DIP

Once you get used to the idea of the four elements and what they mean in your ground condition, you can use this quick dip as an instant check in any situation. This checkup is great if you are feeling bad or if you find yourself in a tough situation.

Simply pause for 20 seconds. If you are with someone and need an excuse, look out the window, adjust your shoe, or walk to the bathroom. Ideally, close your eyes for these 20 seconds. Take four long, deep breaths. As you do so, get in touch with your inner ground condition at this moment. Which elements are extreme right now—either too much or too little? What do you need to get back into balance quickly?

be poor and the soil would be exhausted. This is what happened to Steve. In his previous company he drove himself hard throughout his 20s, and at 28 he was invited to step up from marketing manager to general manager. It was a business with a great brand name, but it was a mess in every other respect.

Steve grabbed at a chance that was too much too soon for him. Within a year he had gone from feeling fired up to being burned out. Neither he nor the business performed well, and he was left feeling bitter and depleted, with his self-confidence withered.

Moving to a marketing manager position with a larger corporation had looked

like a sensible sideways step, a semi-fallow season to renew his fertility—but it turned out to be another setback. My predecessor had become disillusioned with the whole business world, and he had dumped his cynicism on Steve like acid rain during the year before he left. Steve had hoped he would succeed my predecessor, but he knew he was in no condition to do so. He was dried up, as barren as baked mud.

After several weeks of getting more and more wound up, I had to accept that my irresistible force had met an immovable object. I couldn't impose the effect that I wanted on Steve, so I turned my raw, impatient energy to the sales force, where there were some quick wins to keep the boss off my back. I still had a clear vision of how Steve could be, but I had no sense of how to make it happen.

The Recovery Cycle

I used to seek Steve out at the end of the afternoon and sit in his office, telling him about my ideas and enthusiasms, hoping that my own inspiration would gradually revive him, breathe some air into him. I also made a point of appreciating him—for what he was, for qualities such as clarity and straight talking, not for achievement. I sensed that if I tried to force output from him, Steve would close up completely, whereas if he felt warmly valued, with no instant return expected, he would start to open up like a field ready for sowing. Gradually, trust and empathy developed between us.

A few months later, Steve and I were working very well together. We had a direct and effective dialogue; he shaped and sparked my ideas, and I did the same for his implementation. He had forced me to learn a principle that I apply now in any working relationship, even with seemingly compliant people: I don't get sustainable results or the full picture by imposing my will; I need to leave space to hear the other person and to collaborate.

After a year of working together, I appointed Steve as one of three regional managers responsible for a sales force of 80 people. He was cerebral in his approach, and marketing work had reinforced this. Sales management drew him into the feeling side of his nature, as well as the physical, practical side. He had new ways to grow and to develop qualities he had been neglecting, which is similar to the way a farmer develops specific qualities in the soil by planting certain crops. A year later I was promoted, and Steve succeeded me. He did well as marketing and sales director and was later promoted to a managing director position.

The 4 Elements

Although I wasn't using the Natural Advantage model when I worked with Steve Worowski, this model fits with the successful approach I evolved. When we first met, his ground condition was very poor. His organic content—his creativity, motivation, and initiative—was low. His soil depth was good, so his potential was high, but the soil structure was awful, what a farmer would call compacted. When soil is compacted, it has been squashed down; there is little air content, and it has no openness, so the ingredients for growth can't get in. It takes time, patience, and persistent effort to help closed ground open up, as I eventually realized.

Sustainable growth needs to draw on all four elements: earth, water, air, and fire.

With Steve, I took off the pressure for big thinking and a high level of output. Letting him work on the smaller issues was like growing a restorative, undemanding crop on a field. Spending time hanging out with him was similar to using an aerating roller to open up the soil. Gradually he started to absorb appreciation and inspiration, like sunlight and air, and the momentum and vitality of his natural system revived. Steve's soil type, like mine, is basically sandy. His inherent reserves are low, but he can be highly productive given good inputs of fertility. When he and I started working well together, we developed habits that raised both our fertility and our output.

Steve's main assets were his physical and mental energy, which equate to the earth and fire elements, but his approach had left him physically drained, feeling like earth that has had its fertility exhausted. His overuse of fiery mental energy had left him dried up and burned out. Steve's ambition had drawn him to a high-pressure job in a struggling company, and you could say he'd given it everything he'd had, but he'd done so in a way that completely ignored renewal. Sustainable growth needs to draw on all four elements: earth, water, air, and fire.

26

Exercise: Ground Condition Test

This exercise will help you gauge the balance of the four elements in your ground condition. It is a good tool to come back to regularly. Allow yourself about 10 minutes for this exercise.

Take a couple of minutes to relax and turn your attention inward. You may find it helpful to close your eyes. Now, imagine that you are a piece of earth. Let your awareness sink down into this piece of earth and get a sense of its condition. Is it depleted or rich? Wet or dry? Dense or airy? Hot or cold?

Imagine how these qualities apply to your own ground condition right now. Then use the format below to document your ground condition. The ideal range is between 4.5 and 6.5 on a scale of 1 to 10.

You may like to imagine how you would manage a piece of earth with these ratings and see what this suggests for improving your own ground condition. Stay aware of these ratings as you read more about managing ground condition and the four elements in Chapters 1 and 2.

Earth	1	2	3	4	5	6	7	8	9	10
	Lack of humus and nutrients means low growth potential							Excess of humus and nutrients; soil is too rich, unbalanced		

Water	1	2	3	4	5	6	7	8	9	10
	Too dry; rigidly unemotional							Waterlogged; swamped by feelings		

Air	1	2	3	4	5	6	7	8	9	10
	No air; growth stifled by lack of inspiration							Too much air; all vision, no substance		

Fire	1	2	3	4	5	6	7	8	9	10
	No heat; growth limited by lack of mental fire							Too hot; excess of mental energy creates burnout		

Optimum ground condition with all four elements balanced

**Optimum
4.5–6.5**

Soil Types

The ground condition of any farm or garden is fundamentally shaped by its soil type, such as clay, chalk, or sand. Each soil type has characteristic strengths and problems and will suit some crops better than others. As the Natural Advantage process has evolved, I've developed a sense that the main soil types equate to temperament or personality types in people. There are six main soil types, all with human equivalents.

Sand. Sandy soils have an open texture, and both water and organic matter tend to drain through them quickly. Basic fertility is low, but sandy soil can be highly productive if organic matter is regularly added. This equates to people who are potentially fiery and creative but lack follow-through and stamina. They need frequent refills of fertility and good composting to avoid burnout. Steve Worowski is an example of this soil type.

Silt. This is the fine-textured, fertile earth found in river valleys. It is so fine that it lacks structure. It becomes clogged with water and is too dense for air and heat to circulate. A silty soil is like a person who is highly intelligent but impractical. An example of a silt temperament is Phil Morris, managing director of Alibi Publishing, profiled on page 37.

Clay. A dense, heavy soil, clay can easily become waterlogged or hard and dry. Its inherent fertility is fair, but it can be developed through cultivation, drainage, and adding humus. In people, this equates to a temperament that is rather serious and has difficulty in handling emotions. Alison Martin, whom you will soon meet, has a clay temperament.

Loam. Loam is a mixture of the three soil types mentioned above. These combination soils tend to have better structure and fertility than the single-soil types. Although they can be highly productive, loam soils still need considerable care and cultivation. The human equivalent is a temperament that is more complex, more versatile, and more productive than the others.

Chalk. In a chalky soil, the topsoil is thin and alkaline, which limits the range of plants it can support. Chalk soils tend toward dryness because water drains right through them. Their fertility is fair, but it can be developed by adding organic matter. A person with a chalk temperament may be a maverick, with a risk of seeming dry, sour, and unemotional.

Peat. Peat soils have high organic content and good structure. They retain moisture, but they also drain well. However, peat is highly acidic, which means that it stifles biological activity. If left to itself, peat soil will usually be quite dead and unproductive. Someone with a peat temperament is usually intelligent and talented but risks being bitter, disaffected, and unable to apply their potential to their work.

Using soil types as a model for different human characters offers another simple and revealing way to understand both the needs and the potential of your ground condition. In gardening, it is clear that some crops will thrive in one soil type and fail in another. As you explore your own soil type, consider whether your work outputs suit it and whether you have a balance between crops that are demanding and those that are restorative for your temperament.

Send in the Pigs

I met Alison Martin in one of my workshops at Magdalen Farm on how to fulfill yourself sustainably in work. When she spoke about why she'd come to the program, she said: "I'm not at a crossroads: I'm at the end of the road, suicidal. I'm sick of my work, and I'm propping myself up with antidepressants, cigarettes, and wine. I feel like my job is killing me." Alison was 40 years old, a successful middle manager with a high-pressure job in hospital administration. But her skin was sallow, and she wore a tense, negative expression. In ground condition terms, I felt she was a clay type, waterlogged, bogged down, and swamped by negative feelings.

As the weekend went on, Alison reached the same view of her ground condition as I had reached. She questioned Peter Norman, the farm manager, about the boggy field at the west end of the farm and how he was dealing with it. "The land there is clay," Peter explained, "so it's got a tendency toward waterlogging, but we can improve it over time. The main structural change is drainage; we're putting in a network of field drains to draw off the excess water. Another thing we do is turn the pigs on it."

I could see Alison wince at this. We were standing by the field, and it looked like a complete mess, a chaos of mud, with vast sows wallowing in it, grunting happily. Peter grinned at Alison. "Sometimes in farming, when you've got a bit of a mess, the way through is to make a complete mess of it. What the pigs do is churn up the clay really deep so you get more organic matter mixed down into the soil. They open up the structure so the air gets in. Wet clay is awful for persistent weeds such as docks, but the pigs root them out. We also add light compost, such as vegetable waste, which breaks down into humus and makes the soil less dense."

Mapping the Terrain

Soon after this, Alison approached me. "Alan, I'm really excited by all this; I can see there's something here for me, but I can't make it out yet." She shook her head crossly. "It's ridiculous—I don't know anything about this farming stuff."

"You don't need to be a farmer to work this out," I said. "It's about you. Start with putting your attention fully into your body, and feel how it's in a similar condition to the field. The water saturating that clay is like the negative feelings that are bogged down within your physical self."

There was a tense pause. "Okay," she began slowly. "There are old feelings in me that have been down there for years: rejection, self-dislike, depression. And it feels really stuck, sticky like clay. It's awful, it's literally like a bog. These are stagnant emotions, and there's nowhere for them to go."

We stood silently for a while as the pigs grunted on around us. Eventually she looked up and continued, "But on a farm if you've got a bog or a muddy field, you take an overview, you look at the contours, where the land slopes, and how to channel the water."

Alison thought further, then smiled. "Yes. I am quite capable of mapping out these stuck feelings, and figuring out how to move them. It's like engineering for feelings, isn't it?"

"Brilliant," I said. "That's exactly it. It's using your mind to create the channels and direction by which the feelings can move, and as they flow, they become clear and useful; this change is like the difference between stagnant and running water."

Although Alison thought she already knew her story and the causes of her stuck feelings, it felt quite different when she mapped them, spelling out the whole sequence of relevant events throughout her life. Doing this harnessed her brainpower and her problem-solving talents, which up until then had had no way of engaging with her emotional stagnation.

Avoiding Stagnation

A few weeks later, Alison phoned me. "I've figured out the pigs," she said proudly.

"Tell me."

"Well, I remembered how you took me through the drainage thing, and I applied the same method. I got back into that con-

2-MINUTE *CHECKUP*

LANDSCAPE PORTRAIT

This exercise will help you explore the ideas of ground condition and soil type.

Picture yourself as a piece of land—a garden, a field, a farm, or a country landscape. This may be an imaginary place or one that you already know and love.

As you picture this landscape in your imagination, explore its qualities. Does it feel fertile or depleted? Overexploited or underused? Well cared for or neglected? See if you can imagine the soil type of this landscape. What does it need to be both fertile and sustainable?

nection between my physical self and that muddy field, and then imagined what the pigs would mean for me. My first reaction was that I felt like screaming. It was an invasion; they were going even deeper into the crap, opening up the soil, exposing everything, churning it over."

"So what did that mean for your situation?" I asked.

"It meant that mapping the territory was only a start; I had to let myself express these feelings, taking the risk of being really churned up. That'd be far better than staying stuck in them. So I've arranged some counseling sessions, and it's incredible how much lighter I feel for letting this stuff out."

Alison needed to be "lost enough to find herself," as Robert Frost so aptly put it.

Part of her story dealt with her parents, who insisted that girls should always be smiling, sweet, and subservient. By now, she could see that water was useful when moving, but it was a problem when stagnant. She began to express her feelings at work, instead of bottling them up. The ground condition model gave her a new and ongoing approach to managing her feelings—using her mental power and handling surprises with resilience. As she put it, "Whatever comes up, if I take it back to my ground condition, I get a simple sense of what to do."

Alison's experience is typical of many people who have used the Natural Advantage process. Making the link between ground condition in the soil and in your own nature can yield new understanding and resolution, even for deep-rooted issues. Most of us have some sense of affinity with the soil, and the ground condition model has an evocative power to show us what it means to work as a natural system. With practice, it becomes quick and easy to assess your ground condition and to form a clear view of what you need to renew it.

Personal Energy Management

There is a saying that the best way to learn quickly is to make a lot of mistakes in a short period of time. My own learning about ground condition started in earnest when I worked my way into health problems in 1994.

From 1976 to 1990, I was continuously involved in senior management positions, most of them business turnarounds. A 60- to 80-hour work week was my norm, and I felt the stresses of these jobs intensely. Yet my health was excellent. Although I was not consciously managing my ground condition, I did so intuitively. Many elements of good ground maintenance came to me naturally.

To start with, there was a sound rotation cycle in my work and nonwork activities. Every job involved managing large teams, so I had a range of contacts. This large-team management work rotated with intense work on individual tasks. I was also traveling a lot, and long hours on planes and trains were my recovery cycle, my time to relax and to reflect on and digest the long hours of continuous output. My children were young during these years, and my family life was absorbing and satisfying, forming another part of the renewal cycle.

I was also acutely aware that working these hours would wreck me unless I maintained my physical health. Frequent exercise was a priority, and I was careful about diet and alcohol. A strong sense of purpose and inspiration in each job kept my energy renewed. I had a vision of what I wanted to achieve for the businesses and the people in them. I was also clear and positive about my own career goals—immediate fulfillment and future progression.

In 1994 my situation was very different. I had no business structure, no boss, no budget, no job description. I was working alone and with a small group of people at one location, Magdalen Farm. My kids were engrossed in friends, not family, so I had lost that counterbalance. I became emotionally tied up with the short-term problems of the project. My vision and perspective were overwhelmed by a sense of having to scrabble for survival. So I became hooked on pushing for results, not feeding the soil, in myself and in the rest of the team.

Although the number of working hours was saner, I was not maintaining my condition, and my physical resources became exhausted. I was swamped, waterlogged by the emotional reactions that the project and the people brought up in me: intense anger, fear, and bewilderment. All my mental firepower, which had worked well in large businesses, seemed irrelevant in this chaos, just as growth stops in sodden soil because the heat, water, and air can't circulate.

In 1994, when I fell ill with candida, I realized that I had to take my health seriously. In ground condition terms, candida is a sign that humus and biological activity are low, that the natural system has lost its resilience to new challenges. From this crisis I developed a strong interest in what I call *personal energy management*. My approach built on books such as Stephen Covey's *The 7 Habits of Highly Effective People*. Covey writes of four types of human energy: physical, emotional, mental, and spiritual. I developed a detailed set of methods to manage these four energies.

In hindsight, I can see that in the 1980s I used the routines of the job, the needs of my children, and my liking for fixed habits to create a style for my work and life that was sustainable but in fact was quite rigid. My style was outside in, not principle-based. Nowadays, my work has few routines and is largely self-directed. I have grown my approach outward from the principles. Although I still have episodes of fatigue, my work style is now largely sustainable and pretty resilient to changes.

Feed the Soil

Most individuals and organizations are preoccupied with the crop, the outcome of their work. It's as if we are so overwhelmed by short-term economic pressures that we can't step back and balance the equation between roots and fruits. The principle of cultivating good ground condition in organic farming points to the basis for human sustainability at work. It fits one of the basic principles of organic gardening: If you feed the soil, the soil will feed the plant. If we focus solely on feeding the plant, we lose the capacity to create a different output, to overcome unexpected problems.

One of the important features of fertile ground condition is structure. Good structure is permeable—air, heat, and water can get into the soil, and excess water can drain through it. The soil has enough openness that roots can penetrate deep down into it, and it has enough strength to support the root structures firmly.

The illustration below also shows the importance of depth. The most fertile part of the soil is the topsoil, the layer that contains *humus*, or organic matter. The depth of topsoil is a measure of how much available fertility the soil has, of its capacity to absorb more organic matter, and of its resilience. For example, a deeper layer of topsoil can support plants longer in a drought. The us-

able depth of soil is greater on organic farms, and the cultivation methods mean that plants can also access moisture and nutrients from the subsoil.

One of the beautiful elements of natural systems is symbiosis, an association of two organisms that support each other. The two basic issues to consider in managing ground condition are structure and fertility, and there is a symbiotic link between them. Improving structure helps the earth's capacity to produce fertility and supply it to a plant. In the same way,

HEALTHY SOIL

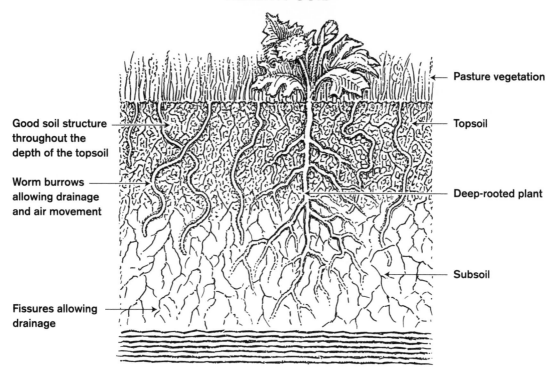

A cross section of healthy soil reveals the qualities that make it conducive to healthy plant growth, productivity, and sustainability. Good structure allows air, water, and heat to penetrate deeply.

actions to raise fertility will help develop soil structure, the texture and resilience of the soil.

Improving Structure

The most common structural problem with soil is compaction. This means that the soil is too dense, and air, water, and heat cannot circulate. Compaction inhibits the biological activity in the earth, and hence, fertility drops. It is more difficult for plant roots to penetrate compacted soil, and it is less rewarding as well because there are fewer nutrients. These problems are worse on intensive farms: Conventional farmers feed the plant, not the soil, and do not concern themselves with soil structure. Fertility is added at the surface, which encourages plants to develop shallow root systems instead of building structure by rooting deeply.

Compaction is one of the most common problems in the human condition, too. I see this in people at work. When output is forced by artificial pressures at the surface, it is shallow. There is a lack of real inspiration in the work, just as there is a lack of air in compacted soil. As a result, the water element—feelings about work—cannot circulate. You see an example of this condition in the case of Steve Worowski.

One of the ways an organic farmer or gardener cures compaction is by planting crops that will do the job for him. Vigorous, deep-rooting plants penetrate the soil, opening up the structure and unlocking its fertility; an example is the chicory plant. Another method of improving structure is mechanical cultivation. Magdalen Farm has 50 acres of permanent pasture along the river Axe. The silty soil can't be plowed because the fields are liable to flood, which would wash away the topsoil. Silty soils are fine-textured and prone to compaction, so a spiked roller towed behind a tractor was used to open up the soil, letting in more air and increasing productivity. A third structure-improving method is to rely on the weather. Heavy clay soils are especially prone to compaction, but over time, this can be remedied by simple weathering—a repeated succession of wetting and drying, freezing, and thawing.

All three methods to renew compacted soil have parallels in human ground condition. Growing a restorative, undemanding crop on a field is like letting a person rebuild confidence and vitality gradually, through working on smaller projects that restore a sense of capability and harness all four elements. Using mechanical cultivation to open up the soil structure is equivalent to undertaking a variety of deliberate interventions to bring more air, more inspiration, to a person or team. These interventions can include team building or visioning or the more informal approach I took with Steve Worowski. Using the weather to break up the soil is similar to the way a person encounters situations that confront him or her with a condition that forces change. The pressures of Alison

> Compaction is one of the most common problems in the human condition.

Martin's job and her visit to Magdalen Farm combined to bring her to the point of seeking a different, better way of life.

The other common structural problem in soil is waterlogging. Heavy clays in particular are liable to retain too much water, thus suppressing air circulation and biological activity. One solution is the use of field drains, a network of pipes that will remove some of the water and channel it elsewhere. Adding organic matter to lighten the soil will also help, as will growing crops or employing mechanical cultivation. Alison Martin is an example of how this applies to human ground condition. Her decision to open up old, stagnant feelings and get counseling to process them successfully is similar to the way recycling decomposing waste into fertile organic matter that can lighten the soil—and the soul.

Building Fertility

Developing fertility is the second main aspect of cultivating good ground condition. In organic farming, crop choice and rotation cycles play a central role in this. At Magdalen Farm, several fields were exhausted from producing demanding crops such as grains and potatoes for too long. These fields were reseeded as clover pasture and were kept for a few years as part of a longer rotation. Nitrogen is the most important nutrient required for plant growth, and demanding crops consume a lot of it. What is remarkable about clover is that it actually draws nitrogen from the atmosphere and fixes it in the soil through its root system. The seed mix for these clover pastures included deep-rooting herbs, such as chicory, so that the crops improved soil structure as well as fertility.

Fertility can also be developed through adding manure and compost; the growth potential in waste products is harnessed and applied where it is most needed. Although organic growers prefer to avoid importing fertility, this is sometimes necessary, especially in the early years. Organic manure can be added to speed up the renewal process. Organic standards also permit some use of natural additives to correct mineral deficiencies; these additives include seaweed, lime, or rock phosphate. These are quite different in function from artificial fertilizers, just as a vitamin supplement and a pep pill are different. Additives on organic fields are designed to work gradually to improve ground condition, not to act directly on the plant in the kick-start method of artificial fertilizers.

How do soil fertility principles relate to human ground condition? They highlight a basic principle of sustainable productivity at work: cultivating underlying fertility, not depending on external spot applications to force a particular crop. To improve fertility, you create resources in yourself that are both adaptable and self-renewing. Human ground condition, like healthy soil, has inherent vitality to meet the unexpected and to produce growth despite a variety of problems. The methods of achieving this draw on several other Natural Advantage principles, which are explained in the following chapters.

Ground Condition in Organizations

The ground condition concept works for teams and whole organizations, as well as individuals. While soil types and condition will be more diverse in a group, there will also be a collective ground condition that usually reflects that of the group leader. The chief executive's outlook shapes the ground condition of the whole company. When I worked for businessman Richard Upton, his approach was to apply intense pressure to achieve current-year results and to cut short any debate about obstacles or future implications. This approach was similar to that of an intensive farmer relying on heavy use of fertilizers and pesticides to push his crop. Upton's approach delivered high profits for several years, but it led to deep, underlying problems that emerged some years later.

Although it is hard, it is quite possible for an individual or team to work sustainably within an overall culture that is depleting the ground condition. The key to working sustainably in such an environment is to operate according to dual standards. Provided that you meet the output demands, you can usually do it your own way if you get on with it quietly.

A few progressive companies already monitor and manage aspects of ground condition. For example, BP runs regular staff attitude studies that include some questions in these areas. The concept of the learning company has parallels with the ground condition model; the methods applied in developing learning organizations are relevant to creating productive ground condition.

Humanizing Corporate Culture

Companies may acknowledge that improving the quality of working life is desirable, but this acknowledgment won't necessarily place the issue on a company's action agenda. However, there are now numerous examples of businesses that have improved performance by humanizing their culture. One such company is Wyeth, a leading international pharmaceuticals supplier. From 1994 to 1997, Wyeth implemented a major program of training and process development, with the aim of increasing effectiveness and the capacity to handle change. One important feature has been training in interpersonal skills—including assertiveness, influencing skills, and conflict resolution—which has enabled a deeper level of personal involvement and collaboration. The principle that each individual has primary responsibility for his or her personal development and learning has been firmly established, and managers hold annual employee reviews to agree on a personal development plan for each individual.

Stephen Isherwood, Wyeth's company training and development manager, says, "We have seen many benefits in both business performance and personal effectiveness . . . Continuous change and learning are now accepted as the norm. Development objectives are agreed between the participant and the manager before attending a training course. Afterward the ability of the participant to deliver enhanced performance and the agreed objective is reviewed and evaluated. The results from this support my view that the steps we have taken at

Wyeth to humanize our culture and increase personal involvement have contributed significantly to our business performance."

Loosening Up

When my consulting business, Working Vision, was asked to facilitate a culture change program for Alibi Publishing in 1998, I could see that this assignment would be both exciting and dangerous. Alibi was a profitable, expanding company of 150 people, publishing several specialty magazines for the information-technology sector. The firm was dominated by Phil Morris, a forthright but likable accountant. He had been brought in as a trouble-shooting president in 1995, at the age of 33. As Phil put it, "I've turned a blooming shambles into a winner, and I know it's up to me. I've got a smashing team here. They'll do anything I tell them, but that's the point: Till now, I've done all the thinking and telling."

Phil had a sharp mind, good judgment, and terrific vitality, so his dominating, directive style had produced results. However, in ground condition terms, his approach was disastrous. The entire organization depended on him for the input to generate the output, and everyone knew it. As one of the directors said, "Just occasionally, Phil asks us what we think. He hardly waits for a reply, and we know it's not worth bothering. He'll have thought it through better than we ever could."

Phil had been asked by Alibi's parent company to focus on overseas acquisitions and development. His brief directive to us was, "Develop my guys so they can run this business sustainably without me."

My colleagues and I began with a detailed check on ground condition, holding individual interviews with Phil, his 11 direct subordinates, and a sample of people at other levels. Just as the soil on conventional farms becomes lazy and inactive because fertility is applied at the surface, so it was with Alibi. The soil structure was compacted, with little air or water, and with no inspiration or feeling in the people. The level of humus and biological activity, the vitality and initiative, was low.

We diagnosed the soil type for Phil and the overall company as silty. Phil himself had a strong vision for the business and intense personal ambition. These qualities created air within his soil to make him highly fertile. However, the rest of the organization had problems typical of silty soil—poor structure, low air content, and low productivity—despite high potential. We designed a mix of workshops and individual coaching for Phil and his management team. A crucial part of this was running sessions for the group without Phil so that they could develop their own ground condition and ease out of their dependence on him.

Until then, disputes between members of the team had always been resolved by Phil. Gradually we encouraged each individual and the whole group to develop a personal vision and purpose for the business, and a sense of his or her ability to

> **We encouraged each individual and the whole group to develop a personal vision and purpose for the business.**

pursue these. We were effectively opening up the soil structure and letting in air and inspiration. We coached the team to start voicing issues directly with each other, and we trained them in such skills as assertiveness and conflict resolution. They began to acquire a mental tool kit to handle their feelings effectively. The process also developed the structure of their ground condition, building a combination of openness and strength. Through a live-action simulation and a forum session on their current business issues, we built the team's ability to look at problems and conflicts and to use them constructively. They learned to compost their waste, which meant that the humus level and biological activity improved for the group and for individuals. (To read more on composting, turn to Chapter 3.)

Our initial summary of the atmosphere at Alibi was that it had a banter culture: arid, cerebral, and devoid of feeling. We sensed that Phil and several of the directors didn't know how to handle emotions. Another step in improving ground condi-

tion was to introduce moisture, the feeling element, into the culture. We began by developing the mental abilities to handle emotions, which acted like channels for water. Then we used a series of experiential exercises, including some physical activities involving risk and trust. Gradually, the loud people who used humor to avoid emotion became quieter, and the silent ones started to voice their feelings. We knew we had crossed a watershed when the loud ones themselves started to open up about their areas of vulnerability.

This program produced a lasting change in the ground condition at Alibi. The biggest problem, as I had feared, was Phil himself. Whenever short-term performance wobbled, he reverted to directive mode. It took several stormy run-ins between him and me in front of his team before he learned the art of constructive conflict. Phil told me, "You guys have earned your brass, having your heads bitten off and coming back for more. But I got the message: It's about finding answers, not winning debates."

Ground Condition in Daily Practice

The key to achieving sustainability is to take its principles to heart, so that they shape your daily activities from the inside out. Setting outside-in targets and adopting techniques such as vowing to check your ground condition every morning may help you break bad habits, but these acts alone are not sustainable. The best way to take these principles to heart is to keep using

them: Play with them, and try them out in real-life situations—your own and the organization's—until you have experienced how they work. In this way, these principles of sustainability create natural structure and become part of your own living system.

Remember that all seven Natural Advantage principles are interdependent and mutually reinforcing. Trying to cultivate your ground condition without enabling it through the other six principles will not get you far.

The Chinese believe in taking medicine when you're healthy—the idea is to avoid getting ill in the first place. In the same way, the ground condition principle works well as preventive maintenance, sustaining fertility at high levels. The model also offers a clear blueprint for recovering vitality, but remember that this will need to be maintained.

Openness

Ground condition is more than simple fitness. The specific aspects of soil quality can give you tailored guidance on addressing your own particular situation. If you get lost, go back to the analogy. Picture yourself as a piece of ground, and see what your soil condition is calling for. Once you have read the whole book, you should find that the other principles enable you to resolve your current need in a sustainable way.

It is important to see the limitations and the strengths of the organic farming model. A person is more like a farm than a field—each person is capable of producing several crops, on different cycles, in parallel. The living earth has an intelligence and an adaptability that echo the human, but on a lesser scale. The level of conscious intelligence, will, and potential for change in people and organizations is immense; it exceeds the scope of any model.

Good structure is essential in accessing the soil's fertility, and the same is true for people at work. In the human context, good structure means cultivating a combination of openness and strength and ensuring that the elements required for growth are both present and accessible.

Resourcefulness

The other main element in good ground condition is fertility. Humus, or organic matter, typically makes up only 3 to 5 percent of soil, so a small change in this level has a major impact on both the resourcefulness and the output of the soil. This is a valuable pointer for each of us and for organizations. While the juice, the life energy, may appear to be a small part of the whole picture, its importance as a catalyst deserves great attention.

Fertility also requires the presence, in balanced proportions, of the four growth elements. The implications of this for people at work are explored in Chapter 2.

The potential for change in people and organizations is immense.

Organic growers check ground condition frequently, and it will help you to do the same. As you learn this new vocabulary, it can give you quick and vivid feedback on how to maintain good ground condition and high vitality. Use the Ground Condition Test on page 27 to check your own ground condition. With practice, you should be able to do this just by sensing your ground condition, without needing pen or paper. Although you can push yourself to achieve output in the short term, remember that this won't be sustainable unless you keep cultivating your underlying ground condition.

Exercise: Know Your Ground

Knowing your ground is one of the major processes in this book; it can help you deepen and consolidate your knowledge of your own ground condition and relate this to the output (or crops) you want to produce in your work.

In the Natural Advantage workshops I lead, this exercise is one of the most powerful experiences for many people. Allow 30 to 40 minutes for it, and if possible, set it up as a walking visualization, as described below. If this isn't possible, simply sit and picture the process described below.

To prepare for this exercise, find a clear space inside or outdoors—at least 10 feet by 10 feet. Find a piece of rope, string, or thread, and use this to divide the space in half. To do the exercise, have a friend read the following instructions to you, pausing where marked until you are ready to continue. If this isn't possible, read the instructions to yourself.

Stand up and walk to position X on your ground plan. Take a few deep breaths, and relax into your body. *(Pause.)* Now imagine that the space you have created here represents your field of activity: a piece of earth that represents you in your work. The area to your left, above the line, represents the air. The area to the right is the earth. And the line is the surface of the ground. You are looking at a cross section of your field of activity, and you are standing on the line where the earth meets the air. To your right is a cross section— your earth, your ground condition going down from the surface, through the topsoil, to the subsoil below. *(Pause.)*

Take a few minutes to fully create this picture. Imagine that it represents you as a productive system in your work. *(Pause.)* Now walk very slowly to your right, going down into your earth. How deep is your topsoil, and what is its condition? Does your ground feel tired or ready for more action? *(Pause.)* Now walk further down into your earth, into your subsoil. What's it like down here? Is it stony, rocky, or sandy? Is it full of water or dried out? Can this subsoil support your growth, or does it need some attention? *(Pause.)*

Now walk to the bottom of your ground plan, the lower edge of your subsoil, and turn to face upward, toward the air. Your productive resources are laid out in front of you. How do they look? How do they feel? *(Pause.)* Now, start to imagine yourself as a plant. Picture what kind of productive growth you want to achieve through this ground. Take a few minutes to see if you can picture what kind of plant you are. *(Pause.)* Next, start to picture your root system. Is it deep and extensive or shallow and limited? Can your roots gather all the moisture and nutrients you need from down in the soil? *(Pause.)* Start moving slowly up through the earth as you explore this question. *(Pause.)*

Now approach the line. See how you feel about appearing above the surface, about being visible. How does the air above you feel? Is the atmosphere welcoming or hostile? Is it polluted or clear? *(Pause.)*

Next, imagine what kind of growth you are achieving above the ground. This may be a tree trunk, a plant stem, or the leaves of a flower or vegetable. *(Pause.)* Is your growth above the ground strong or weak? Does it feel in balance with the root system that supports it? *(Pause.)* Start to picture any fruits, flowers, or edible produce from your plant. Are they large and abundant or small and sparse? Are they full of color and flavor or not? *(Pause.)*

Move around your ground plan. Witness yourself as a productive system, and stand back to see what perspectives you get. *(Pause.)* You may want to move slowly through the whole process again to learn more about it and how the different parts connect with each other. *(Pause.)*

When you have finished, you may find it useful to draw what you have seen. Take time to understand and interpret it. You may find it helpful to talk about it with a friend or counselor.

chapter 2
NATURAL ENERGY

IF WE ASK WHAT MAKES the conventional farm unsustainable, a prime factor is its use of unnatural, forced energy sources. Factory farming takes most of its energy from nonrenewable resources, whose residues pollute the earth and groundwater. Consider the parallel in the workplace: Where does your personal energy come from? Often work output is fueled by stress, fear, or pressure.

In both cases, forced energy stimulates the problems as much as the desired crop—it reduces the natural capacity for self-renewal, pollutes the outputs, and saps the underlying resources. The organic way is less controllable, and it may be more labor intensive, but it yields better-quality crops and renews the means of production. This second principle of the Natural Ad-vantage grows directly from the first. Natural energy inputs are essential both to create good ground condition and to use it. In this chapter, we move on from the un-derlying conditions for growth to the en-ergy inputs that create the desired output.

Natural Energy Productivity

From the mechanistic viewpoint, energy is simply an input to achieve a desired output. A sack of fertilizer pushes out the crop. A gallon of gasoline gets you to the shopping mall. Setting a deadline and pres-suring your subordinate produces the re-port you need. From the natural systems viewpoint, it is clear that energy doesn't

THE NATURAL SYSTEM

Natural
energy
outputs

Clean processes

Reusable "waste"

Desired outputs

In a natural system, ample energy is supplied by abundant natural resources and composted "waste," while the output is nonpolluting. Organic farming and gardening follow this model.

44

THE MECHANICAL SYSTEM

Desired output   Desired output   Desired output

Forced inputs   Forced inputs   Forced inputs

Buildup of polluting waste

In a mechanical system, such as the conventional farming model, energy needs are met from the outside as forced input (synthetic fertilizer). This approach short-circuits the natural cycle of growth and produces a build-up of polluting waste.

disappear; it simply changes form. When energy is used in a process, the residual energy tends to disperse. This explains why the polluting residues of fossil fuels are so hard to clean up.

The organic growing model shows that if you harness natural energy in natural processes, the output and residues can also be clean and nonpolluting. The so-called waste residues can move on through the cycle, and natural processes can renew the value, the utility, of these dispersed forms of energy. Examples of this are biological activity in the soil and the ability of plants to turn carbon dioxide into oxygen and carbon. It is important to see that energy flows as a cycle, not in a linear way. This cycle is the start of raising energy productivity.

In a natural system, most of the energy need is met from recycling and from abundant sources (see the illustration on the opposite page). In a conventional, mechanistic, linear system, most of the

energy inputs have to be expensively fabricated and tailored to the purpose (see the diagram above).

It is useful to explore the parallel between plant growth and human productivity. The inputs to the plant include clean, renewable energy, such as sunlight, and "waste," such as carbon dioxide and waste matter in the soil. The processes by which the plant grows are clean, efficient, and nonpolluting. The outputs of the plant's growth typically include a useful crop, such as tomatoes or wheat; desirable by-products, such as oxygen; and "waste" that is biodegradable and reusable. If we superimpose these stages onto human endeavors, the cycle could work as it appears in the personal energy cycle on page 46.

Our basic model for translating the natural energy principle from organic farming or gardening to the workplace will be the four elements that were introduced in Chapter 1: earth, water, air, and fire.

THE PERSONAL ENERGY CYCLE

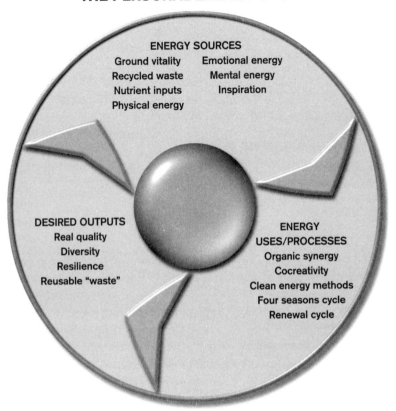

The Natural Advantage applies the principles of the organic method to produce clean and reusable human energy.

Considering these four elements in plant growth provides specific pointers on cultivating natural energy productivity in our work. In the same way, intensive farming methods show how conventional workplace cultures diminish natural vitality and raise dependence on forced energy inputs to achieve results. A fuller exploration of natural energy principles is provided in "The Natural Step," starting on page 191.

Human Energy Elements

In farming and gardening we are essentially dealing with physical energy flows. For example, an organic grower can calculate a fertility budget by estimating the inputs and outflows of key nutrients such as nitrogen to check if the overall energy cycle is sustainable. With people at work, it's more subtle: We need to consider both tangible

2-MINUTE*CHECKUP*

WARM SHOWER

This exercise takes only a few minutes, but it's a great way to get a natural energy boost when you need one. Do the exercise standing up, if possible.

Take a couple of deep breaths to reduce any tension you are feeling. Then remember a time when you felt warmly appreciated for something, maybe an achievement at work or a friend saying why she likes you. Let yourself experience fully this feeling of being appreciated. Notice how your body posture changes—you may even feel a warm glow spread throughout your body. Drink this in, enjoy it as you'd savor a warm shower, until you feel fully invigorated.

and intangible energy, and the interplay between them. If you're feeling emotionally stressed, this adds to the demand on your physical energy resources. Conversely, if you feel appreciated, this can enhance your physical energy, much like raising the biological activity in the soil.

The four types of human energy we will consider in this section are as interdependent and synergistic as the four elements in ground condition and plant growth.

Physical Energy = The Earth Element

The biological activity in the earth is a kind of natural power station. It draws energy from air, water, sun, waste, and minerals. These are converted into fertility—energy in a form that's usable for plant growth. The earth is the growth medium in which the inputs combine, and healthy ground condition requires all four energy elements.

For human ground condition, the nature of our physical inputs, especially of food and drink, has a major influence on our physical energy level. When we rely heavily on kick-start inputs, such as sugary foods and caffeinated drinks, this creates the same problems as artificial fertilizer in the earth. The price of the short-term boost is that our ability to renew our own vitality becomes progressively clogged.

There are many other ways to cultivate physical energy besides choosing a good diet. Aerobic exercise, which gets the circulation moving, has a significant benefit, as does relaxation. Most of us carry a lot of stress in our body, and stress impairs physical vitality when it's not released. Even body posture can be important: Good posture can improve our physical energy level, just as good soil structure helps fertility. Everything you do to improve the other three energies will help your physical condition, too. If you feel positive, think clearly, and have a strong sense of purpose and vision, imagine how this can enhance your physical energy—and imagine how the opposite would reduce it.

The earth is also the source of a wide range of minerals required as nutrients for plant growth. Particular crops need specific nutrients—cabbage and green vegetables especially need calcium, and sugar beets require phosphorus. Healthy soil delivers a variety of nutrients better than synthetic

THE HUMAN ENERGY CYCLE

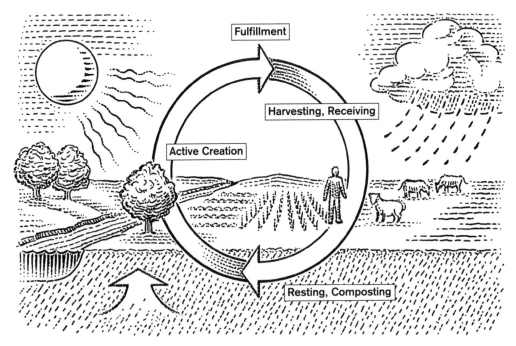

The natural cycle of life provides us with a basic blueprint for human energy sustainability as well. The four types of human energy combine to create a cycle of growth and renewal as shown here.

inputs and depleted soil. The parallel for human health is the minerals and vitamins we need in order to function effectively. Stress reduces our reserves of these. And the level of pollutants most of us have to deal with in our air, food, and water also put heavy demands on these reserves. As a result, mineral and vitamin supplements are probably advisable to sustain physical ground condition.

In cultivating your physical energy, it's important to be observant and responsive. Many people respond to their physical ailments the way an intensive farmer treats weeds, simply grabbing a means to suppress the symptom. An organic grower

knows that a specific weed has a specific message; it's saying something about the condition of the soil and the response it requires. In the same way, if you know how to observe your physical condition, you can learn what you need to maintain your energy.

If you are willing to observe and respond to minor ailments, you may avoid some major ones. For example, when working under pressure from a deadline to complete part of this book, I developed mouth ulcers. Not only did this tell me in broad terms that I was working unsustainably, but it also had specific messages about my energy flows. On the physical level, it showed me that I needed more rest and more vitamin B. It also highlighted an emotional energy issue for me, a reluctance to receive nourishment and new ideas.

Just as ground condition shows the state of all four elements, our physical body will reflect issues from all four types of human energy. If you are mentally stagnant or emotionally unsettled, this affects your physical energy, and your body can highlight the issue for you if you observe it closely. This is a big subject in its own right; a good doorway to the topic is a personal development book called *You Can Heal Your Life* by Louise Hay.

Emotional Energy = Water

In relation to the growth of a plant and the life in the soil, water has two essential functions. First, it is a transmitter of energy and nutrients: It carries them down into the earth and up through the plant. Secondly, the hydrogen and oxygen in water are an energy source in their own right. However, water can also carry problems, such as diseases, or excess nitrates from artificial fertilizer. The system can be parched or swamped: Too little and too much water both cause problems.

These properties of water provide suggestions for emotional energy in human systems. The root meaning of emotion is outward movement. Our feelings are a significant means of transmitting energy and nutrition, both within the individual and between people. If I have a sense of purpose about a project, I can communicate it to myself and others with feeling, with love and appreciation. This positive emotional energy will nourish work output, just like watering a plant. I could also express this vision to myself with anger and self-criticism: "It's about time you put your back into something, you lazy time-waster." This self-criticism would be like water carrying the kick start of artificial fertilizer through the plant; it might prod me into action but unsustainably.

Feelings can also operate in any of these ways in our interaction with others. At Alibi Publishing, the productivity of the whole organization was limited by its dry ground condition, a culture focused on mental energy, where feelings were not expressed. The first step in addressing this was to develop the senior team's ability to handle emotions. We trained them in ways to let feelings flow through their work, without swamping it. As a result, productivity rose, nutrients could move through the system, and people could interact more easily with one another.

Water is a power source on its own, and so are emotions. For example, appreciation is one of the best natural energizers.

In contrast, strong negative emotions, such as fear and anger, can be seen as waste. They have high energy content, but they need to be recycled to be useful.

If you feel that your way of working or the culture in your organization is too dry,

> **Positive emotional energy will nourish work output, just like watering a plant.**

what can you do about it? It's easy to foster a climate of appreciation at work. The key is to develop the habit of appreciating more than you criticize. Appreciate yourself and others. This is likely to start a virtuous circle, a progressive spiral in which the working culture becomes more positive, more flowing, more fertile. In *Emotional Intelligence,* Daniel Goleman discusses a number of research studies on how people learn best: It's by feeling recognized and appreciated for what they're doing right—however limited this may be—and not by being criticized for what they've done wrong.

One of the barriers to positive emotional energy is that many people find it difficult to give or receive praise. A common reason for fearing praise is the expectation that it will be followed by criticism or a request for something. If you can start to change the expectation, you should start to change the experience, too.

Water tends to spread, to permeate. In some situations, this is a useful quality, but it can also cause problems. In everyday life, it is essential to channel water through plumbing and drainage systems. The same is true of emotional energy. We can easily be swamped or flooded by feelings if we can't manage them. We may require a better drainage system: In human terms, this equates to methods for managing emotions, such as assertiveness and conflict resolution. We may also require a better balance between the elements. If a

piece of ground is waterlogged, air and warmth will help dry it out. In your work, engage your sense of purpose and perspective and your mental skills to help you clear out an excess of emotion.

Mental Energy = The Sun

In this model, fire, or sun, equates to mental energy. We often take too narrow a view of the mind's potential. Mental energy, in the full sense, includes not only logic and analysis, but also intuition and imagination and the ability to combine them all. The sun's energy animates the life in the soil and the growth of the plant. In the same way, it is mental energy that enlivens our ground condition and fuels our output. Mental energy turns an idea into action, an inspiration into a tangible product.

Does this mean that all we have to do to fulfill a vision is to think about it? No. Mental energy in the full sense is fiery—there's more to it than just thinking. It includes the heat of our will, our intent. It includes the bright light of insight, understanding, the flash of intuition, as well as the creative spark that ignites a process. It also includes the power of fire to consume and transform. To be productive, fire needs air, physical fuel, and something to heat—often, water. If we can integrate our mental and emotional energy, the result is powerful, like steam.

If you look at the images you associate with fire, they should give you guidelines

One of the barriers to positive emotional energy is that many people find it difficult to give or receive praise.

for generating and managing mental energy. The image I find helpful is to imagine my brain as a wood-burning stove. If the fuel is too wet, it's hard to start the fire, and then I get choking smoke instead of useful heat. Conversely, if the fuel is too dry, I get high heat for a while but no sustained output. This metaphor highlights the subtle interplay between mental, emotional, and physical energy. We often think of emotion as impeding our brain, which it does at the extremes. However, the most productive mix for plant and human growth is moderate amounts of both heat and water. When it's used well, emotional energy can enrich our mental processes and our overall productivity.

Fire also needs air for combustion. To get the fire started and burning strongly, I need to open the stove's dampers wide and provide plenty of air. And to kill the flame, all I have to do is shut off the air flow. For me, this is a clear model of the connection between mental and inspirational energy. When I want to animate a new project, I need a strong sense of purpose and vision, and I need to convey this to my team to get their fire started. The vision needs to blow through and fuel the mental process, or you don't get productive heat.

Like fire, mental energy needs to be contained and directed to be of most use; without this, it can be highly destructive. This means regulating and balancing the

> **Mental energy is fiery—the flash of intuition, the creative spark that ignites a process.**

supply of all four elements so that you get the amount of firepower you need for the job at hand. It also means developing a range of mental tools, such as analytical and intuitive methods, and ways to combine them. You can explore this further through the books mentioned in "Resources" on page 211.

In Chapter 1 of this book you have already seen examples of the extremes of mental fire. Alison Martin was so swamped by negative feeling that her mental fire had been extinguished; she was unable to use her intelligence to dig herself out of work and personal stress. Steve Worowski represents the other extreme. By overusing his mental powers, his whole ground condition had become burned up and dried out. He drove himself to a state in which his physical resources were exhausted and there was little air or water left in the soil. He had lost his sense of purpose and his capacity for feeling. In this state, more fire, or mental effort, will only aggravate the problem. It takes rest, careful cultivation, and an inflow of air and water before the fire can be rekindled productively.

Inspiration = Air

In organic growth, air has two essential functions. First, it is an enabler. Healthy soil has about 25 percent air content, and these spaces enable water, heat, and air to circulate and interact with the earth to generate growth. Secondly, air is a source of fertility. It's understandable but ironic that humans often equate air with oxygen. In fact, 78 percent of our atmosphere is nitrogen; in organic growing, air is a major source of this nutrient to fuel production.

The air element equates to inspirational energy, a sense of higher purpose, wider perspective, and vision. What the organic model highlights is how inspiration is needed to enable our fertility and productivity. It also shows us that vision and purpose are powerful energy sources, fuel for growth. Think about outstanding achievement in any field—business, sports, the arts, or your own work. Inspiration is part of the power we need for peak performance.

Consider the qualities of air and how these also describe inspirational energy. Both air and energy are invisible, intangible, yet are always around us, available. If we are tense or defensive, our breath is usually shallow and we don't access its full potential. As with water and fire, both intent and technique can help us harness the power of air more fully.

In my own energy management, I find the link between inspiration and breath very helpful. When I notice myself tensing up, taking several long, slow breaths has many benefits. It immediately gives me a sense of expansion and relaxation, helping me to see the situation in better perspective and to connect with my intention and purpose. Breathing more deeply adds oxygen to the bloodstream. This enhances brain activity, giving me extra mental energy. It also helps to release any physical and emotional stress I am feeling.

2-MINUTE *CHECKUP*

AIR LIFT

This is a quick way to give you a natural boost of inspirational energy. It's best to do this exercise standing up—ideally, out of doors, if you are in an area with clean air.

Take a few long, deep breaths to relax any tensions you are feeling. Now remember a situation in your life when you felt deeply inspired. See if you can find a time in your work when you felt a strong sense of vision and purpose, or find a scene from your personal life. Picture the scene and the setting as vividly as you can, and experience the feelings again.

Notice how your body posture changes and how your whole body feels. Imagine this sense of inspiration circulating around your bloodstream, through your whole body, as you continue to breathe deeply and slowly.

Enjoy this sense of inspirational power, and anchor it in your body as you consider your current work situation.

Accessing your inspirational energy can be as easy as breathing, but technique and process are also important. It's helpful to find a visioning process that works for you, that enables you to find clarity and purpose even in complex and confusing situations. You may need to cultivate your ground condition and soil structure to be able to harness the air element. For example, compacted soil has little air circulation; this usually equates to physical tension and depletion, which may need a concerted program to resolve. Relaxation, massage, yoga, or tai chi could all be helpful. Waterlogged soil also has poor air circulation, which is like a person's being swamped by emotion; professional counseling can help in clearing the situation. You'll find a good example of harnessing inspirational energy in the Caradon story later in this chapter.

Dirty Energy

During the workshop at Magdalen Farm that Alison Martin attended, she got into a lively discussion about energy and farming with Peter Norman, the manager. Alison attacked the question head on.

"Peter, I can't see what's wrong with putting fertilizer on your crops. Surely it's just like having a bit of sugar on your breakfast cereal? I mean, it's just an energy boost, giving nature a helping hand."

Peter smiled and shook his head. "No, it's more like having a bowl full of sugar and nothing else. How would that feel?"

Alison, Peter, and I had taken a stroll after lunch. It was a sultry June day, and we were leaning on a gate, looking at the hills rolling down to the river.

Peter led us down the lane, across a cattle grid, and onto the farm adjacent to Magdalen. "What we've got here," he said, "is a 30-acre field of intensively farmed wheat. Come and see—I'll show you what's really happening."

At first glance, things didn't look so different from next door. Alison stared at the wheat around her. "These plants are going on fine. What's the problem?"

Peter gave a dry laugh. "Look closer and you'll see." Alison knelt beside him and looked closely. "Ugh! Some kind of tiny insect, lots of them, crawling all over the plant."

"They're aphids," Peter explained. "The nitrogen fertilizer they put on this crop is like an overdose of artificial energy. It's dirty, it's polluting, and it's in an unnatural form. It kick-starts the plants but it also kick-starts the problems. Like these aphids. They suck the sap from the wheat, they encourage fungi, and they carry viruses."

"But you could sort this out with a pesticide, surely?" Alison offered.

Peter laughed wryly. "Sure, and that's what they do here; we're only seeing aphids because we're up in the corner where the spray can't reach. At Magdalen Farm, we have a lot of ladybugs and ground beetles that eat the aphids. The pesticides here kill the predators as well as the pests."

We stood silently, taking it in. "And here's another problem," Peter said. "What do you see between the rows of potato plants?"

"Well," said Alison, "there are a lot of weeds growing in this corner, and there are dead weeds all over the main part of the field."

Peter nodded. "One of the problems with nitrates is they make everything grow. In fact, the weeds grow faster than the plants because they're good at using whatever energy is around. This guy's weed problems are much worse than Magdalen's. So he has to dose his land with herbicide and pesticide. If you try to quick-fix your first problem, you just get into deeper trouble."

"And I suppose he'd get resistant strains of weeds, just as he would with the insect pests?" Alison asked.

"Exactly."

Diminishing Returns

Alison stood up, dusting herself off gingerly. "OK, Peter, I'm getting the picture, and it's pretty grim. But if fertilizers are part of the dirty energy problem, where does your clean energy come from?"

"In any sustainable system, energy use is crucial, right?"

Alison nodded impatiently. "Sure."

"So what do you think a sustainable approach would look like?"

Alison thought for a minute. "I guess you'd use renewable energy sources. You'd recycle energy, and you'd minimize use."

Peter smiled. "That's exactly what organic growers do, and this guy's doing the complete opposite. The raw material for his fertilizers, herbicides, and pesticides is basically fossil fuel. Plus there's the energy used in processing, transporting, and spreading the stuff. So the main energy he uses for his outputs here is imported."

"How do you mean?"

"I mean it's not compatible with natural systems," Peter explained.

"Feed the soil, and the soil will feed the plants?"

"Yes," Peter continued. "These artificial fertilizers are soluble chemicals—it's like giving a human being a massive intravenous dose of one growth nutrient. What would happen if you got all your food that way?"

Alison shuddered. "I guess my digestive system would just stop working."

"Exactly." Peter gestured at the field. "With these synthetic inputs, the plants in the soil get lazy, and the residues actually suppress the biological activity. Check it out."

Alison took his spade and dug a sample. "I can see it for myself. The topsoil's shallow. This earth feels pretty dead. There's not much humus, hardly any worms or insects."

Peter nodded. "After years of importing dirty energy, this is what you get: The ground's polluted, the fertility's at rock bottom, and you're into diminishing returns."

"I don't understand the last bit."

"Every year the fertility in the soil gets smaller, and the residues increase. So the bang for the buck from your artificial fertilizer goes down; you put ever more fertilizer on the field each year to keep forcing the yield."

> In any sustainable system, using renewable energy sources is crucial.

"So it's a vicious cycle," Alison said. "Where does it end?"

Peter shrugged. "What you're seeing here is so-called normal farming. Sometimes it really crashes. Maybe you get a resistant pest or weed that wipes out the whole crop. Or the water board jumps on you because of nitrate pollution. Sometimes it just keeps getting worse in a subtle way."

Conversations like this are typical of the way I developed the Natural Advantage model. After the visit to the neighboring farm, I spent time with Alison looking at the energy sources she had been using in her work and the potential alternatives. We could both see that she faced the same problem as an intensive farm: growing dependence on forced energy inputs, declining productivity and quality, and a rising need for artificial additives to suppress the problems. As Alison put it, "I'm seeing my craving for red wine, cigarettes, and tranquilizers in a different light. My energy system is unsustainable."

Forced Energy Systems

There are some common aspects to the energy systems in conventional and organic farming. For example, sun and rain are clearly essential to both. However, the key source of energy and fertility is different. In conventional farming, this source is artificial fertilizer. This approach does not stimulate the natural cycle of growth; rather, it short-circuits and inhibits the growth cycle. Applying a narrow range of nutrients at the surface means that plants do not root deeply; nor do they draw in a wider range of other minerals from the soil. This makes them more vulnerable to extreme weather conditions. Chemical analysis shows that conventional crops have less iron, calcium, protein, and vitamin C than organic crops.

What energizes you? Does your output well up naturally from within you, like plants growing from fertile ground? Or is your production driven by synthetic pressures? In many of the people and organizations I see, output is largely forced.

An easy test of this is whether your main motivators will lead to renewal—or to depletion and pollution. Here are some of the artificial fertilizer equivalents that I see in the typical work situation:

- Fear of losing face, losing your job, or simply losing control
- Systematic pressure through performance culture, controls, targets, deadlines, and aggressive bonus schemes
- Competing for power or prestige
- Pressure from managers, supervisors, or shareholders

By contrast, the main energy sources for organic farming and gardening are natural, plentiful, and free: sun, air, water, waste, and the biological activity in the earth. For many of these forces, the supply can't be controlled but can be shaped, and an organic grower ensures that these resources are harnessed. This is more a matter of stimulating and shaping natural processes than forcing, and it starts with cultivating ground condition.

The plant waste and animal manure on organic fields is a major energy source. Recycling this as compost provides natural fuel for the earth and avoids the costs and problems of disposing of the "waste" while importing artificial fertilizer. Growing crops that renew the energy resources in the soil is another part of the organic way.

Natural Energy in Organizations

The principle of using natural energy to achieve sustained production applies to organizations as well as to individuals. However, applying the organic way is more difficult once we move beyond the individual. Many organizations develop norms, cultures, and operating methods that tend to institutionalize a mechanistic approach.

Although command-and-control hierarchies are unfashionable, newer approaches are often unsustainable. Empowerment and self-direction can leave teams and individuals under even more stress than before because of insufficient skills and support. The pressure for performance keeps growing, and there may be less scope to define expectations and negotiate an acceptable workload. On the other hand, dispersed power structures create more scope for groups or individuals to reshape their way of working.

In moving an organization to natural energy methods, delivering results remains a paramount concern. Unless top management and stakeholders are exceptionally understanding, predictable outcomes are still required. The challenge is to achieve them through organic methods that are inherently less controllable.

There are many ways to make this difficult transition possible. It can be done by evolution, not revolution: developing the skills first, trying new approaches, operating on dual voltage—following two paths at once, delivering results the old-fashioned way while learning new techniques. The key deliverables can be used as a touchstone, a sanity test of each new move. It also helps to form a vision of improving results through natural energy methods, not just maintaining them. Over time, the organic way can achieve higher output, more value, better quality, and closer customer dialogue. You'll find advice about the transition process in Chapter 8.

Seeking a Balance

Most organizations have two main energy problems. They are dependent on forced energy inputs, and they have an imbalance between the four energy elements. They are preoccupied with mental and physical energy, with thinking and doing. In terms of the four elements, there is too much earth and fire and not enough water and air. As a result, the culture, the ground condition, is hard, hot, dry, and compacted. There is little space for the flow of feelings or for the expansive energy arising from genuine vision and inspiration.

The way to correct this energy imbalance is through a mix of intent and technique. If top management or team leaders can change their habits, this change will permeate to others. When people can express and receive feelings, both positive and negative, the ground condition of the organization becomes more fertile and receptive.

Many organizations produce vision, purpose, or value statements. Sadly, many of these are just another synthetic, external input and are regarded skeptically by most people, both within and outside the organization. Often such statements are developed by a handful of people acting unilaterally and in isolation. For a vision to energize an organization, there needs to be scope for people at all levels to contribute, to feel part of a creative dialogue. Too many vision statements grow from mental energy, not from the heart and soul, not from the emotional and truly inspirational levels. The question of how to create and work with a sustainable vision is explored further in Chapter 4.

Applying the Principles

Caradon has been described by a leading venture capitalist as "the most successful management buy-in ever." I was a cofounder of this major building materials group and president of its largest operating division. Within two years we achieved a dramatic turnaround in the business—in profits, market position, morale, and personal fulfillment of the people involved. How did we achieve this? Part of the answer is by applying natural energy principles to our work and to the whole organization.

The Caradon story began in 1985. At that time I was president of Lumex Corporation, an ailing American division of Redland, a major British multinational. My boss and mentor at Redland, Peter Jansen, had a superb eye for acquisitions. He had realized years before that Reed, a large publishing group, would eventually simplify its portfolio and sell off its building products division. He cultivated contacts within Reed and was eventually offered the first look at Reed Building Products when they decided to divest it in 1985.

Peter asked me to look at Reed Building Products with him. We were excited by the prospect. The business was performing poorly, but we could see its potential. In ground condition terms, Reed Building Products was fertile but sleepy soil. We felt inspired and enthused: We could see what the business needed, and we had the vision and skills to achieve it.

Redland turned down our strong recommendation to buy the company. Soon after, Peter hatched the idea of a buy-in, supported by the venture capital. He invited me to join him as his number two, as executive vice president of the group and president of Twyfords Bathrooms, the largest operating division. It was an exciting moment, and I felt completely sure about saying yes to the proposal.

We started Caradon in fall 1985 with $12 million of share capital and $90 million in loans. In the previous year, Reed

> **Too many vision statements grow from mental energy, not from the heart and soul.**

Building Products had made gross profits of $12 million. Two years later, profit was $27 million, and we had repaid a large part of the loans. Less than two years after its founding, Caradon had an initial stock offering, and the offering price was 40 times oversubscribed. The original share capital of $12 million was now worth $228 million, and it rose rapidly thereafter. Caradon went on to become one of Britain's top 100 companies just nine years after it began.

The Power of Clean Energy

Peter Jansen and I both had a highly intuitive approach to our work. This grew from principles that were largely unarticulated, and neither of us was much into formal values statements. Our approach can readily be understood in terms of clean energy principles and the four elements.

Air. The business inspired us, and we inspired it. We felt a passion for the people, the products, brand names, factories, and the customers they served. We had a vigorous, clear sense of vision, seeing the fuller potential in this situation.

People are often demoralized when the business they work for is sold. The reverse was true with Reed Building Products. As many of the employees explained to us, for several years they had sensed that the previous owner had no vision or purpose for the company. Now they knew that their leaders had put their houses on the line to buy into the business. The Caradon era was welcomed as a breath of fresh air.

Bringing air into the organization involved opening it up, creating a more free-flowing culture, with direct personal contact. The previous style had been impersonal and hierarchical, with a preference for written reports. In the early years the Caradon head office had three key people: Peter Jansen, Danny Cohen (our finance director), and me. We moved around the organization a lot, extending our roots into it and opening up the soil structure in the process. We made a point of expressing our enthusiasm about the people and the business, and gradually our inspiration permeated to them. Being shareholders as well as managers, we could link the vision and purpose of the organization as a whole to the operating companies and their particular issues.

Water. The culture we inherited was dry. The language its head office spoke to the operating companies was mostly financial and technical. In contrast, we expressed our feelings and asked others to tell us theirs. There were stacks of issues and inefficiencies to address, but we were working with good-hearted people.

Intriguingly, Caradon's massive debt created camaraderie. No one reproached the new leadership for it. They understood that we had taken a carefully judged business risk and backed it with our personal financial commitment. There was some fear and insecurity about whether we'd succeed and what changes would be needed. But the fear led to action, not rumors and inertia. We encouraged people to voice their fears and anxieties; they learned that these would be heard and considered, with no attempt to reproach or suppress them. By hearing and exploring the negatives, it was possible to clarify and recycle the energy they contained.

One of the qualities of the early Caradon years was flow, a relatively easy forward flow in business initiatives, decisions, and communication. I attribute this largely to the way we brought the feeling element into the culture so that this energy was available to all of us as positive energy. Even the need to lay off several hundred people early on did not knock the appreciation culture. We spoke face to face with the people who were leaving, valuing what they had contributed and admitting our own sadness at having to make the cuts. The response from almost of all those leaving was support and understanding for our approach.

Fire. The amount and quality of mental energy that Caradon applied to turning its businesses around was outstanding. Peter, Danny, and I all had different styles. Mine was like the fire of a blowtorch, probing into blockages, heating up the facts of a situation to expand and reshape it. Peter's fire was more like lamplight, gentle but penetrating. His style was to ask a few questions, but the right ones, and to keep them burning steadily until they were answered. Danny was like an inviting fire in a cottage hearth. He had a conversational style that people warmed to. They would open up naturally to him, and his gentle questioning would elicit crucial information very effectively. People knew that both Peter and Danny had an iron fist inside the

glove; if the easy style didn't work, they would be firm in confronting the issue.

All three of us were keen to stimulate and harness the knowledge and intelligence of the whole organization. We did this with our direct subordinates and encouraged them to do the same. We also chatted with people at every level. The soil structure and the culture opened up so air could circulate and the fire could burn more brightly. The business turnaround was good not only because of strategic thinking at the top, but also because we harnessed mental energy at every level and enabled a mass of operational improvements. This happened through culture and example, and through project teams, consultants, and suggestion schemes—real ones with genuine recognition and rewards.

> **What this soil needed was more biological activity so that the whole organizational organism could become more dynamic.**

Earth. When Caradon began, it had high potential fertility. People were more dormant than depleted. Along with air, water, and heat, what this soil needed was more biological activity so that the whole organizational organism could become more dynamic. We stimulated this in many ways. Exploring previously ignored problems and tapping unused intelligence throughout the organization was similar to activating and recycling an immense pile of waste.

We created a high degree of movement—new connections that often had no immediate performance goal, but that paid off handsomely by stimulating ground condition. For example, Peter, a golf lover, introduced a Caradon Golf Day, which brought together people from all levels and parts of the organization. At Twyfords, I organized visits to the factories for our employees' families and for our customers. Such initiatives created a ground swell that was more valuable than any amount of top-down directives. The whole organization became enthusiastic, with many individuals and teams improving the infrastructure of the business, much as biological activity conditions the soil.

Natural Energy in Daily Practice

Learning to apply clean energy principles in your day-to-day life is like learning a new sport. It takes time and practice to get your eye in, to learn what to look for, and to develop your range of responses. Don't fade if making your early moves feels as if you're taking three steps forward and two steps back. You probably have a range of habits and dependencies to change—not to mention those of people around you.

Asking yourself "How's my energy?" may be too loose to be useful. Checking your ground condition, including the four energy elements, can be a quick and practical approach. Using the tangible analogy of earth (physical), water (emotional), air (inspirational), and fire (mental) should help you with action as well as understanding. Following through on the analogy can give you specific pointers on how to manage your natural energy.

Exercise: The Personal Energy Audit

This audit is designed to give you an overview of your main energy inflows and outflows so that you can set yourself priorities for managing your energy better and so that you can identify issues that may need further investigation. The audit is not intended to be exhaustive and is not a substitute for professional help where needed, such as a comprehensive medical health checkup, advice on diet and exercise tailored to your needs, or counseling regarding major emotional issues.

Use the checklist on pages 62 and 63 to assess the main energy inflows and outflows in your working life. The specific items listed are not meant to be comprehensive; space is provided for you to add other items that are significant for you. *For each item, rate it on a scale of 0 (no flow) to 10 (major inflow or outflow).* As you go through, place an asterisk in the Review Priority column for items you feel need your urgent consideration. Remember that some items may be both a source (inflow) and a use (outflow) of energy.

Initially, do these ratings for your current way of working. You may wish to repeat the process to see how much impact a different approach would have. Also, remember that outflows include those that are desirable and productive *and* those that are a dissipation or misuse of energy. The processes in which you use energy should be considered outflows.

For example, Rick Martin is an architect. His work is not very physically demanding, so he rates it as a small outflow (2). However, he considers his long commute to cause a significant outflow of energy (7). His downtown offices are designed as a conge-

nial, physical environment, so he rates his workplace as giving him an energy inflow (3). Rick rates his diet as mostly healthy, more than offsetting the occasional beer and burger, so diet rates moderately high for energy inflow (6) with only a low rate of outflow (1) for the unhealthy items. Rick is aware that he often feels tense at work, which makes his breathing shallow, so he rates this as a low energy inflow (2) and marks it as a review priority. Rick jogs or works out at a gym several times a week; he feels that this generates a lot more physical energy than it consumes, so he rates his energy inflow relatively high (7) and his outflow as low (2).

When you have finished, add your inflow and outflow scores for each of the four energy types, and then total them. If you are running an energy surplus, congratulations! If you are running an energy deficit in your work, ask yourself how this deficit is being supplied. Are you making high-energy demands in the rest of your life to fund the deficit in your work, or are you exhausting your energy reserves?

As you review your audit, look particularly at items you have marked with an asterisk for further attention. Choose up to five of these as specific priorities for immediate action. Consider how you would like your energy habits to change in these areas, how you can get more advice or information, and how you can set about making a change.

When you start to convert to sustainable methods of work, I recommend that you use the Personal Energy Audit as a way of measuring your progress and steering your priorities. It can also help you make major choices about your job or lifestyle.

The Personal Energy Audit—*Continued*

PHYSICAL	Energy Inflow	Energy Outflow	Review Priority
The activities of your work itself			
Other activity related to your work, e.g. commuting, preparing for work, winding down afterward			
Diet: "healthy," sustaining food/drink "unhealthy" food/drink			
Breathing			
Exercise			
Relaxation			
Other			
Subtotal			

EMOTIONAL	Energy Inflow	Energy Outflow	Review Priority
Self-appreciation or putdown: supporting or blaming yourself when results are not "successful"			
Appreciation or negativity from your boss			
Appreciation or negativity from colleagues at work			
Feelings expressed toward you by people you work with (colleagues, customers)			
The general attitude to feelings where you work: Can feelings be voiced, or are they suppressed?			
The emotional rewards or pressures of your job			
The emotional rewards or pressures of the whole organization			
How do you respond to unexpected changes at work? Are they typically a stimulus or a stress for you?			
Support/antagonism from family and friends			
The emotional rewards or demands of your leisure time/hobbies			
Other			
Subtotal			

MENTAL	Energy Inflow	Energy Outflow	Review Priority
Does your job, and the way you choose to do it, stimulate or exhaust you mentally?			
Does the organization you work for stimulate or exhaust you mentally?			
Is your habitual way of thinking positive and creative, or do you tend to worry and fret and focus on the negatives?			
Do you use both logical and intuitive skills in your work, and integrate them?			
Do uncertainty and conflicting data stimulate or dissipate your mental energy?			
Do your activities outside work (family, friends, hobbies) stimulate or exhaust you mentally?			
Other			
Subtotal			

INSPIRATIONAL	Energy Inflow	Energy Outflow	Review Priority
Do you have a sense of purpose and inspiration in your work?			
Does the organization you work for have a true sense of purpose and service that helps inspire your work?			
Do you have a mentor, boss, or colleague at work who is a role model for you in bringing spiritual energy to work?			
When your work gets demanding or exhausting, can you re-energize yourself by remembering the point of it all?			
Do you have a sense of purpose and inspiration in your life generally?			
In your free time, do you choose activities that inspire you (nature, music, meditation), or do you choose distractions or compensations for stress and fatigue?			
Other			
Subtotal			

GRAND TOTAL _____

chapter 3
COMPOSTING WASTE

THE MOST ABUNDANT AND VALUABLE WASTE in our lives, and in many organizations, is not what goes out in the trash or up the smokestack. Rather, it is human energy waste. The way individuals and organizations operate can create alarming amounts of waste that pollute the atmosphere and our ground resources. I am not talking about environmental waste; I'm talking about the mechanistic use of our human resources and how this approach pollutes the climate of an organization.

One of the basic principles of an organic system is that there is no waste. Every output becomes a useful input. This is not recycling as we know it—reusing scrap paper, glass, or cans. Traditional recycling is a mechanical system, in which you get out less than you put in. And you use substantial energy to achieve even that.

The difference in a natural system is that recycling can be synergistic: You get out *more* usable energy than you put in, and the energy achieving this is mostly clean and costless. To emphasize the difference from mechanical recycling I use the term *composting*.

Composting is by far the most important way an organic grower recycles waste. It involves transforming animal and plant waste into a major energy source for future growth. In essence, composting is a biological process that can be initiated and shaped by human intervention. Using it requires care in collection, handling, and application, but the principles and methods employed in organic growing show how we can harness the fertility of our waste issues at work. As you adopt the principles of ground condition and natural energy in your work, you will develop the capacity to compost human energy waste as a major source of fertility.

This chapter considers four types of human energy waste, aligning with the four elements: physical, emotional, mental, and inspirational. In this context, we can define waste as energy whose form impairs our productivity and sustainability. The waste we are considering here is primarily intangible, although negative energy, such as anger or anxiety, often creates physical stress.

Fire Yourself Up

My personal development time is my research-and-development lab. It's my chance to explore way-out ideas, some of which I refine for the business world. In April 1999 I spent two weeks in Hawaii, learning from a kahuna. This is the name given to teachers of the Hawaiian native tradition, a set of principles evolved through generations of tribal culture and through living closely with the land and ocean. In my first few days with my teacher, Kahu, I was forced to realize that my outlook was narrower and more Western than I had thought.

"Alan, you keep asking how to," Kahu said. "You're looking for techniques again, trying to box me up and pin me down. You should be looking for the goddamn principles." He slammed his fist on the wall—as often, moving from gentle to fierce without pause. Slowly I learned to listen, fully listen, instead of seeking the next cue for a clever question. I realized that whether Kahu was talking about cooking fish, making love, or designing buildings, the principles were visible and they were common to everything.

Each morning we were asked to spend several hours performing strenuous, repetitive physical exercises. I longed for a crisp kickoff presentation, with overheads, to summarize the objectives. All we were told was that this was preparation. After a couple of days I told Kahu, "I can't go on with this. My whole body is aching. I'm exhausted."

Kahu looked keenly at me. "Do you know what I do when I'm tired and flat?" I shook my head. "I get myself angry."

I was stunned. "You mean, you deliberately make yourself angry?"

Kahu flashed me a roguish grin. "Sure. If I've got a big session and I'm down, it's the fastest way to get some energy. Try it. Try getting mad about how pointless these dumb exercises are, and see if it gets you moving." He went off, laughing, to have a coffee break, leaving the group to repeat the same movement for another hour or two.

Keep Moving

The main principle behind the exercises Kahu gave us was to keep moving. "Whatever comes up, whatever you feel, bring it into the movement, don't stop."

Now that I let myself, I got really furious about these exercises, being left in a room to do them for hours with no explanation. The effect of this anger on my body was powerful and actually delightful. Instead of dragging myself through the movements slowly, with aching limbs, my whole body was energized. The movements became easy, and by lunchtime I felt refreshed, not depleted. I thought how differently I'd have handled this in a typical workshop. I would have sneaked out of the group and gone for a coffee break, with my negative feelings festering, suppressed.

A Time to Rant

A few weeks later, I had the chance to apply Kahu's teachings in earnest. I was immersed in writing this book, and I felt completely stuck. The writing was going slowly and lacked sparkle. The publisher was niggling, and I felt tired, dejected. Then I remembered a scene from my favorite Marx Brothers' movie, *Duck Soup*. Groucho Marx, as Rufus T. Firefly, President of the tin-pot republic of Fredonia, winds himself into a fury over a trifling insult.

I strode up and down the length of the room, ranting grandly, trusting that my secretary next door would understand as usual. "This is pathetic," I told myself loudly. "A man of all my talents floundering around like this! Eight pages in two days! It's appalling; I can do better than this. Just watch me!" If a waterlogged field gets air and warmth, it becomes highly fertile very quickly. In the same way, by applying purpose and mental energy to my dejection, I got myself moving productively. My feelings of discouragement were useless waste, but there was plenty of power in them to be harnessed.

The Alchemy of Compost

The ancient alchemists sought to turn base matter into gold. Composting achieves this. It starts with rubbish, animal excrement, rotting vegetable matter, straw, even weeds. All this "waste," which is useless in these forms, ends up as humus, which is highly fertile, rich in biological activity, and able to renew the earth's vitality. Composting has many hallmarks of a natural process. It is complex in detail, but simple in concept; it's powerful and clean; and it's synergistic— you get more out than you put in. One study found that it takes one-fourth as much compost as ordinary manure to produce the same yields.

Think about all the stress, conflicts, and failures that are never faced, and of all the things that workers murmur about to their buddies but never say to their bosses. Like most so-called waste, human energy waste is full of energy and value, and we just have to figure out how to convert it.

The composting cycle in organic growing provides a superb blueprint for recycling human energy waste in the workplace. In growing, this is a physical process that needs to run its course over several months. With human energy waste, the process can take anywhere from seconds to years. It can be applied to minor operational issues or to such fundamentals as the purpose of your work.

In the work context, composting is a process that individuals and teams can learn to apply themselves. However, it is a powerful transformational process requiring experience and specific skills. It may be wise to get professional aid to help you recycle the most difficult waste: emotional and spiritual issues and interpersonal conflicts. I offer direct guide-lines for going through the process yourself, but use discretion about when to do so unaided.

There are several methods of composting. Some depend on the use of air: They are aerobic. Some depend on excluding air: They are anaerobic. The temperature in the process may be cool, warm, or hot. I have chosen to talk here about hot aerobic composting because it offers the best parallel for the human system.

7 Tips for Successful Composting

This summary of the main principles of hot aerobic composting shows how they apply to human energy waste.

Collection

To get the benefit of the composting process, waste materials have to be gathered and brought together. This is a significant investment of labor, and when you're dealing with animal excrement, it may not be very pleasant! In the same way, your first step is to identify and gather the waste in your work. This requires patience, good observation, and resilience. Your waste may include difficult feelings and project failures that have a pungent smell and that you would rather bury.

Finding your waste takes both peripheral and focused vision. You need to see where the waste has been buried and suppressed or thrown out to the edges of your ecosystem, the equivalent of waste ground where trash gets dumped. Start with physical waste, reviewing tensions and ailments. Then consider mental waste: contradictions, unresolved questions. Why did that project fail? Why did that customer really switch his or her account? Facing such questions reveals their emotional content. Many issues that may seem entirely rational also involve our feelings. Observe your feelings as clearly as you can. This is all part of the collection stage.

Next gather the emotional waste, identifying the tensions and where you feel stressed in your work. Delve into this, identify the sources of the tensions, such as particular responsibilities or relationships. Keep breathing as you do this, aerating the compost. Explore any negative feelings, such as fear, anxiety, uncertainty, and anger, that you have in your work. Use as much mental clarity as you can to understand the causes of these feelings. Think of these waste feelings as a flow of energy that has been impeded, and see what outcome would unblock that energy. What is it your energy wants to flow toward? Maybe you're angry because someone has not acknowledged you, or perhaps you're fearful because you

Keep believing that there's gold in your muck, a positive reason for the upheavals.

haven't faced the implications of losing your job and the constructive alternatives this could open up.

Negative inspirational energy can be the most depleting and the most difficult to face. A sense of pointlessness about your work is like a major pollution problem—pervasive and hard to clear. Use the parallel with air pollution. It can arise from a single main source, such as a dirty factory, or from a diffuse problem, such as road traffic. Either way, a systemic change is probably needed, a switch to clean energy sources and processes, including recycling.

In counseling it is often said that when you express a problem, you're already halfway to resolving it. Gathering and identifying your waste issues is a significant step in the recycling process. It helps to record and describe the issues in detail; record both the facts and your feelings, and don't just use shorthand labels. Avoid judging yourself or the issue as much as possible.

Heaping

The waste needs to be heaped up so that there is a sufficient mass of material for the biological processes to start and sustain themselves. If the heap is too low, the process may not begin. If it is too high or dense, parts of the heap will lack air and the process will be incomplete.

Pile your problems on top of each other and heap up the waste. Spreading your negatives thinly or scattering them at the edges of your field will not recycle the toughest ones and won't give you the maximum juice. Adopt Peter Norman's approach of sending in the pigs: "Sometimes in farming, when you're in a bit of a mess, the best way through is to make a complete mess, churn it all up good and proper." You are initiating a process that may be scary, that is beyond your conscious control, but that can really move you forward.

You build your compost heap by facing your waste issues fully and deeply. Be prepared to face them all, whatever aspect of your work they relate to, whatever type of energy level they represent. If this leaves you feeling overwhelmed or in despair, allow the feeling, observe it, and don't deny it or judge it. Keep your sense of purpose and perspective; remember that you are more than your feelings. Adapt this Buddhist mantra: "I feel fearful, but I am not my fear." And ensure that you have support available to you.

What do you want to achieve? Know that you have the power to choose.

Air Supply

A plentiful supply of air is essential to fuel the biological activity in the hot aerobic composting process. If the air supply is inadequate, some or all of the heap will not reach peak temperature, desired breakdowns will not occur in the waste material, and weed seeds will not be killed.

At the most basic level, this means that when you feel strong emotions, keep breathing! It also means that you have to sustain your composting process by af-firming your sense of purpose and perspective. Keep believing that there's gold in your muck, a positive reason for the upheavals. You need inspirational energy to fuel this transformation.

Water Content

The ideal moisture content in a compost heap is quite high: 55 to 70 percent. As with ground condition, too much or too little will stifle activity. If the heap is waterlogged, air is excluded, and the compost pile will not heat up.

Relating this to your work, if you are too dry, if you deny or repress your feelings, the composting process will be inhibited. Exploring the issues with a friend or counselor may give you the encouragement and safety to get your feelings flowing. Conversely, if you are swamped by your emotions and the compost heap is soaked, the waste will rot, not transform. In this situation, your compost needs more heat and air: mental clarity, constructive inquiry, and a sense of perspective.

Heat

High temperature is central to this process of transforming muck into gold. Microorganisms combine with air and moisture to generate heat through decomposing the waste. As the temperature rises, the more complex material is broken down and becomes fuel to continue the process. At its peak, the heat may reach 160°F.

Relating this process to the four human energy elements, it highlights the importance of our intelligence in composting our energy waste. The process should generate heat—mental energy—which can then take the process further. You should find that composting your waste issues generates fresh understanding, which allows for clear thinking to move you forward.

Turning

To get the full benefit of the process, it is common to turn the compost pile after a few weeks. Turning means inverting the compost to aerate it. This is done in the cooling-down phase and initiates a repeat of the cycle. Turning the compost heap increases the air supply and renews the recycling process. The effect is to achieve fuller breakdown of the waste and to raise the humus content. In your own composting program, this means reviewing your progress occasionally, bringing in the qualities, air, purpose, and perspective.

My experience of human energy composting is that the process runs its own course and has its own momentum. It can be distressing and tiring, but I have learned to trust the process. It's important during such times to take care of yourself: Rest when you can. But as with most organic processes, you can't fully control it. Periodically I am aware of things churning away within me, and sometimes I have to give it my attention. But I don't have to make it happen, and I can't force the pace.

Application

The timing and method of applying compost are important to derive full benefit from it. The aim is to incorporate the compost into the soil as quickly and fully as possible. In this way, the extra humus acts as a catalyst for the rest of the soil. The ideal season for application is autumn—the compost will stimulate further buildup of fertility in time for the demands of spring crops. Frequent spreading in thin layers is preferable to one heavy application.

The main moral of this for workplace waste is about timing. It is best to recycle your waste some time before you place a peak output demand on yourself. Allow time for absorption.

Make Friends with Your Weeds

In conventional growing, weeds are simply seen as undesirable waste products to be stamped out as fully as possible. For the organic grower, weeds are a good example of the gift in the problem. I remember asking Peter Norman at Magdalen Farm how he deals with weeds. He replied, "The first thing to understand is the message. When you get a particular species of weed in a particular place, it'll tell you something quite specific that you need to respond to. For example, if I see buttercups or coltsfoot, I know the drainage is poor. If I see nettles or docks, it tells me the nitrogen level is high."

The conventional grower's approach to weeds treats them as an enemy to be eliminated. The organic grower treats weeds more like the mainstream treats a dissident minority group: They may seem antagonistic to the mainstream, but fruitful coexistence is possible. Weeds can actually assist the main plants. Sometimes they attract pests away from the crops; often they are home to predators that will consume the pests before the pests consume the main plants. Hence, organic growers will leave wide field margins for the weeds to grow, and they may even include weed strips interspersed in large fields.

Can you see a parallel here for your work? Do you or your organization stamp out anything or anyone that diverges from the immediate output task? If you find a dissident voice in yourself or your team, I suggest you treat it in the same way the organic grower handles weeds. Learn from it, tolerate it, keep it within reasonable bounds, and see how to use it instead of eradicating it. The alternative is likely to be progressively declining fertility and rising ground pollution.

Fertility from Conflict

Financial Friends was a small client for me, just a two-person partnership, but their problems looked so thorny that I was drawn by the challenge. Phil and Marion Wood had started this business while they were married and had set it up as a formal partnership when they divorced, four years before I met them. Their business was financial advice, selling pension plans and life insurance to private individuals. Marion dealt with generating sales leads, handling inquiries, appointments, and paperwork. Phil met with the clients and wrote the proposals.

"I never thought I'd say this, but I'm sick of this business." Phil sat slumped behind his desk. "I've no taste for it any more. It's messing up my whole life. It's depressing me.

Marion sat stiffly, her arms crossed, and looked at him witheringly. "You always get so dramatic, you take it all personally. I wish you'd face the practical side." She turned to me. "The basic problem, Alan, is that the business is underperforming. I think it's due to some kind of communication block between Phil and me. That's what we want you to fix."

I had a strong sense of two people hooked on their own, irreconcilable scripts. In ground condition terms, Phil was waterlogged, and Marion was dry and as hard as rock. It was a daunting task to engender openness and flow so that they could explore the real issues and communicate with each other. I suggested that the best next step was an individual session for me with each of them, and they welcomed this idea with relief.

As I prepared for my session with Marion, I was unsure how to reach her.

FLAME WEEDING

This is another useful way to compost negative energy, especially unsettling emotions. With practice you can use this in real-time, whenever difficult feelings come up for you.

Imagine there is a flame above your head, a violet-silver flame. As you become aware of negative feelings or other tensions, see where they are located in your body. Then, as you breathe in, imagine lifting this negative energy up above your head and into the flame, which will transform it. As you breathe out, imagine clean, positive energy coming down from the flame, and flowing into your body as you exhale and receive this composted energy.

Beneath her hard crust of logical criticism, I suspected she had buried a lot of feelings about the marriage and the business partnership with Phil. I took my usual park-and-ride approach: using my conscious mind to clarify the question, and then leaving my subconscious to come up with an answer. That afternoon, driving in sultry June weather, I started to think about thunderstorms. When it gets really hot for a while, summer storms can blow up and give you torrential rain. I started laughing; I realized that this gave me an approach with Marion. I could see how a natural process could help her open to the water element and start moving feelings that were clogging and polluting her system.

Stoking Up a Storm

When we met, I was even more analytical than Marion. I plied her with questions, and we piled up a stack of observations on the problems of the business. Most of them were caused by Phil. Although she stayed sharply logical, I could sense that Marion was getting increasingly tense and heated as the issues were heaped together. I sought to step up the heat and to lead her toward expressing her feelings. Aiming to pile the waste higher, I voiced my own emotions about it strongly. At the same time, I made a link to the air element and the overall vision of the business. My guiding image was of the hot, sultry wind that often precedes a summer storm.

"Marion," I said, "I feel really upset by all these concerns you are listing. These are major problems, serious."

"Very serious." Marion was twisting her hands as she spoke.

"I've got to tell you, I feel really worried for the future of the business. You and Phil have both put so much into this partnership, it's got so much potential, but it's obviously under serious threat."

"Very serious." Marion was staring into space.

"What also really upsets me, Marion, is how this affects you. Where does this situation leave you? I can't imagine how you're feeling."

"Feeling!" The storm broke. She leapt to her feet, shouting, picked up the vase from her dining table, and threw it so hard that it shattered against the wall. "Feeling! I want to kill him! How can I get it right with a man like that?"

For some time Marion stormed on, alternating between expressing her rage at Phil and weeping with a pent-up mixture of sadness, pain, and frustration. Remembering how the heat needs to rise in the early stage of composting, I urged her to let the feelings flow instead of trying to calm her down.

As Marion became quieter, I raised questions about purpose and perspective to aerate and turn the compost. "Do you still have a sense of vision for Financial Friends?" I asked her. "How would you like to see the business develop from here?"

These questions certainly renewed the composting process. I was impressed that Marion was already combining feelings, thoughts, and perspective. "Alan, the point is, Financial Friends *is* Phil and me. You can't have a vision for this business without a vision of how the two of us relate. That's what I feel desperate about."

"Desperate?"

"Well, desperate in my confusion. I have this sense that we have negative patterns between us that go back for years, and we're exhausted from them. But what I can't see at all is, can both of us change enough to make it work properly?"

Stir Things Up

The ferment intensified again. I felt I was coaching an improvisational jazz quartet, using my questions to draw in whichever of the four elements seemed faintest.

Marion started pacing restlessly around the room. I took this as a good sign that her energy was getting moving. "It's always been like this with Phil. I try to do my part perfectly. Then if there's any problem, it must be his fault."

I nodded. "So how do you feel toward him now?"

She clenched her fists. "Angry! Oh yes, angry. I'm furious, in fact."

I stood up and came closer to her. "So what I suggest is intensify the feeling. Picture the scenes that upset you, remember how the business is suffering, and feel your fury. Speak to him."

She kept pacing the room, and I could see the tension rising in her body until at last she started shouting. As the raw rage passed, the fertile insight that emerged was: "I can't achieve anything except through you, Phil."

At this point, I intervened. "So you're still furious, but now you can see why. Right?"

She nodded. "Right."

"Keep feeling the fury, and ask yourself a question. Forget Phil: What would you like to do with this anger? You've got this terrific energy you've unleashed: How do you want to use it? Imagine that you can achieve things without him. What do you want to achieve? Keep walking, keep feeling the anger, but breathe it, circulate it."

She looked puzzled. "What do you mean, circulate it?"

I came over and stood next to her. "Where in your body do you feel the anger?"

She held her stomach. "Here. Definitely."

"OK. So as you breathe, imagine breathing this anger up your spine, through your brain, down to your heart, and back to your stomach. Think of the anger as steam: It's scalding, but there's a power you can harness. Picture these questions like the pistons in a steam engine: You feed the anger in, and you can get forward motion out."

There was a long silence. Marion walked slowly around the room. I could actually watch the cycle of her breathing in, moving the energy up, confronting the question, and then releasing the energy to continue the cycle. After a while she sat down, eyes closed, still composting. Eventually she opened her eyes and smiled at me.

The fastest way to get some energy is to make yourself mad.

"This is such a relief," she said. "At least I've got past blaming someone else. I can see that I'm quite skilled and capable, though I have blind spots, too. I'm no good at selling. But I don't have to depend on Phil for it." Her energy was shining as she smiled at me. "When I know I have the power to choose, it gets clear. We could bring in a second sales consultant, and I can channel the leads through that person. Or we could dissolve the partnership, and I could use my skills elsewhere."

"And how do you feel about those options?"

"I'm happy with either of them. I just feel confident I won't have to live with the crap any more."

Draining the Swamp

My initial session with Phil was quite different, but also fruitful. What he needed was air and drainage, not air and water. Feeling swamped by a sense of helplessness and hopelessness was a familiar and even comfortable place for him, his way of escaping blame. He was reluctant to open to a sense of purpose or perspective, which would aerate the compost heap.

I helped him find purpose by asking him to remember the vision and excitement he felt at the start of the business. I also pressed him to face the implications of things going on as they were. We began to analyze his feelings and the repetitive patterns between him and Marion. This helped to drain off some of his emotion and bring his mental energy to bear, raising heat to help the process.

When the three of us met again, the energy of the session was clean and vibrant. They both wanted to move forward, to agree on an overall goal for the business and on steps to achieve it. They could see that when Marion denied emotion and Phil drowned in it, the issues never got faced. "I'll tell you what, Marion," Phil said. "I'd like to agree to a no-blame clause between us."

Marion smiled. "What do you mean?"

"Let's say we won't blame each other for the fix we're in. We are where we are. I want to decide where we go next, not whose fault it was in the first place."

My work with Financial Friends is ongoing, although it's progressing slowly. It is too soon to say whether sustainable principles will take root in the business. There have been some lasting changes in Marion; she is stronger in herself, more independent, and able to use and express her emotional energy. She has also found some independent channels for her abilities. Although Phil has responded positively in our sessions together, he has been reluctant to change his old habits. It is still easier for him to wallow in helplessness than to come out and face the issues. The potential synergy of the partnership has not yet been achieved, but like many natural processes, change on this scale has its own pace and can't be forced.

Storming Forward

Virosoft had all the signs of a successful company: office lights burning until 9:00 P.M., flashy cars out front, marriages seething, and people suddenly becoming ill. I had been asked to work with the executive board to improve their effectiveness as a team and ease the organization's growing pains. The company had a highly profitable niche in the software business for virus checkers. It was my first experience with a firm that was doubling in size each year.

The company was the brainchild of Aziz Khan, a brilliant and charming software engineer in his mid-30s. A Pakistani immigrant, he started Virosoft in 1993 when he was only 31. As I got to know Aziz, I could see that his complex character had both blessed and cursed the company. He integrated three different aspects. First, he was likable and approachable: He saw Virosoft as a family and he lived it. People of all ages and at all levels talked of him as being like a brother. Aziz was also a technical genius: He had created and patented a breakthrough in virus checkers, under the nose of far larger competitors. His third strength was a natural commercial awareness. He came from a family of merchants and traders, and his instinct for the customer was superb. He cheerfully admitted that he supervised the finances by watching the cash balance, as if he were running a market stall, but it worked.

The Unhappy Family

In the first three years, Virosoft had grown from 6 people to 14, then to 30, then to 60. During this time Aziz was able to provide the necessary linkages himself. By 1997 the organization was expanding, as planned, from 60 to 130 people, and Aziz was busy with international growth. At this stage, everyone was frustrated. People diverged in their views of the problems and potential solutions, but a sense of confusion and "stuckness" was pretty universal.

Aziz hated conflict. On a one-on-one level he could charm his way through it, but he suppressed any debate at board meetings. He had no idea how to lead an unhappy family, let alone one this size. After our groundwork, my colleague Gill and I met with Aziz alone. It took some tough talking and frequent reminders about the profit problems to persuade him to face these issues with the board. Over half of Virosoft's whole team were engineers. As Gill and I considered how to create a common language for the company, we felt it needed both technical rigor and human content. We decided to use Myers-Briggs, one of the leading psychometric tests, since it would provide objective measurements and descriptions of personality differences.

In our first workshop with the executive board, our aim was simply to start creating openness, safety, and understanding. We had already debriefed and coached each director on personal profiles. In the workshop we didn't name the individuals, but we showed the team their collective picture. For example, of the twelve board members, seven were mainly led by thinking, and five were led by feeling. Six preferred a structured approach, while six preferred a fluid, pragmatic approach. Eight judged themselves mainly by their own internal standards, and four, by others' views of them. We emphasized that there were no value judgments in these classifications, and it was not better to be one type or another; they were simply different.

The effect of this analytical clarity was like warm sun on frozen ground. The mood of the group lightened and opened. Individuals started to disclose their own profiles. There were laughing exchanges across the table, as different types understood the reasons for previous misunderstandings.

Addressing the Waste

It was in the second workshop that we initiated a composting process within the team. To maintain the airflow, to give overall shape and purpose, we anchored the session on the needs of the business. We had observed that generally the waste issues, the problems, were being ignored.

> **The waste issues, the problems, were generally being ignored.**

Individual vice presidents were doing their own thing, tackling the urgent and not the essential, or escaping on overseas trips. We asked each of them to come to the meeting with a list of their nine most important issues: three for the whole business, three for their departments, and three for their own work. We deliberately didn't ask them to bring solutions: We wanted to stoke up the sense of frustration as the fuel for deeper change.

At the start of the workshop, the finance director raised a question: "If some of our issues involve a disagreement with someone else here, do you want us to explore them?"

"You mean, is it OK to acknowledge conflicts between you?" I replied.

"Yes." There was a tense silence. Everyone looked at Aziz.

Aziz paused, sighed, and then spoke out. "Look, you know I can't stand conflict. To be honest, I feel sick at the prospect of sitting here with you openly disagreeing with each other." He shook his head and sighed again. "I know Alan and Gill believe we're stuck because we won't face differences. I guess we can't resolve them till we face them. So, yes, I do want you to acknowledge the conflicts. We're just going to have to trust each other. I mean, that's how it should be in a family." He reached out and grasped the hands of the colleagues on each side of him. Suddenly we had a circle of hands all round the table, and the alchemy had begun.

The Negative Brainstorm

Gill and I encouraged the team to treat this as a brain dump, a kind of negative brainstorm. We asked them to name their issues and own their feelings about them. "If you have feelings toward a colleague here," I said, "express them, even if they're negative. The one ground rule I ask you to follow is to speak in 'I' not 'you' statements. To say 'I feel angry and let down by you' is your opinion, to which you're always entitled. To tell someone 'you're annoying and unreliable' is a foul, so avoid it."

"And another thing," Aziz put in. "I want you to treat me as one of the team for this session. If you've got a conflict with me, tell me. Just because I couldn't stand it before, don't hold back from arguing with each other now." He grinned and held up a hand. "I've still got a few nails left to chew."

After that, the heap gathered rapidly. We asked people to voice issues as they arose. This enabled them to start with the easier issues and voice the emotive ones as they felt safer. Gill and I encouraged them, urged them to voice their feelings,

and threw in a dash of reason or purpose as needed to keep us on track. Often the response Gill or I gave to issues was analytical. We wanted to encourage the vice presidents themselves to be observant and to relate their problems to the needs of the business. We knew that a group of 12 people who were mostly new to voicing or responding to strong feelings about their work would find this process powerful and difficult. We chose to err on the side of safety, even if the compost did not reach peak heat this time. Sometimes we needed to fuel the fire, but more often we showed the others how to manage it.

At one point Salim Hussain, the technical director, got quite angry about his conflicting goals. He pointed at the sales director and at Aziz. "You two have pushed me into an impossible situation, and I'm damn well sick of it."

"Will you spell out what's upsetting you, Salim?" I asked.

"For one thing, you"—he nodded at Aziz—"tie me down with all these clever calculations. Engineer man-weeks, project time-weeks. You pin my bonus and appraisal on completing the development projects on time."

Aziz spread his hands wide in a peaceable gesture. "But Salim, you agreed to all that with me. Where's the problem?"

Salim almost sneered at him. "I suppose you think that's all we do in my group, develop new software? Well it's not. Because you"—he turned on the

> **The one ground rule is to speak in "I" statements, not "you" statements.**

sales director—"are always on my back, telling me you need us to give your customers technical support. You have no idea how much time these queries take." He turned to the group. "And as long as Mr. Big Promises keeps putting our name on the line...."

"Hang on, Salim," I intervened. "I can see you're upset, but can you back off calling names? Stay with how it feels for you."

Salim looked at the sales director. "I'm sorry."

"It's okay," he nodded.

"Salim," Gill asked, "how much of your department's time is this customer support taking up?"

Salim frowned. "It's over 30 percent."

Aziz exploded: "Thirty percent of your whole capacity! No wonder you're behind on development projects. Why haven't you raised this before?"

Salim gripped the table tensely. "Look, you don't like conflict, you don't like problems. I'm trying to please everyone, so I just do the best I can."

Trusting my intuition despite my ignorance, I asked, "Are the customer queries mostly on one product?"

Salim looked surprised at the question, but answered. "Yes, they're nearly all on Maxim One."

"And is it certain types of installation?" the sales director asked.

"Sure." Salim was becoming calmer as he moved back into technicalities. "It's the bigger, older installations, hybrids."

The operations director interrupted. "Surely they're using it beyond the spec?"

He looked sharply at the sales director. "Have we checked that?"

The sales director colored. "I don't know. I'll certainly see."

"If that's the case, can't we sell them an upgrade?"

At this point, I intervened: "I'd like each of you to give me a one-word snapshot of how you're feeling at this point."

They answered: "Angry," "tense," "mad," "frustrated," "I wish I wasn't here," "overwhelmed," "angry."

"Thank you," I said. "So there are quite a lot of strong feelings and tension in the room. I hope you aren't finding that surprising or alarming because I certainly don't. You've been doing superbly at handling some highly charged issues, and I really want to show my appreciation of how well you've all dealt with this. At this stage, I'd like to ask you to join with me in attempting a way of harnessing some of this negative energy. Are you willing to try something?"

There were cautious nods. I went on: "This is a short exercise I call stand-up comics. The aim is to get the tension moving and start composting it into positive energy. Can you all stand up, please? Now, let your body stretch, ease the tense parts. And try making some funny faces and a few sounds—it all helps to get the energy moving. Aziz will show you how."

Aziz leapt to the challenge, and soon they were all groaning, grimacing, and laughing at one another. The atmosphere in the room eased dramatically.

"Excellent," I said. "And now, stand tall, with your knees relaxed, and take some really long, deep breaths, right down into your stomach. Imagine you're breathing right into your tension, and on the out breath, imagine the tension becoming a positive flow of energy, up your spine and through your brain. Try the principle of 'don't get mad, get moving.' Imagine how you want to use this energy productively; let's put it into the business of this session."

As we moved the workshop on to solutions, the level of participation and the quality of people's interactions were impressive to all of us.

Sweet Release

After this workshop, I questioned Salim, "Were you intending to discuss your workload in that session?"

He shook his head, smiling gently. "No way. Until now I've always kept my trash in the can; showing it to colleagues just gives them the ammunition to shoot at me. But today, I was somehow carried along by the heat of the group, and I'm glad."

Over a period of months, we brought the principles of open communication and composting into the Virosoft culture. Initially our focus was on Aziz and his team, combining one-on-one coaching sessions and a series of group workshops, where we addressed business issues, team dynamics, and the link between them. As the new skills and cycles took root with the vice presidents, we moved on to run cross-functional three-day workshops that included every manager and supervisor. The first evening of each workshop was a composting session, which we invited one or two vice presidents to attend. The energy and the information released in these sessions were tremendous, and the benefits continued long after the workshops.

Composting Waste in Organizations

In any energy process, the ideal is to use clean fuel and clean methods that achieve the result without pollution. The typical approaches in many organizations are far from this: They often rely on forced-energy inputs. These processes may seem logistically efficient, but they make poor use of human energy, and they generate waste problems that are rarely addressed.

Corporate Waste

Here are a few examples of how energy waste can arise in working relationships:

- Back-biting between production and sales departments, blaming each other for delivery problems
- Unresolved tensions between an old-school, highly analytical boss and an intuitive, creative subordinate

- A project team making superhuman efforts preparing a bid for a major contract, but finding it awarded to a competitor
- Two managers jockeying for position, competing for power, both wanting to succeed the current chief executive
- A company hitting quality problems, with sales dropping, and with 20 percent of the workforce suddenly cut, leaving the rest of the workers feeling insecure

I have seen two main obstacles to the composting approach in organizations. One is the reluctance of key individuals. Phil Morris at Alibi Publishing, described in Chapter 1, admitted to me, "I have one speed, and that's fast-forward." He did not have the patience or the skills to slow down and compost the fertile mess of divergent views, dissatisfactions, or setbacks. The other obstacle is that the culture and habits of many companies institutionalize waste suppression. A performance culture can easily be a pretext for ignoring the deeper issues. When results go off plan, pressure is applied simplistically to push them back on plan, instead of understanding and using the divergent influence. It is much like the way an intensive farm suppresses the weeds instead of learning from them and using them.

Human energy waste is one of the biggest potential energy sources for an organization. There are also many other forms of corporate waste that can be composted. One is failure: a job assignment that didn't work out, a product launch that failed, a project that is abandoned. It takes resilience and patience to acknowledge and explore such setbacks, but they can be a valuable source of fertile humus to improve performance.

Corporate Composting Processes

Although the habits and processes of conventional organizations such as Virosoft may perpetuate waste suppression, there are proven processes that can develop composting skills and help the habit to take root. Here are some examples:

- Training in assertiveness and conflict-resolution skills
- Using a facilitator to help a team process waste-energy issues, as in the Virosoft case; ideally, this should be combined with individual coaching sessions to develop and practice the relevant interpersonal skills.
- The creation of peer support groups as a way of learning relevant skills off-line and providing mutual support to apply these skills
- Establishing forums for open space, two-way dialogue, both vertically and horizontally through the organization
- Telephone support lines and face-to-face sessions with independent counselors
- An all-hands meeting: periodic gatherings of everyone who works in the organization; while these are sometimes used only for top-down messages, they are more productive but less predictable if open questioning and debate are encouraged.

Composting Waste in Daily Practice

As you can probably see, the first three principles of the Natural Advantage are interdependent. You need to start cultivating your ground condition and converting to natural energy in order to compost your waste effectively. Recycling requires a number of new habits. The first is to notice and gather waste, instead of ignoring it and pushing it away. The Personal Energy Audit on page 61 can help you locate your waste, as can the guidelines mentioned earlier in this chapter.

The tool kit in Chapter 9 includes two methods that can help you with composting: connected breathing, and negative energy recycling, a valuable tool for changing unhelpful patterns.

As you start to gather your waste, you should find that some of it recycles almost instantly, without the need for a composting process. Simply noticing and naming a problem can be enough to show you how to use it. However, some waste is more difficult to compost, and you may have to live with the discomfort of the process for some time. This is where the techniques of creative tension, described in the next chapter, are useful.

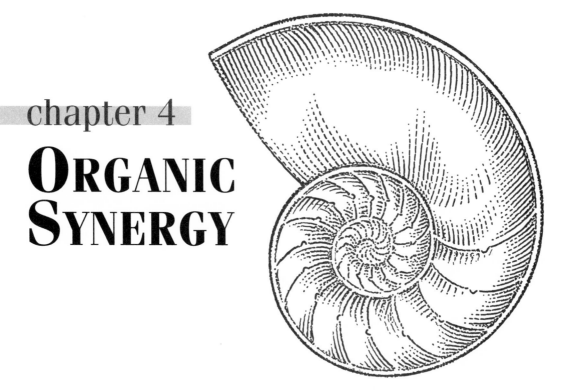

chapter 4

ORGANIC SYNERGY

THE ORGANIC WAY is not about letting nature take its course any more than it's about forcing output. Rather, it's about harnessing and shaping natural resources and processes to grow value. The key to achieving this Natural Advantage is what I call *cocreativity*: the art of creating output by cooperating with natural forces instead of overriding them. Working cocreatively means integrating apparently conflicting qualities, such as push and flow, activity and receptiveness, the planned and the unexpected. In this way, we come to find the gift in the problem that often emerges from the synergy of uncertainties.

The idea of bringing polarities—apparently opposing qualities—together in our work is not a new concept. For example, the "both/and" approach, being both active and receptive, is something we are now familiar with. However, cocreativity is more similar to multiplication than to addition: A × B, not just A + B. It is the process of integrating opposing qualities that cultivates the synergy between them.

Synergy is when 1 + 1 = 3: When you use a problem to move you to a more fruitful outcome. The root meaning of *synergy* is "energy together," and it is a characteristic of natural growth: By combining energies, the whole is greater than the parts. The idea that the output can be greater than the inputs may seem contradictory, but in natural processes, the quality, the usable energy of the output, can far exceed the energy of the inputs. This helps to explain how organic synergy regenerates resources: Composting and building soil life are two examples of this process.

Many individuals and organizations try to eliminate uncertainty, to push it out of the picture. They seek to control people and events to achieve results according to a preordained plan. This mechanistic approach is exhausting for all those involved, and it cannot continue to deliver results in a world as changeable as ours. This approach is especially tough on the leaders, who are expected to know how to overcome every challenge to execute a plan, often by any means necessary.

Cocreativity and synergy offer a sustainable alternative. The approach here is like sailing a yacht instead of steering a powerboat. It's an art and a process, as well as a technique.

The Art of Organic Synergy

"We have been growing herb plants for over 15 years now, starting with a few excess plants from our own garden," explained Alex and Hilary Duthie in a 1996 feature story that appeared in *New Farmer & Grower* magazine. "The range of varieties we grow now numbers about 400 . . . We have tried as many different organic growing media as we can get hold of . . . [and] pests and diseases are not a great problem. The rusts which plague conventional chemical herb growers just do not seem to appear."

You won't find the words synergy and cocreativity on most organic growers' lips; nor will these words show up in their handbooks. Yet these concepts are fundamental to their ability to work successfully with nature. Kahu, the teacher I met in Hawaii, urged me not to box him up or pin him down, not to dissect lived wisdom into a list of techniques. The principles of organic growing can't be reduced to a formula any more than art can; these principles are more like the quality of good ground condition—a living organism with natural vitality and adaptability.

Living with the Land

Traditionally, growing skills have been passed from generation to generation. The young farmer learned a mass of information and skills by experience, living with the cycles of the land for years. Then came modern intensive farming, what Peter Norman calls recipe farming: "You just call up your feed and chemical suppliers, and they send you a mix. The last thing those big chemical companies want a farmer to do is think creatively; they want to be paid for that."

Although organic growing builds on traditional methods, many of these methods have to be continually reinvented. For one thing, there are always new pollutants, pests, and weather conditions to deal with. And as Dirk Hoostra, my partner at Magdalen Farm, used to tell me, "Every piece of land is different. You have to live with it for years before you understand it." Also, the land area in the United States that is farmed organically more than doubled in the mid-1990s, and many of those coming into organic farming didn't have the benefit of growing up in farming families and acquiring years of experience. Add to this the staggering variety of food that consumers now demand, and the broad range of distribution channels, and you'll see why farmers have had to learn fast.

> If you can relax into uncertainty and cultivate receptive observation, synergy will emerge.

Dealing with Uncertainty

All growers have to cope with major uncertainties, but their responses can be very different. The conventional grower seeks to turn a fluid, natural system into an artificial, mechanical one. By chemically controlling fertility and the suppression of pests, he tries to regulate the situation and impose a predictable result. This goal echoes the intent of such business practices as total quality assurance, process re-engineering, and other schemes that seek to sanitize the messiness of real life and codify it into orderly but artificial stability. The trouble with this approach is that you usually need a mess to create synergy.

Organic growers produce results amid more uncertainty and with less control than any other managers I know. This requires skills such as observation, humility, and inventiveness, along with traditional management qualities such as drive and intelligence. It's certainly not an easy thing to learn the art of organic synergy just from reading about it in a book, and so I have included two longer case histories in this chapter to illustrate the concept in practice.

The Organic Way

The personal growth of Dirk Hoostra, described in the next section, is typical of the organic way. The incidents illustrate the organic principle that by staying with the mess of setback and uncertainty, you reach a synergistic solution: one that addresses root causes, not symptoms, and promotes the harvest of practical knowledge from a problem.

Weeds and pests are a good example of problems that can be solved with this kind of solution. An organic field may seem to be vulnerable because it doesn't use chemicals to suppress weeds and pests. In practice, a cultivated natural system will keep the problems in manageable proportions. The biological activity in healthy soil is resistant to threats, just as a healthy person's immune system prevents infection from taking root. Weeds and pests will be present, but they don't take over. It may look messy, but the problems also serve a purpose; they actually contribute to the resilience and productivity of the land. And the organic farmer uses them for feedback, adjusting the system as necessary.

The equivalent for you and your work is to cultivate your natural resilience and trust your full array of talents, instead of relying on logic to master every problem. If you can relax into uncertainty and cultivate receptive observation, synergy will be able to emerge, whether through intuition, emotional intelligence, inspiration, or gut feeling.

Becoming Cocreative

Dirk is the farmer who converted Magdalen Farm to organic methods. When he joined us in 1991, he was a painful example of macho management. Our situation was of the mad leading the myopic as I attempted to manage Dirk in setting up an organic farm from scratch, but it forced us both to quickly learn about cocreativity.

Dirk was 30 years old, tall, a big, red-faced Dutchman. He was fearsomely strong, in physique and in will. His iron drive was invaluable but also caused a lot of problems. Dirk had worked on organic farms and had run an organic market garden, but he had no formal training and had never managed a whole farm, let alone started one. And we were literally at ground zero. We had the fields and a few buildings, but no tractors, no equipment, and no livestock.

Dirk spoke English like a mouthwash, rolling the words around his mouth and spitting them out. He and I liked, respected, and annoyed each other. We were both good at being the charging bull—dominating the situation, imposing our will, making things happen. So Magdalen drove the two of us crazy; we were trying to push forward with so little understanding or control. How do you buy a cow? What do you do when your wheat crop is full of weeds? We were both so inexperienced that we hardly knew where to start.

The Raging Bull

For the first few weeks, Dirk raged like a penned bull. He was furious at the problems of getting the farm set up, furious at me and at things in general.

"Alan, I never was in such a situation like this," he told me. His previous experience had the backing of a wealthy owner, so all the equipment had been new and had run perfectly.

It only took us one phone call to the nearest tractor dealer to discover that buying new equipment for Magdalen was way beyond our budget. "I'm sorry, Dirk," I said. "We'll have to find our way through this together. I guess you'd better try the farm sales." These are the auctions of equipment and stock at a farm that's being sold. It took us into the world of conventional farming, but there seemed no choice.

After a couple of forays, the raging bull was even angrier, and hurt, too. Dirk took me into the yard to show me the baler he had just bought from a farm sale. He had jacked up one side. "See this? They just fixed the drive chain with wire. The first time you use it on a field, it will break. These guys must think I'm a joke. They just made a fool of me." He was fuming and close to tears.

"I'm really upset by this, too, Dirk," I said. "We'd better have a talk with Norman Hale." Norman was a long-established organic farmer who lived nearby, and he'd been a helpful friend when the Wessex Foundation was buying Magdalen Farm. As Dirk told his tale, Norman shook his head and frowned.

"Something doesn't stack up here," Norman said. "You might think it'd be the law of the jungle at a farm sale,

Make friends.

Take your time.

Make it personal.

but it isn't. Leastways, not if you treat them right. Why don't we do the next one together?"

Treating Them Like Muck

Two weeks later there was a major sale offering several items we needed. It was a daunting scene. A field full of equipment and farmers, most of whom seemed to know one another, and the conversations about equipment were beyond the ken of Dirk or me. Norman turned to him. "To start with, Dirk, try it the way you've been doing it. I'll stand by and listen."

Dirk checked his catalog and walked up to the farmer who was selling the equipment we wanted. The farmer was talking to someone else, but Dirk simply interrupted. "Hey, you got this muckspreader. Does it work good?"

The farmer, clearly surprised, nodded. "Yes…"

"So you won't sell me no junk?" Dirk asked. "No problems, eh?"

"Well, it's in pretty fair condition, I'd say—" the farmer began.

"Okay." Dirk ticked his catalog and walked away. We came over and joined him.

Now it was Norman who was upset. "Dirk, you talk about them treating you like muck. That's how you treated him."

Dirk was open-mouthed. "What the hell do you mean? I just ask him a couple of questions. That's normal, isn't it?"

Norman shook his head. "Look, if you sell something to a friend, you don't screw him, right? You need to make friends with this guy. Take your time, make it personal. Understand him. Get him talking about his farm."

"You think I have time to think about his farm?" Dirk was getting angry.

Norman stared back at him keenly. "If you want to learn about farming here, you'd better find the time. I mean, your trouble, both of you, is you don't even know what questions to ask. Yes, get him talking. And make sure you listen."

"Hey, I listen OK." Dirk's face was fiery red by now.

Norman shook his head. "You just fired questions and interrupted him. Let him say what he wants, let him ramble, and the facts you need will come out. Hear his story, and tell your own."

"Tell my story?" Dirk was baffled. "I just need . . ."

Norman leaned toward him. "Actually, you have a pretty interesting story to tell, trying to start a farm from scratch. I mean, you really need help. And if you tell your story, you'll start getting it."

I could see Dirk's expression change. Something in him relaxed. He was finally hearing the message.

"Come on, we'll try it out," Norman continued. "You can meet a couple of the farmers I know here. If you treat them right, they'll treat you right."

After that sale, Dirk virtually collapsed. He could see that his rigid, hard-driving mode was not successful or appropriate. He despaired. He fell ill for the first time in years. His partner, Marika, and I had to persuade him to stop. Then we had to coax

Something in him relaxed. He was finally hearing the message.

him to start again. Dirk gradually realized that we wouldn't call him a jerk if he didn't get things right the first time. He found that he could look foolish and make mistakes and still survive.

Columbus Style

For several months after the farm sale, I saw Dirk veering between attack and despair, but something was emerging. His hard side was becoming gentler, and the soft side was gaining strength. He and I coined the term "Columbus style" for this new approach. We were sitting on the lawn beside the farmhouse, enjoying a sunny early evening in September.

"You know, this is pretty funny, you and me," Dirk noted. "We're tough guys, we're like Marines. You give us a map, we'll go anywhere."

I smiled. "Sure, if we only knew where to go, we'd storm our way to it."

"So with this crazy farm, we don't have a destination." Dirk started to laugh. "You know, the trouble is we're off the map."

I nodded. "It's like Christopher Columbus. We're beyond the known world, sailing west . . ."

He grinned. "Yeah, the crew is nervous, the boat leaks, we might die before we find land . . ."

"It's running on faith, Dirk," I said. "At least now, we know that we don't know."

Dirk's biggest achievement at Magdalen Farm was starting the dairy herd from scratch in 1992. He bought the livestock, built the facilities, and set up the routines.

Dirk's approach to starting the dairy herd was cocreative; he was a very different man from the raging bull at the farm sales a year before. Now, he showed subtlety, ingenuity, and immense patience. It took patience with the cows, but even more with the authorities, who had to approve the milking parlor for health and hygiene.

The government inspector was suspicious at first. He was cynical about organics, and he saw us as a bunch of amateurs. He began by telling us that our plans were impossible and unacceptable, and he threw the rule book at us. Far from getting angry, Dirk met him with a kind of youthful charm. He spent time explaining what the project was about, and eventually, the inspector was so supportive that he sketched out a design for us and explained how to do it economically.

Learning from Agnes

A few weeks after milking had started, I arrived at Magdalen Farm to find Dirk still in the dairy parlor long after he should have finished. He was sitting in a stall with one of the cows, massaging her teat. "What's up?" I asked. I was struck by how peaceful Dirk looked, with his head leaning against the cow's flank.

Very gently, he moved his head, signaling me to come nearer. "I'll talk to you later," he murmured. "If I talk now, I won't be with the cow."

I went to the farmhouse kitchen. Marika explained to me, "We have a cow with mastitis."

I winced. Mastitis is one of the main threats in organic dairy herds. It is an infection of the udder that is painful for the cow and affects milk quality. One reason conventional dairy herds are dosed with antibiotics is to avoid mastitis, although this creates a number of other problems. When Dirk came in, I could see he was tired and distressed. "I just don't know if it's working," he said. "We have to wait till morning—then we'll know."

"Did you get the vet in?" I asked.

Dirk nodded. "Sure. He told me to use antibiotics. I said to him—"

"But hang on," I interrupted. "If you do that, the milk's not organic grade. I mean, surely we—"

"Hey, hey, Alan. Relax." He put a hand on my shoulder and smiled. "You didn't let me finish. You don't listen enough!" He laughed. "We didn't use antibiotics, not yet, anyway. I talk also to Norman. He tells me how they do it with no drugs. That's why I massage the teat. See, it helps the circulation and that helps to fight the disease."

"We also use a homeopathic remedy we get from Norman," Marika added. "The vet says it's okay to try, but he comes in two days; if Agnes isn't right then, we have to give her antibiotics."

In the end, Agnes had to be treated with antibiotics. "We were too slow to see the problem," Dirk explained to me. "It pisses me off, but we just didn't have the experience."

A few weeks later, at one of our progress meetings, Dirk said, "You know, the mastitis problem with Agnes really taught us a lot."

I nodded. "How did it help?"

"Marika and I were so upset we didn't ever want this problem again. So what we did," Dirk went on, "is go to Norman's farm and shadow his dairyman. Two times we went there, both of us, and we watched everything. Now, we know what we're looking for—lots of things about hygiene, and we learned about stress."

Put Yourself in Their Hooves

This was a new idea for me. "Really? Stress for cows?" I asked guardedly.

He nodded enthusiastically. "We bought these cows out of three different herds. They don't know each other, and that's hard for them."

Marika added, "We have five cows who all try to be boss. They all push to be the first one into the milking parlor."

I shook my head. "So what do we do about stress in cows? Run a team-building workshop?"

Dirk laughed. "Well, Marika and I just put ourselves in their hooves. We pretend we're the cows. Now I don't push them around so much. I don't swear at them any more. And we give each cow more space." It was winter, so the cows were housed indoors, on straw. "We moved some cows to the second barn. And we made it easier. We gave them extra straw for the past four weeks. That doesn't cost us much, and already they're giving something back."

"What do you mean, giving something back?" I asked.

Dirk grinned. "The yield goes up. There's more milk each day."

The Gift in the Problem

I have described Dirk's progress at length because it shows how cocreativity can develop. When Dirk came to Magdalen, he only had one response to problems: to narrow his focus and push. It didn't produce lasting satisfaction for him, and it didn't solve the problems. While you move toward sustainability, you have no choice but to learn cocreativity. And as Dirk's experience shows, the tensions of trying to achieve results without control or clarity can help to teach you how.

Dirk's drive pushed him to keep facing the problems, and slowly he started to integrate active and receptive skills. He learned when to push and when to yield. And he gained the crucial habit of relaxing into a problem and exploring it observantly, instead of tensing and forcing. The result was that he created organic synergy out of a series of difficulties. The way Dirk handled the farm sales, the dairy parlor, and the mastitis all took us further forward than we could have hoped for. In each case, he eventually found the gift in the problem.

> **While you move toward sustainability, you have no choice but to learn cocreativity.**

I often find that external issues are enlarged reflections of my internal ones. Dirk's raging-bull style showed me my own tendency to push too hard. The finesse in receptive skills he developed, and the way he combined this with determination, taught me a great deal. I also learned from the way his partner, Marika, changed while at Magdalen. At first, she was too passive to be cocreative. What she had to learn was how and when to push.

Part of my own payback from the mastitis problem came months later, when Phil Morris asked me to "clean up" the newly formed customer support group at Alibi Publishing, described in Chapter 1. "We've got the mother of all bottlenecks down there, Alan," Phil fumed. "It's clogging the whole system. If they can't sort it out, I'll go through them like an enema, so help them." This sounded like the antibiotic option, so I tried Dirk's gentler methods. For the customer support group, this meant giving space, support, and attention, and disclosing the real problems. It also meant taking the pressure off and rebuilding their vitality so that they could work out the problems for themselves.

Achieving Organic Synergy

My experience of teaching co-creativity and synergy is that the concepts are understandable and attractive but elusive for most people. Each of the following is vital for achieving synergy:

- Building up creative tension: exploring, facing, and feeling the intensity of two or more apparently conflicting aspects of a situation
- Staying with the tension and relaxing into it
- Applying both intuitive and analytical tools, such as creative conflict resolution, to explore the tensions further and to open a way to potential outcomes
- Using a range of creativity-building methods to stimulate insights and ideas that may provide the solution

The following section describes some of the main ingredients of organic synergy: using creative tension, drawing on both sides of brain, and creating working vision. The Diamond Process (described on page 94) applies this approach, as do other methods covered in Chapter 9.

Creative Tension

The ability to meet high levels of uncertainty in a positive manner is central to the remarkable resilience of organic growers. The cocreative response to tension, uncertainty, or contradictory data is to explore it and relax into it. You can play with the tension, making a joke of it, as I did by hamming up my frustration and doing my Groucho Marx act in the incident described in Chapter 1. Although the idea of relaxing into tension may feel strange, it's taught in many Eastern philosophies. Buddhist meditation masters will suggest that you witness your tensions and breathe into them. Tantra, the Indian approach to aligning sexuality and spirituality, teaches that the fullest ecstasy arises when we let go into a high state of arousal, riding the tension instead of discharging it.

The nature of a cocreative process means that we cycle between the polarities, or extremes; we repeatedly immerse ourselves in each of them. We develop strength, creative tension, and the potential for integration by moving between them. The synergistic quality arises because we deliberately use and harness the tension to move us forward.

The Cocreative Brain

One way of developing cocreativity is by understanding and engaging both the left and right sides of the brain. Roger Sperry, an American psychologist, won the Nobel Prize for medicine in 1981 for his research on the different characteristics of the left and right hemispheres of the human brain. The talents of the left side include logic, verbal reasoning, and numerical reasoning—the ability to analyze a complex situation, to dissect it into parts, to identify linear chains of cause and effect. Many people would see such skills as the sum total of mental ability, but this is only half the story.

The right side of the brain offers such gifts as intuition and imagination; it is more visual, spatial, and conceptual. While the left brain can dissect a complex situation, breaking it into smaller parts by analysis, it is the right side that gives us synthesis, creative vision, the fresh combination of parts to move us forward.

The right and left sides of the brain equate to the archetypal feminine and masculine qualities that Chinese philosophy calls yin and yang. The yin, feminine, includes receptive, yielding, intuitive, unconscious, and integrating qualities. The yang, or masculine, includes active, conscious, penetrating, rational, testing, and distinguishing or separating qualities. Most people habitually use one of these sets of qualities—one side of the brain—more

THE COCREATIVE BRAIN

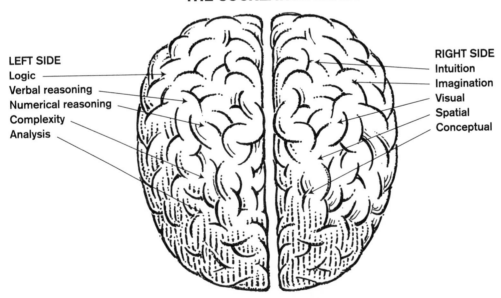

LEFT SIDE
Logic
Verbal reasoning
Numerical reasoning
Complexity
Analysis

RIGHT SIDE
Intuition
Imagination
Visual
Spatial
Conceptual

Much has been made of the differences between left-brain and right-brain approaches to solving problems. In fact, sustainable success requires the development and integration of both sides of your brain.

than the other. Yet all of us have the potential to develop and integrate both. Doing so raises our energy productivity, our adaptability, and our cocreativity.

Working Vision

The debate has been running for years over the importance of vision and how to achieve it. Much of the confusion arises from conflict between left-brain and right-brain approaches and the failure to realize that a working vision includes and integrates both sides.

Sustainable success requires vision and clarity in both everyday operations and overall strategy. The way to achieve this is by combining focused vision and peripheral vision, which equate, respectively, to the active/left brain and receptive/right brain. They also represent two of the main schools of thought regarding "the vision thing." The left-brain approach to vision sees it as deduced from analysis: objectively assessing capabilities, opportunities, and stakeholders' needs. The vision is then logically cascaded into a strategy and into action plans. By contrast, the right-brain approach sees vision as creative and inspirational; it arises intuitively from those involved, from their picturing the qualities of the desired future. The most viable and appropriate visions arise from integrating these two approaches. For example, Dirk Hoostra created a productive dairy herd at Magdalen by integrating driving ambition with observation of details.

Think about your own typical ways of exploring a situation. Is your way of seeing driven by your desired outcomes, so you hone in quickly on the details you judge to be important? Or is your typical way of looking soft-focused, receptive, scanning the scene for the information that presents itself?

Whether you favor the focused or peripheral approach, cultivate both types of vision, alternate between them, and then seek to combine them. While the concept of the left and right sides of the brain may still seem abstract, noticing and cultivating these two ways of seeing is a practical way to develop them.

> **The cocreative response to tension, uncertainty, or contradictory data is to explore it and relax into it.**

All the visioning methods I use involve the breath in some way. At minimum, they all begin with some slow, relaxing breaths to engage the air element more fully. The specific methods include the following:

Meditation. Sitting in silence, focusing on the breath, and opening receptively to clarity and direction

Visualization. A range of guided journeys, often in natural settings, to explore a situation, face and release negative feelings, reach a vision, and integrate it into practicality

Vision questing. A process found in Celtic, Native American, and other traditions. It involves spending time alone in an isolated natural setting, calling for your vision, and finding guidance and support from your surroundings.

The Diamond Process

The Diamond Process offers a road map for the cocreative approach. I developed this process as a way of teaching managers how to handle high levels of change and uncertainty synergistically. It is relevant for issues that are mainly practical, mainly emotional, or mainly inspirational. It can be applied quickly or in depth.

THE DIAMOND PROCESS

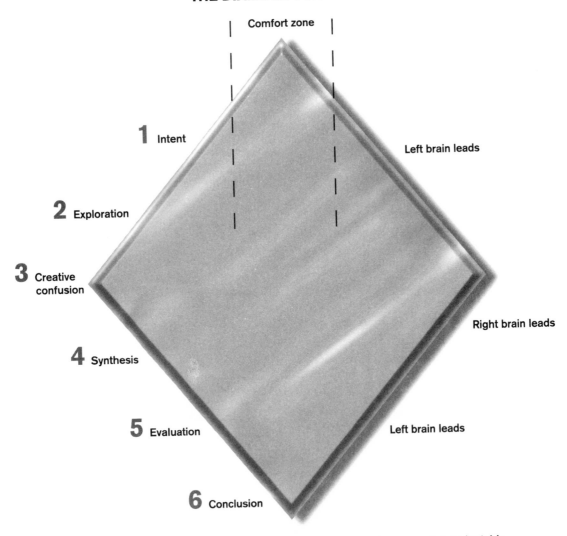

How most change takes place: From an intent or question arises uncertainty (outside the comfort zone) that, with the help of both left-brain and right-brain activity, naturally moves toward a resolution or conclusion—and the process begins anew.

The shape of the diamond symbolizes the shape of most change processes. There is a starting point: an intention, a question, or a partial understanding of the situation. From this point, the picture widens into growing uncertainty, confusion, and contradiction. A successful change process then finds new insight that gives clarity and focus, bringing the process to a finishing point, which in turn will typically be the start of another diamond.

The six stages in the process can be explained as follows:

Sometimes just closing your eyes, breathing peacefully, and waiting enables you to find the synergy.

1 Intent

You plant the seed for this process by stating and affirming your intent. Even if your aim is as vague as "to understand my confusion," it helps to state this goal explicitly. Feeling your tension and affirming your desire to reach an outcome raise your energy and motivation for the process. Another benefit of doing all this is that it engages your subconscious and unconscious mental capacities in the process. The same approach is expounded by W. Timothy Gallwey in *The Inner Game of Tennis;* the conscious brain specifies the goal, but the brain never prescribes how to achieve that goal. The brain briefs the unconscious to find the solution.

2 Exploration

In each phase of the Diamond Process, both sides of the brain contribute, but one takes the lead. In the exploration phase, it's the active, logical, left brain that leads. Exploration is the stage for gathering data, exploring a wide range of information sources, analyzing what's going on, and looking for parallels and lead indicators. One aim of the exploration phase is to go well beyond your comfort zone, which is the habitual frame of reference and limiting beliefs that we use to reduce the confusions of real life to a manageable level.

3 Creative Confusion

If your exploratory work has been done well, it will naturally propel you into confusion. Real life is full of changeability and contradiction, to an extent that can be almost intolerable. As the poet T. S. Eliot said, "Humankind cannot bear very much reality." The word *confusion* literally means a flowing together, and the aim in this stage is to relax into the tension and uncertainty, to feel the intensity, and to stay with it. This stage is the transition to leadership by the right brain, the receptive principle.

4 Synthesis

This is the phase when you open receptively to the "aha!" moment, the creative insight that produces a way forward from the creative confusion. Like any right-brain process, you can't force it. There is a saying, "In sleep, sex, and fishing, the more you try, the less happens." The same applies here. Sometimes just closing your eyes, breathing peacefully, and waiting enables you to find the synergy. If not, this is a good time to go for a walk, have a bath, make a meal, or play some music; do something enjoyable and stay observant for the answer when it's ready. If you'd like a specific method for this stage, try the Witness Triangle, described on page 176.

5 Evaluation

This is where the left brain takes the lead again. You have a vision of an outcome: It may seem obvious or crazy. Either way, you need to check out the practicalities, do the sums, ask the awkward questions, understand the implications. Few of us have 100 percent infallible intuition, and you may have to return to an earlier phase of the cycle.

6 Conclusion

Your evaluation may wholly support your new vision or may highlight doubts or risks. Before you go ahead, return to the right brain; sit with your potential decision, see it in perspective, and ask if it inspires and motivates you. This is the stage we often include before an important decision by saying, "I'll sleep on it."

It is sometimes appropriate to cycle back within this process and repeat some stages. For example, confusion may raise more questions to explore. Or you may alternate for a while between confusion and synthesis. It is also cyclical because the conclusion to one diamond often becomes the starting point for another and the process begins again.

Dancing with Worms

In 1983, at the age of 35, I achieved my ambition of becoming a division president. However, the business involved was hardly a star prize. The Lumex Corporation was like a small, scruffy, leaking tramp steamer; it was a money-losing operation with a few hundred people. It looked out of place in the parent multinational, Redland, whose bigger divisions were like cruise liners: upmarket, smooth, and profitable.

Peter Jansen, my new boss, was disarmingly frank about Lumex: "I know you'd like to run a business where you can be creative with marketing and product design. This isn't it. Quite honestly, we know Lumex is a mess, but we have no idea how much of one. If you can clean it

up, I'll find you something to run that you'll really enjoy."

The Lumex Corporation was an assortment of businesses that made highway maintenance products. It had a small office in Chicago and four plants scattered across the country. The company was in its second year of losing money. "My hunch is that the true losses are worse than reported," Peter told me. "It's worrying the head office, and I want you to get them off my back."

Facing the Fog

I started at Lumex with a naive confidence that I could easily manage a turnaround business in America. I had dealt with several money-losing operations, and with a Harvard M.B.A. and four years of working for Procter and Gamble, I thought I knew American culture. In practice, Lumex was a rude shock, a nightmare. In other turn-arounds, it had been easy to find the tags—the slack cost controls, the quick sales opportunities—but not here.

At Lumex, my first impression was fog. There were no usable facts in the puff and jargon I encountered. I felt desperately frustrated, eager to act decisively, to be the hero. But I could find neither the sword nor the dragon. By month four I had found a few people in the business I could trust with senior roles. But it was clear that the new team consisted of steady-handed operators, not strategists or leaders.

By month six the operational problems were largely identified and costed. We were producing reliable financial reports and forecasts, but the picture horrified Redland. Losses were running into seven figures, and that wasn't the worst of it. The biggest concern was that there was no end in sight. Even after six months I could not come up with any strategy to make the business profitable. I felt appalled at my failure. Peter Jansen had been completely supportive, but he told me, "You'd better know that there are some senior murmurings around here that you're not up to the job. I know it's been a hell of a time for you, but I'd like you to set a target time for proposing a strategy."

My heart sank. I responded, "How about three months from now?"

> **I felt desperately frustrated, eager to act decisively, to be the hero.**

Despite my track record, Lumex looked hopeless. Its main business was supplying road-marking paint to state highway authorities. These authorities specified the product formula precisely and took the lowest price from sealed bids. Most of the cost was in purchased raw materials. There was almost zero opportunity to add value to sales or to reduce costs. The volumes were so large that any diversification would be a drop in the bucket. Competition for these contracts was severe, and the profit margins were thin at best. If your material costs or factory yields were even slightly out, you lost money. For these reasons, the business was almost unsalable. Closure was the obvious option, but the shutdown costs were so high that it was better to find a way to keep going.

Meeting Up with a Frog

Having committed to my deadline, I felt like the youngest son in so many fairy tales—the foolish youth who undertakes the impossible task. He typically wanders aimlessly, sometimes desperately, until a chance meeting with a frog solves his problem. Since all my strategic analysis and direct efforts had failed, I decided to go and revisit all the sites. It was not entirely random, but I set forth in a receptive, observant spirit. For once, I did not have lists of sharp questions to ask: I felt that those might prevent me from finding the unexpected.

The tension between my desire to push ahead to a solution and the apparent impasse on all fronts felt unbearable. At times I lapsed into my usual ways of avoiding tension: despair or distraction. I would give up and let go, feeling hopeless and overwhelmed. This allowed me to rest and release some of my stress. At other times, I would distract myself by getting busy with simpler tasks that I could achieve. This gave me some diversity in my work and renewed my vitality. However, most of the time I kept myself in the tension between the active and receptive modes, and it was from this tension that the creative leap emerged.

In the space of three weeks, I revisited all our factories. I also went to meet customers and suppliers. I attended an industry conference and met our competitors for the first time. This had to be approached carefully, because antitrust law was actively enforced, and Redland was determined to avoid any hint of price fixing. The seed of a solution came from a titanium dioxide supplier in Pittsburgh. "Of course, Al, the key to your business is freight," he said.

In the past, if someone's views contradicted my prejudices, I had found a way to devalue them. I could easily have written this guy off as a has-been full of irrelevant folklore. Not now: I was open to clues. Maybe this was the frog!

I sat up. "Freight? What do you mean?"

He pushed his steel-rimmed glasses back up his nose. "Sure. Your product is about the cheapest damn stuff you can buy in a barrel. The cost of trucking goods in and hauling 'em out is a big number. You won't make much profit shipping more than 500 miles from a plant."

After that I could hardly wait to finish the conversation and get hold of a map. There were so few competitors in this game that I could plot every location from memory. Suddenly a picture emerged. I could see that our plant in Tennessee was hopeless. The population within 200 miles was quite small. Competitors were better placed for the big markets in Georgia and Texas, whereas Milwaukee looked like a good location. Our problems there were an oversized, antiquated plant and a competitor only 100 miles away.

I can still recall sitting with the map, my concentration drifting. An idea shot through me like a bolt of electricity, startling in its power and simplicity. If we could buy our competitor's plant in Green Bay and simply shut down our old plant in Milwaukee, we would be 800 miles from the nearest competitor. I was pretty sure that the freight costs of competitors would enable us to add a few percent to our profit margin. And so it would prove.

I took my ideas to my Lumex team, who welcomed them with relief and helped to refine them. Once we had a clear vision of a solution, we went for it like a tornado. The numbers worked. Peter Jansen and Redland gave it their backing. I estimated what our competitor's factory had cost to build and what it was worth to us, and I drove a good bargain.

> **In the tension between the active and the receptive modes, the creative leap emerged.**

Following Through

Two other finds from my visits added to the successful turnaround strategy. One was poaching Anna Santini, the general manager of our largest and most successful competitor. Anna was tired of the politics in her parent company. She liked my enthusiasm and the semi-independence she'd gain from having a boss in Britain. Anna was naturally cocreative. She had superb observation and intuition, but she was tough, too. She had a degree in chemistry and had always wanted to manage a factory. To get there she'd had to join as the plant manager's secretary and prove herself at every step. Having her as president of Lumex was an immense relief for all of us.

The other breakthrough came from an impulsive decision to attend a Milwaukee Chamber of Commerce dinner. Because we sold our products over a wide radius, no one had ever bothered to attend. By attending, I met the presidents of two other businesses in Milwaukee who were big buyers of the same raw materials. We re-alized that our seasonal demand cycles were complementary. It became obvious that we should pool our purchases, and this would add several percentage points to our margins.

I had realized on day two of my time with Lumex that it would never be Redland's kind of business. It would have to be sold, but first it had to be salable. The losses in year one were ugly. But from early in year two, Lumex USA returned to profit, and I was able to start seeking a buyer. The American business was eventually sold as a management buyout to Anna Santini and the team I had helped build.

My experience at Lumex, like Dirk Hoostra's at Magdalen Farm, forced me to learn cocreativity. Both of us were determined to achieve sustainable results in a situation we could neither understand nor control. Without toughness, we'd have failed. Without receptiveness and subtlety, we'd never have found a way through. By staying with the tension of uncertainty, the gift in the problem eventually emerged.

Organic Synergy in Organizations

Developing cocreativity is even more beneficial and challenging for groups than for individuals. The culture and dynamics in many work teams inhibit this kind of process. Mechanistic approaches, using controlled inputs to force a predetermined outcome, will promote conformity, however much they claim to empower.

Some of the leading management thinkers of the past decade have argued for the move toward organic synergy, albeit in different language. One example is Stephen Covey, in *The 7 Habits of Highly Effective People*. His Habit 6, synergize, offers valuable guidelines and examples on how to apply it in organizations. For example, appropriate reward and recognition systems are an important factor. Covey comments:

I did some consulting for another company that wanted training for their people in human relations. The underlying assumption was that the problem was the people.

The president said, "Go into any store you want and see how they treat you. They're just order takers. They don't understand how to get close to the customers...."

I persisted, and within two days we uncovered the real problem. Because of the job definition and the compensation system, the managers were "creaming." They'd stand behind the cash register and cream all the business during the slow times....

So the managers would give all the dirty jobs—inventory control, stock work, and cleaning—to the salespeople....

That's why the department heads were tops in sales.

So we changed one system—the compensation system—and the problem was corrected overnight. We set up a system whereby the managers only made money when their salespeople made money. We overlapped the needs and goals of the managers with the needs and goals of the salespeople.

And the need for human relations training suddenly disappeared. The key was developing a true win/win reward system.

2-MINUTE CHECKUP

BOUNCING BACK

Use this exercise if you feel depleted in your work and need more renewal and support.

Take a few long, slow, relaxing breaths. Now, start to picture all the inner and outer resources available to you in your work. You may want to draw a picture or diagram of them. As you make this review, look for the extra resources you need. Scan through the diversity of your own skills and activities. Scan through the diversity of your colleagues, clients, and other contacts. Recognize and enjoy the resilience your network gives you. Also, think about how you can add diversity and increase this resilience further.

Chaos theory is also relevant, suggesting that the most productive, creative, adaptive systems embody "bounded uncertainty": They have processes that can structure and channel fluidity, rather than suppressing it. This is akin to the cocreative notion of integrating the active/structured and receptive/fluid qualities.

In addition, Peter Senge's book *The Dance of Change* overlaps with the cocreative approach, although he uses this term in a narrower sense than I have. For example, he comments, "Leadership grows from the capacity to hold creative tension," and he cites Martin Luther King as one example. He reports the views of a number of successful change leaders;

these views include the importance of persisting receptively amid ambiguity and lack of clarity.

The Push-and-Flow Culture

Appropriate culture and values are the ground condition in which cocreativity can take root and flourish in an organization. This means fostering values that may seem opposed to each other: for example, cooperation with competition, high trust with high challenge, and push with flow.

Caradon was a good example of this: There was a strong drive for performance, along with a deep willingness to listen, flow, and adapt to achieve it. We created an esprit de corps in the group as a whole, which balanced rather than swamped the pride that people felt for their operating company. Competition and comparison are natural drives, and we harnessed them in encouraging each business and each team to progress. However, we also created processes for collaboration between companies. Several Caradon companies had related product lines and served the same customers. In the past this had just created tension; now, much of this tension was converted into fruitful synergy.

A cocreative culture is likely to be values led, not results driven. In *Built to Last: Successful Habits of Visionary Companies*, James Collins and Jerry Porras reveal that only 3 of the 18 sustainably successful companies they studied began with a specific product idea. Most developed around values, around the kind of company they wanted to be. This contrast between values-led and results-driven cultures also typifies the difference between organic and intensive farming.

A good example of cocreative culture is given by Bill Hewlett, cofounder of Hewlett-Packard, and is cited in *Built to Last*:

When I talk to business schools occasionally, the professor of management is devastated when I say that we didn't have any plans when we started—we were just opportunistic. We did anything that would bring in a nickel. We had a bowling foul-line indicator, a clock drive for a telescope, a thing to make a urinal flush automatically, and a shock machine to make people lose weight. Here we were, with about $500 in capital, trying whatever someone thought we might be able to do.

Another crucial ingredient in the cocreative culture is the willingness to face conflict and resolve it constructively. Consider Virosoft, profiled in Chapter 3. Aziz Khan had built a values-led organization with diverse talents and temperaments. He had assembled the ingredients for highly productive creative tension, but he had suppressed them because of his reluctance to face conflict openly. When he signaled his willingness to change and we provided the skills, Virosoft rapidly became a cocreative culture. The business started to find its synergies and improved its results and its resilience in the process.

Propagating the Skills

Some of the most frustrated chief executives I meet have a clear vision of future direction. Their problem is that because they can state the vision, they expect the organization to move straight into action for it. In my experience, culture, skills, and processes all have to evolve before vision and action will align. Although there's an element of alchemy at the heart of cocreative processes, there are a number of skills that can stimulate this alchemy and remove the barriers. These begin with assertiveness, the ability to express, hear, and stay present with emotions. As Thomas Crum says, "In order to have conflict resolution, you've got to have conflict."

Without assertiveness, there is no creative tension, no dialogue to develop— only suppression, blow-ups, or walk-aways. When I led the assertiveness training session for the directors at Alibi Publishing, I was unsure if a busy, hard-nosed senior team would be receptive to it. I was impressed by the eagerness with which they took in and used these methods. Another example is Intel, which runs management classes in what they call "constructive confrontation."

Consider an episode in Philip Carroll's transformational leadership at the oil company Shell, quoted in *The Dance of Change:*

Eighteen months into the process, after a series of regular off-site meetings to talk about our values and plan the transformation together, it began to dawn on the members of the Leadership Council: We didn't have the basic skills to listen to people and let their ideas make an impression on us. . . . We could not even engage ourselves in discussion. Some of us shut down in the face of disagreement. Others tried to win every argument. . . . It took in-depth reflective work and a series of private meetings for us to learn to listen more effectively. As that started to happen, people throughout the organization began to gain confidence in our efforts. I began to hear, for the first time, talk about the process of transformation from people out at off-shore drilling base camps, or at refineries.

Processes for Uncertainty

The difficulty in describing processes to engender synergy is that they're often nonspecific and may seem vague. The drive for action and focus in most organizations is so intense that the main need is often to provide space for receptivity. An example is the peer group review process at energy giant BP–Amoco. The 200-plus business units form part of peer groups, and managers from these companies meet in self-facilitated sessions once a year. These provide an open space for exchange of experiences, mutual observation, and identifying the often-subtle cues for an issue that has to be addressed. At the end of each peer group review, the session is joined by a member of BP–Amoco's executive board so that the experiences and impressions can be transmitted directly.

Processes to cultivate observation, peripheral vision, and receptiveness to soft data can be developed within existing formats. Here is an example from Intel vice president David Marsing, quoted in *The Dance of Change:*

In staff meetings we'd say, "How's the factory doing?" Everybody wanted to shoot his hand up with a quantitative indicator. "No," I said. "Don't give me any data. How does it feel on the floor, working with your people? How does it feel to be in some of the key meetings?" The first few times we did this, people looked at me as if to say, "Where is he coming from?" But we deliberately made it a regular practice—conducted with such repetitiveness that it became integrated into our everyday work life. Then they began to look forward to it. They also began to interact differently with their people. This subtle twist, just a simple little thing, started to get people to exercise their observational skills, and use a different part of their brain....

I decided to personally practice enough so that I could integrate and embody these skills in myself. This meant establishing a routine of meshing intuitive and analytical behavior, acting and reflecting, listening and advocating, "task" work and process work, and analytic problem solving and systems thinking, without having to consciously think about it. I now believe that my ability to tap into the organization's potential was a direct result of developing a strong ability to integrate these tools.

Organic Synergy in Daily Practice

What is most important in achieving this quality of organic synergy is a deeply felt understanding of the principles, as well as the learning skills that enable it. With time, cocreativity becomes more of a habitual instinct than a technique. It starts with the basic response to uncertainty; when you feel yourself tensing, don't push, don't give up—relax and explore.

The Diamond Process, described earlier in this chapter, gives you a basic route map for applying cocreativity to generate synergy. The organic growth tool kit in Chapter 9, starting on page 171, offers several tools to help in this process, as well as advice on further reading. These tools include the following:

The Witness Triangle. A simple method using physical movement and visualization to explore two positions that are in tension and to find a third point, the synergy that builds on them

The Aikido Approach. Pointers from this Japanese martial art, which is based on the principle of using conflicting forces constructively

Negative Energy Recycling. A way of turning negatives into positives that includes physically moving the negative energy away from the body and then replacing it with new positive behaviors

Creative Conflict Resolution. A detailed guide to a process that can be useful in finding the synergy in conflicts, either internal or external

chapter 5
RIDING THE CYCLES

ANY SUSTAINABLE SYSTEM, whether it's in your personal life, at work, or in the garden, will be based on natural cycles and will be cultivated to achieve productive goals. A cycle is a recurrent succession of things. The root origin of the word is the Greek *kuklos*, meaning "circle" or "wheel," although often a cycle is best pictured as a spiral, since it creates renewable, forward, or upward movement, not just repetition. The earth actually gains in vitality by being cycled in the right way. So do batteries. And so do people.

The main benefit of aligning with cycles is to generate high output in a way that is renewing and balancing. Cycles establish sustainable rhythms that can help us handle the pressures that pull us toward depletion. They can also raise our resilience to change. Without renewing cycles operating in our lives, it's perfectly possible to dissipate the benefits of clean energy inputs. Have you ever returned from a thoroughly refreshing vacation only to feel that the effect has worn off two weeks later?

The specific cycles that are right for an organic garden will depend on the desired output, or crops, along with soil type, climate, and many other circumstances. In the same way, to gain the Natural Advantage, you need to identify or evolve the specific cycles that are appropriate for your life and work.

The cyclicality of the natural world is inescapable. Think of the daily cycle of light and dark, the lunar cycle of wax and wane, and the annual cycle of the four seasons. If we consider how we interact with friends and coworkers, however, some of our relationships and day-to-day dealings seem anticyclical. There is the pressure of connectivity: If you are reachable almost every waking hour, on your cell phone, by e-mail, and by pager, then you risk being exposed to the pressure almost continually. Likewise, there is a push for longer service hours and 24-hour access to everything from banking to grocery shopping for increased productivity.

Cultivating Cyclicality

The modern trend toward speed, convenience, and disposability make it clear that cyclicality now has to be chosen and consciously created. The pressures toward linear working and depletion won't disappear, but some of the apparent problems that are created as a result can be harnessed to our advantage. Longer hours of service and the explosive growth in communications provide us with resources to configure ways of working that match the cycle styles of different individuals.

This chapter offers both the overall principles of working with cycles and some specific models to consider. It focuses on three main cycles, as follows:

The cultivation cycle. Include all four seasons in your work patterns: spring (seeding), summer (growth), autumn (harvesting), and winter (rest and review).

Renewal rotation. Apply the principle of crop rotation in your work so that a demanding task is followed by a restorative one or a fallow period.

Nutrient cycling. Ensure that fresh energy and nutrients are habitually moved from where they arise to where they are most needed.

Seeing the Cycle

The technical director of Virosoft, Salim Hussain, met me for monthly individual coaching sessions for more than a year. This was part of the program described in Chapter 3. When I arrived at Salim's office for our third session, he looked shocked and dejected. "I've just had my annual medical," he explained. "I have a problem with high blood pressure. And I may be getting ulcers." He laughed bitterly and shook his head. "It's so damn stupid. My wife is a nurse, and she's been telling me for months that I can't go on like this."

"So why can't you go on, Salim?" I asked. "What's dragging you down?"

His face reddened and his hands clenched. "Everything! The job is running me. It's like a treadmill that never stops; in fact it speeds up. If I could . . . hang on." He darted out to bark instructions at a young engineer who had been peering through the glass partition.

"Would you be willing to try something a little unusual?"

He shrugged. "Why not—nothing to lose, eh?"

"Could you ease up and relax for a minute? Let your imagination emerge. See if you can recall a time when you felt really happy in your work, when you could go on forever." To my surprise, he did lean back, and a dreamy smile came over him.

"Oh yes." He took off his glasses and looked at me. "I was a junior lecturer in computing science."

"Did you enjoy the work?"

Salim sat up proudly. "I was as happy as ever. I had research funding, was free to do my own projects, and I lectured for 12 hours a week. It all worked beautifully. When I was stuck on research, I'd prepare for a lecture. When I came back to the lab, often my problem was solved."

Forever Midsummer

At this point, I took Salim through the cultivation cycle (described in detail starting on page 111). I explained the value of including all four stages: spring (seeding); summer (growth); autumn (harvest); and winter (rest and review). When I had finished, Salim grunted angrily. "Well, my problem's clear. It's forever midsummer in my job. Constant push for output."

"OK," I said, "but who's making it that way? Aziz gives you a lot of freedom and respect, Salim. I challenge you to do things differently."

Salim spluttered, called for a coffee, and started thinking.

"Can you think of work you enjoy in each phase of the cycle?" I asked.

Salim tensed up. "Ah, not in spring, no. I don't like starting projects." He looked at me apologetically. "You see, I'm such a damn perfectionist. That's why I hate giving promises."

Light started to dawn for me. "So that's why they always have to chase you to set project timings?"

Can you recall a time when you felt really happy in your work?

He nodded, pursing his lips. "Hmm. Not good, is it? But summer growth, if it's the right project, this is what I love."

"What makes it the right project?" I asked.

"If it's real research, something to stretch my brain. It's all these damn people and logistics that get under my skin."

"So what about the autumn, harvest season?" I asked. "Do you like that?"

He looked uncomfortable again. "Frankly, no. I don't want to sign off on things until they're 100 percent right. The longer you go on with a piece of software, the more you see how it should be done. Always I have to let it go too soon. My God, if you knew all the little bugs in our programs. I could scream."

I nodded. "I can see that's really hard for you. What about winter, rest and review?"

He suddenly looked sad. "In my academic work, I used to love this. At the end of every term, I would tidy all my papers, record the learning points, and just stop." He beamed at me. "It was amazing how fresh I was after every vacation." His smile faded as he realized the implications.

"Salim, if you were more at ease with all four seasons of the cycle, do you feel you'd be more at ease with your work overall? Would it help your stress level?"

He stared at me, almost fiercely. I imagined that his logic circuits were glowing pink as he tried to get past the limitations of the left brain.

"Well, hypothetically, yes. But empirically, the facts are against it. I have never enjoyed these spring and autumn seasons in my work. How could it ever be different?"

Balancing the Cycles

"Salim, if you want to balance the cycle, it's perfectly doable," I said. "You remember we talked about energy cycles in the last workshop? If there's a blockage at any point in the cycle, the flow is impeded, right?"

Salim gave a strange, tense smile. "My God, this is just like my arteries. When the flow is blocked, the pressure rises. Go on."

"So one benefit of tracing the flow through the cycle is to see where the blockages are. Then we can apply a composting process to them."

Salim shook his head. "How do you mean?"

I went on. "Take your resistance to starting and seeding projects. Instead of denying it, you should magnify it, go right into it, and then you can change it. My guess, Salim, is that your block about the spring season is partly because your standing in other people's eyes matters so much to you."

Salim sat up. "Of course it matters."

"Yes, but I'd say you care too much about their opinion of you. And you think it depends on your getting everything right, so you avoid giving commitments. You're afraid of failing, so you don't want to start."

> One benefit of tracing the flow through the cycle is to see where the blockages are.

He leaned forward, staring at me. "But there's no other way, is there? Ever since first grade, it's always been the same: good work, good boy; bad work, bad boy."

I met his glance, choosing my words carefully. "I can see it's a deeply held belief for you, but I'd call it baggage—unhelpful baggage. You're carrying it around, and it's dragging you back. I mean, you talked about empirical data, Salim. Do you really believe you have to get everything right?"

He was wriggling in his chair. "Yes, I have to get it right. No, it's . . . I don't know. . . ."

"Why don't we check it out?" I asked. "Why don't we go and ask Aziz right now?"

In Aziz's office, I explained the situation and simply asked him, "Can you tell us what you most value about Salim?"

Aziz answered readily. "Salim, what I value most about you is your technical genius. I can tell you honestly, I wouldn't sleep so well at night without you here. I just feel that whatever crises we have on the software, you can solve."

Salim frowned at him. "So my value to Virosoft depends on getting things right every time."

Aziz looked at him with surprise. "No. You are a technical genius, but that doesn't mean you have to be perfect. You're allowed to make mistakes sometimes."

"Did you hear that, Salim?" I asked. "Will that help you balance your seasons?"

I could see him relaxing. "Yes," he understood. "I'm allowed to make mistakes."

Rest and Review

"Aziz, there's a second question I'd like to ask you," I said. "Salim and I have been looking at his workload. It's depleting him because it's become monotonous."

Aziz looked startled. "Monotonous? You know, I find that quite insulting. We have an exciting business, growing fast, full of challenges . . . ."

Salim interrupted. "Aziz, that's the problem. It's all challenges. I spend my whole time fire fighting."

I added, "I'm sure you'd get more out of Salim if his work were cyclical."

Aziz was irritated. "You know, I'm really not following this conversation. What do you mean, cyclical?"

"Like growing crops in the field," I replied. "To sustain the output, you need a rotation cycle. The high-output crop is followed by a renewal crop, which restores fertility."

Aziz was getting fidgety. "I don't think I have the time for all this. What bothers me is getting Maxim 3 developed. How does this help?"

"Let's go back, then," I suggested. "You said, Aziz, that what you most valued in Salim was his technical genius. So your main need is for him and his team to resolve your technical problems. Is that correct?"

Aziz nodded. "Absolutely."

I turned to Salim. "And that work is pretty demanding for you, isn't it?"

Salim nodded. "Draining. It's not just technical, it's the people. That's what takes it out of me."

> **The high-output crop is followed by a renewal crop, which restores fertility.**

"OK. So if that takes it out of you," I asked him, "what would put it back? Aziz really needs you to do this work. What would renew you?"

Aziz was at last getting it. "Come on, Salim, just say what you need. We want to sustain you."

Salim looked anguished, like a young boy afraid to ask for what he wants.

"Remember lecturing," I said. "What worked for you there?"

Suddenly he relaxed and smiled. "OK, I'll tell you what would renew me, what would actually keep me going. One thing is being free to do my own research. Not here, but on my own, no interruptions, one or two days a week. I get so much energy from creative time like that. . . . And the other thing is vacations. I'd say I—"

"But you take your four weeks, don't you?" Aziz asked.

Salim shot back, "Do you realize I work a 70-hour week, including all the time at home? You're not getting the best from me, Aziz, far from it. I really need several weeks a year when I stop completely, no thinking, no work, just lying fallow."

I stepped in. "The suggestion I'd like to make is that you appoint a technical operations manager under Salim, to handle the project management and personnel issues. That way, Salim would have time for the renewal part of the cycle."

The appointment was made within a few weeks, and Salim's health and productivity improved immediately. He started to initiate ideas, not just react to requests. He even took up bowling with his team every Tuesday night. He told me, "I'm relaxed enough to talk with them, now that I don't

2-MINUTE *CHECKUP*

CIRCLE OF SEASONS

Take a few minutes to picture each of the four seasons of the year: spring, summer, fall, winter. For each season, consider what you like and dislike, then relate this to your work. In particular, look at which seasons are difficult for you, and why.

Think of the four-seasons model when you find yourself getting stressed or when your workweek has been particularly tough. Keep learning about yourself, and remember that like all natural things, you are part of the circle of seasons.

have to manage everything. And we get a lot of problems solved, just unwinding together." However, it still took some time for Salim to become less of a perfectionist.

"You won't be able to please everyone all the time," I told him. "Sometimes you'll have people hammering at you and you'll just have to say no. Ask them to talk to your new operations manager. Or just don't be here."

He stared at me. "How can I not be here?"

"Lots of ways, Salim," I answered. "And if you're going to stay sane and cyclical, you'll probably have to stay out of this office a couple of days a week. As you said, it's quiet time on your own that renews you. Work at home. Have a second office, hidden in the warehouse. Put your phone on voicemail. You have to create the cycles; if you go with the pressures of the job, they'll exhaust you again."

The Cultivation Cycle: Aligning with the Seasons

The cultivation cycle is the basis of production on any farm, although it's used more fully in organic systems. The cycle of the seasons may seem obvious to you. Yet Salim Hussain's experience of it is typical of many I've seen. Perhaps because the cycle is simple and familiar, applying it to our work can yield surprisingly powerful insights.

This cycle is summarized in the illustration below. As you look at it, consider some of the questions I asked Salim Hussain and explore how you might answer them for your life or work.

THE CULTIVATION CYCLE

It is helpful to think of our life and work following the same naturally regenerative cycle as the four seasons.

111

Aligning your life with the seasons can boost your effectiveness at work and at home. Clearly this is often impossible; as we discussed earlier, you can't control many of the things that happen to you. But ideally you can make allowances based on what you do know, compensating for the unexpected as best you can. For instance, if you know you have a high-output project in the winter, schedule some rest time before and after and plan to minimize other demands on your time during that period. If you expect to do review and maintenance work in the summer, look to undertake a smaller project that will allow you to enjoy seasonal growth.

Keep in mind that even in the organic system, each of the seasons isn't exactly three months long, and activities don't always align with the cycle of the calendar year. For instance, some crops are sown in autumn and harvested in spring. In the human context, there will typically be a number of tasks vying for your attention at different stages of this cycle. And you need to move through the cycle of the seasons according to different timetables. To some extent, you need to honor the cycle daily, weekly, and monthly.

In a business context, the autumn and winter phases are likely to be squeezed. While the activities of these two seasons can be done in quite a short period, one of the crucial aspects of these more receptive seasons is open-space time, when a deeper understanding can emerge as the groundwork and seed for the next turn of the cycle. Recognize which seasons you and

2-MINUTE *CHECKUP*

WINTER CLEARING

Use this exercise if you are feeling overloaded or overheated. Pause, take a few breaths, and picture a clear winter landscape. Perhaps a mountain after a fresh fall of snow or a forest of oak trees in a winter gale that blows around the bare branches. Picture your crowded thoughts and concerns just dropping away or blowing away from you, sense the emptiness of this scene, and feel a sense of quiet renewal arising for you from this winter landscape.

an organization overemphasize and underemphasize; contrasts between the two can be illuminating.

Winter: Preparation

In the cultivation cycle, each season is a prelude to the next. The winter period of rest and review creates the platform for spring growth. The cold weather means that biological activity in the soil is largely dormant. This rest helps build the energy reserves for the intense growth ahead. Freezing and thawing open up soil structures, doing the groundwork for the spring. This is also the time when the farmer reviews ground condition and output needs and plans the spring plantings. Winter is a time for slower processes, such as preparation and integration. Manure applied in the autumn is slowly mixing into the soil, enriching the humus.

In terms of human work, this is the season for rest, renewal, and groundwork. Even a short downtime—a pause for stillness, reflection, and perspective—can be helpful. It's a stage in the cycle when you should review and renew your ground condition, improving structure and mixing in compost, so that you're ready for the coming growth. This is also a time for groundwork in the sense of planning your crop, looking ahead through the whole cycle to prepare for it by making a schedule and identifying skills or resources you need.

Spring: The Delicate Start

Seeding and establishing the crop is a time of intense human activity. Getting the growth process started is the most delicate and crucial stage in the cycle. The soil may need final preparation for planting. Perhaps the soil needs plowing to aerate, stimulate fertility, and improve the structure. Perhaps it needs harrowing, when metal spikes are drawn across the surface of the field to kill weeds and break down lumps of soil. Or sometimes rolling is needed to create a finer, smoother topsoil.

Getting the growth process started is the most delicate and crucial stage in the cycle.

Planting the seed is a vulnerable stage. It offers useful parallels with starting work projects, especially if we look at planting in the garden rather than field-scale crops. Ground condition and planting methods have a significant influence on the success rate of the crop. If the soil is too cold or too dry, the seed will not germinate: The process of growth won't even begin. If the ground is too wet, the seed will rot instead of grow. Some plants will be started indoors, in protected conditions: These seedlings must be hardened off, acclimatized, before they are exposed to outdoor conditions. In this early phase, the plants are vulnerable to weather extremes, such as heavy frost, rain, or drought. Close attention, forethought, and quick response can bring the young crop through such problems; for example, applying a layer of mulch, such as straw, helps to protect the crop.

The right conditions for seeding and growing the desired plants will also stimulate the weeds. Slow-growing crops, which need time to get established, are especially at risk of being out-competed for resources by weeds, which are often vigorous and fast-growing. Hence, this period of early growth is the busiest time for weed control. For some crops, spring will be a time for feeding as well as seeding and weeding. Fast-growing, nutrient-hungry crops such as tomatoes may need supplementary help.

Does this have parallels for your work? Creating a new product or starting a new task is more like cultivating a plant than turning on a computer. Your success rate and speed of growth will be helped by your freeing up time to give plentiful attention to this season of preparing the ground, providing a balanced supply of the four growth elements, protecting the new crop, and dealing with weeds and weather problems as they arise. Watering is especially important—nourishing the new starts with love and appreciation. Bear in mind that problems are likely to grow fast, as weeds do, and draw on the tools of cocreativity to handle them. Recognize that this season demands a lot of resources, so ease up on other demands on your energy, and line up as much support for yourself as you can.

Summer: Letting It Roll

It took several years for me to get used to the ease-up phase of early summer. At first it seemed strange that the most intense plant growth is a time of lower human activity. In northern climes around late May and June, if the establishment work has gone well, the organic grower can, to some extent, sit back and enjoy watching the plants grow. In fact, it's a good example of cocreativity; the active phase in spring cycles into a more receptive time in early summer, which cycles into the active period in mid- and late summer when harvesting begins.

In contrast, one of the risks of the mechanistic approach to work is trying too hard. Having geared ourselves up for intense effort, we keep going until we're exhausted and don't know when to stop. One lesson of the summer season is to know when to stop pushing and allow natural growth to take over. It is quite possible to have recreation and celebration at the height of the growth process and not just at the end.

During summer, most crops should be growing strongly and rapidly, approaching fruition. This is a good example of how fast natural productivity can be if the right conditions are created. However, for some crops, further management may be needed: hoeing out weeds or thinning the crop so that the strongest plants can reach their full potential. In the workplace you don't have to make natural growth happen, but you may need to steer it. And sometimes the number of growth projects have to be thinned down to achieve full maturity.

Autumn: The Harvest

Harvesting, gathering in the completed crop, lasts through summer and into autumn. It is a useful reminder for our work that harvesttime is an extended period. There may be several stages in moving from the crop to the finished product. Consider wheat: Once the plant is cut, the grain must be separated from the husk and the stalk. It then has to be dried before being processed further. Similarly, in your work, allow time to harvest the full value and nutrition from your outputs.

Autumn brings us to completion of the gathering-in phase and the time of harvest festivals. Appreciating and celebrating the fruits of the earth and our labor is another basic element in the sustainable cycle. Then, as plant growth slows right down, we move into the autumn activities of pruning, maintenance, and gathering our stores in preparation for winter. There can be considerable

In your work, allow time to harvest the full value and nutrition from your outputs.

Exercise: Cultivation Cycle Survey

In your living and working cycles, are some seasons exaggerated and others avoided? Do some tasks in each season get fully addressed, while others get short shrift? When the process is forced, parts of the cycle can be overridden or short-circuited for a period of time before the resulting problems become severe or apparent. But to maximize the beneficial effects of the Natural Advantage, particularly sustainable production, significant involvement in all stages of the cycle is required.

The Cultivation Cycle Survey, below, is a simple tool for assessing yourself, a team, or an organization for balance and completeness in the cultivation cycle. Give each item a rating from 0 for total neglect, through 5 for balance, to 10 for major overemphasis. Answer honestly, circle the appropriate number for each cycle, and then consider which steps in the cycle need more of your attention.

CYCLE STAGES

TOO LITTLE ← → TOO MUCH

Ground preparation: Planning, nurturing the starting phase

| 0 | 1 | 2 | 3 | 4 | 5 | 6 | 7 | 8 | 9 | 10 |

Seeding: Using creativity

| 0 | 1 | 2 | 3 | 4 | 5 | 6 | 7 | 8 | 9 | 10 |

Weeding: Learning through problems, maintaining clarity

| 0 | 1 | 2 | 3 | 4 | 5 | 6 | 7 | 8 | 9 | 10 |

Feeding: Raising momentum by support, vision, and appreciation

| 0 | 1 | 2 | 3 | 4 | 5 | 6 | 7 | 8 | 9 | 10 |

Having fun: Enjoying, celebrating, enabling enthusiasm to produce results

| 0 | 1 | 2 | 3 | 4 | 5 | 6 | 7 | 8 | 9 | 10 |

Harvesting: Bringing projects to completion, reaping full benefit for the organization and individuals

| 0 | 1 | 2 | 3 | 4 | 5 | 6 | 7 | 8 | 9 | 10 |

Reviewing: Drawing out the learning and appreciating people

| 0 | 1 | 2 | 3 | 4 | 5 | 6 | 7 | 8 | 9 | 10 |

Maintaining: Preparing/renewing/pruning for future growth

| 0 | 1 | 2 | 3 | 4 | 5 | 6 | 7 | 8 | 9 | 10 |

Resting: Yes, rest!

| 0 | 1 | 2 | 3 | 4 | 5 | 6 | 7 | 8 | 9 | 10 |

work to do at this stage to complete the year's cycle, but the pace can be slower. For example, fruit and root vegetables may need to be packed and stored so that they are available in the winter. It is also a time for pruning—cutting back old growth to improve the coming year's production. And it's a time for checking ground condition at the end of the output phase to see what maintenance and renewal are required.

In the workplace, the autumn season is vital in making the growth cycle sustainable as well as productive. This is the time for reviewing and learning, tending and regenerating your production capacity. This is also when you get the full fruits of your crop—through learning, celebration, and knowing how to process and store some of the output. Without this, you risk getting only superficial satisfaction from the whole growth cycle.

The Competence Cycle

The four-seasons cycle can also be seen as a model for any learning or change process. To explore this, I developed the competence-cycle model (on the opposite page) with one of my colleagues, combining the cultivation cycle with his work on learning competences. While this model can be applied in many ways, one of the most revealing ways concerns a person's overall relationship to his or her job. Some people move through a job cycle too quickly, jumping to another position during the summer phase before reaping the full harvest of its potential. Others stay too long, often stagnating in the winter phase for years.

It is easy to overlook your own shift from high to low competence on this cycle. If your job is repetitious, you may get used to a low level of energy and achievement. Moving yourself from the winter phase and starting the cycle again need not mean changing jobs; you can reconfigure the job or set yourself new learning goals it.

If we consider this as a model of learning and change situations in general, what the cyclical principle emphasizes is balance, and completeness: moving through each stage of the cycle, giving full attention to each in turn, finding an appropriate speed, and keeping moving without rushing or stalling.

Renewal Rotation

The basic principle of crop rotation cycles is to grow a variety of crops on each piece of land. It contrasts with the monoculture on conventional farms, where the same crop is grown on the same land for several years. One of the key organic crop rotations is a cycle that alternates between a high-value, demanding crop,

THE COMPETENCE CYCLE

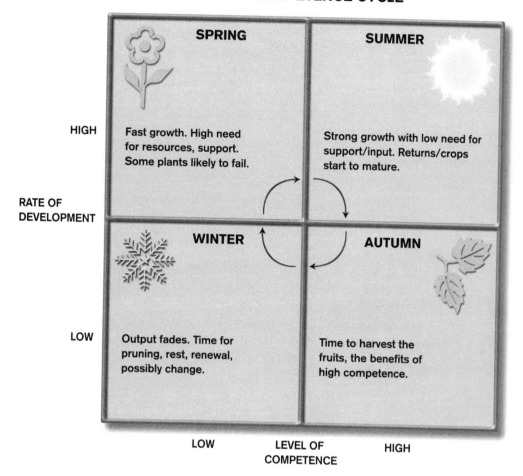

	SPRING	**SUMMER**
HIGH	Fast growth. High need for resources, support. Some plants likely to fail.	Strong growth with low need for support/input. Returns/crops start to mature.
RATE OF DEVELOPMENT	**WINTER**	**AUTUMN**
LOW	Output fades. Time for pruning, rest, renewal, possibly change.	Time to harvest the fruits, the benefits of high competence.
	LOW	HIGH

LEVEL OF
COMPETENCE

Your rate of development and level of competence on the job will wax and wane according to a natural cycle. Recognizing how energy flows from season to season allows you to anticipate change and manage your personal resources.

such as wheat, and a fertility-building crop, such as clover. This cycle takes many forms, some quite sophisticated, with eight or ten courses, and the complete cycle could take as long as 10 years. Besides renewing fertility, crop rotation also achieves pest and weed prevention by natural means.

This use of rotation is an example of increasing the level of change and variation to reduce problems. It echoes a theme in *Blur*, a book by Stan Davis and Christopher Meyer on managing change: They believe that the best way to handle rising speed and complexity is often to increase them even further.

RENEWAL ROTATION

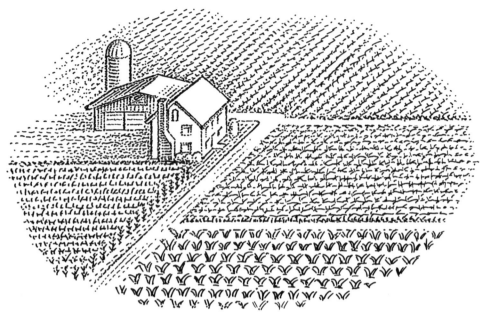

The organic method takes full advantage of the practice of renewal rotation. Besides building fertility, crop rotation also provides natural protection against pests. The potential benefits to your personal ground condition are similar to those realized in the garden or on the farm.

Renewal Rotation at Work

The equivalent of crop rotation in your work could be rotation between tasks, between jobs, or between different modes of working. The potential benefits for your personal ecosystem are similar to those of the organic farm. Rotation between tasks is probably the simplest approach, although rotation between jobs works superbly for some people.

The third option, varying your mode of working, is in some ways the easiest, but it requires more self-discipline. It depends on your own awareness to make the change and alter your habits. A simple way to do this is to notice your customary ways of working and thinking and to periodically choose the less-habitual ones. For example, if you tend to react to problems in a left-brain, analytical mode, try easing off, free-wheeling, or going for a short walk, making space for your right brain to contribute.

Designing Your Cycle

Designing a rotation cycle is a cocreative process. You can analyze some factors, such as soil type, climate conditions, and current market demand, as well as your own working style (see the "Working Rhythms Checklist" on the opposite page), capabilities, and goals. And yet intuition is needed to guess at the uncertainties, antic-

Exercise: Working Rhythms Checklist

The primary goals in creating rotation cycles in your work should be to achieve balance and renewal and to avoid monoculture or excessive repetition. Observe what you overdo, and create cycles to counterbalance this. If you regularly drive yourself too hard and make too many demands on your fertility, clearly you need more renewal activities. Conversely, if you are understretched in your work, you may need to add more challenging crops to that cycle and raise your vitality. You could achieve this through a range of unpaid work and leisure activities.

The Working Rhythms Checklist, below, will help you examine your usual working style. For each pair of qualities, score yourself from 0 to 10, according to which style of working you tend toward. On the blank lines, you can add other qualities you find important or that you're afraid you don't exercise enough.

WORKING RHYTHMS

	0	1	2	3	4	5	6	7	8	9	10	
Active	0	1	2	3	4	5	6	7	8	9	10	Reflective
Production	0	1	2	3	4	5	6	7	8	9	10	Maintenance
Preparation	0	1	2	3	4	5	6	7	8	9	10	Implementation
Broad exploration	0	1	2	3	4	5	6	7	8	9	10	Focused action
Change/risk	0	1	2	3	4	5	6	7	8	9	10	Stability/safety
Independent	0	1	2	3	4	5	6	7	8	9	10	Collaborative
Stretching	0	1	2	3	4	5	6	7	8	9	10	Renewing
Playful	0	1	2	3	4	5	6	7	8	9	10	Serious
_____	0	1	2	3	4	5	6	7	8	9	10	_____
_____	0	1	2	3	4	5	6	7	8	9	10	_____
_____	0	1	2	3	4	5	6	7	8	9	10	_____

ipate future customer needs, and adjust to surprises as the rotation progresses. Consider the following specific methods used in rotation that offer ideas for human activity cycles at work.

Intercropping. This method, also known as polyculture, involves growing two crops on the same land at the same time. Although it can make cultivation and harvesting more difficult, it has several benefits. Typically the overall productive yield is greater. The growth potential of the four elements is used more fully and efficiently, and there's less space for weeds to develop. Particular combinations of plants can be especially synergistic and can prevent pest problems. For example, if onions and carrots are intercropped, the onions repel the carrot flies.

The inference for the workplace is that combining activities can be mutually reinforcing and can raise your energy productivity. An example is Salim Hussain, who intercropped research and lecturing. If one of your main activities draws heavily on certain talents, choosing a complementary task alongside it can be the best way to achieve balance. I have seen a computer programmer take up massage part-time and a management trainer branch into landscape gardening. This is different from renewal rotation because you can sometimes produce two demanding crops together if they're synergistic.

Trap crops. One of the artful ways in which organic growers reduce pests is to start a crop to attract them and then plow it in, killing the pests at the same time. The use of trap crops gives another example of intensifying a problem in order to resolve it.

2-MINUTE *CHECKUP*

PRESSURE BALANCING

When you feel under pressure at work, and at risk of pushing yourself into depletion, try closing your eyes for a couple of minutes. Ask yourself, What would renew me right now? Is there something, however brief, that would restore the cycle, balance the pressure, so I can keep going without exhausting myself?

Learn what works best for you!

I have used this method to good effect when initiating a new project or a new team. Getting them working on a difficult and even provocative dummy project for a day or two brought more of the problems to the surface so we could debug them before getting on with the main work.

Undersowing. This is the principle of sowing the seed for the next crop before the preceding one is fully grown and harvested. In most situations, an organic grower will avoid leaving the earth uncovered, without a crop of some kind. Bare, unused earth is more prone to weeds and to soil erosion. Undersowing maintains continuity of cover and uses the earth productively, as one crop begins before the other is finished. The first crop is usually harvested while the seeds of the new one are germinating underground.

At work, this approach can have the benefits of continuity and extra gestation time. Approaching the completion of a project can be a bumpy period, as people speculate about what's coming next. If the seeds of the next project are sown before the harvest of the last one, it gives more time for creativity to germinate and for new working relationships to put down roots before the next high level of output is required.

Bastard fallow. This is another ingenious method of intensifying the growth of weeds in order to eliminate them. It means leaving a field without a crop, usually just for a few weeks. Various methods may be used to stimulate maximum weed growth during this period: for example, creating a false seed bed, which is prepared and cultivated as if for an output crop, but no crop is sown. The weed seeds are thus given maximum encouragement to germinate. As the weed plants grow, they can be plowed under as compost.

In the work context, this is probably a high-risk strategy. I would only follow it if I felt there was a severe problem with weeds: dissatisfaction, buried conflicts, or energy leaks. An example would be a department left temporarily without a boss. If there are difficulties, this is one way to flush them out; however, it needs to be structured in order to face the problems constructively. A mild example is the workshop we ran for Alibi Publishing without the dominant presence of Phil Morris. His subordinates were not used to resolving their issues directly with each other, but by providing both skills and a safe context, they were able to do so.

The Nutrient Cycle

Cultivating natural systems is a matter of knowing when and how to intervene to harness a natural process with minimum human effort. While a conventional farm depends heavily on importing synthetic nutrients, the organic farm generates its own and operates both horizontal and vertical nutrient cycles to move them to where they're needed.

Some fertility is produced where it's required, such as in growing clover or green manure on a particular field. It is also valuable to have a source of discretionary fertility, which can be moved to where you want it. This process is known as *horizontally cycling nutrients*. For many organic farms, this fertilizer comes from the winter housing of cows. While the cows are kept under cover for the winter, their dung mixes with the bedding straw, composting, to create manure. The manure can then be shifted to where it's most needed—typically, in fields being prepared for high-value crops, such as grains.

The implication for the workplace is to be aware of where you can generate compost and how to shift it to meet your main energy demands. The horizontal cycle means gathering positive energy from one aspect of your life and work and applying it to the current need. For example, a sense of appreciation may be an important motivator to you and may be missing in a current project. If so, harness it elsewhere, and carry that feeling into this project.

Vertical cycling means moving nutrients within the soil. When rainwater passes through topsoil, it carries nutrients down into the subsoil, beyond the reach of many plants. A crop rotation, therefore, should include some deep-rooting crops that will reach into the subsoil and draw nutrients back up. For example, the roots of red clover or field lupines can go down as deep into the soil as 5 or 6 feet.

Digging Deep

People talk of digging deep into their reserves, implying that they are close to exhausted. The analogy with ground condition suggests that if you dig deep, or better still, grow deep, there will be more nutrients available to you. Vertical cycling in your work means drawing such nutrients from deeper in your ground condition— from past experience or from your subconscious.

Harnessing subconscious resources is hard to do directly; it is more a cocreative process, where you consciously identify the need but leave the right brain, your intuition, to get on with the work for you. There are some processes that can help this, equivalent to the deep-rooting plants used for vertical nutrient cycling on the farm. The following paragraphs illustrate how the nutrients deep within the human condition can be brought to the topsoil.

> **If you dig deep, or better still, grow deep, there will be more nutrients available to you.**

Imagining the Future

I was leading a workshop for the sales managers of Homelux Corporation, a market leader in domestic appliances. It was a change-management workshop, using the Natural Advantage, and the main aim was to help the sales management team adapt constructively to a forthcoming reorganization. But there was a sec-ondary agenda: This was mid-December, and it was also the team's Christmas get-together, so I couldn't get too earnest with them.

The team had a pretty successful track record, but their confidence had drained away during the year, as their sales performance had been below target—one of the reasons for the reorganization. Their ground condition was depleted, and I knew that this next round of changes was making them edgy. Vertical nutrient cycling was one of my objectives for the session. Just as a hard rain carries nutrients down into the subsoil, the recent outbursts of criticism and insecurity had washed nutrients out of their topsoil.

I explained to the team that I would like them to explore how they had managed change in the past, to help them develop ways to meet it in the future. I put them in pairs to review the changes they had handled in the past 10 years. To add some fun and to widen the perspective, I asked half of them to be themselves and gave different roles to the others. I gave the most arrogant and ambitious member of the team the role of their president. Twists like these got them laughing and unwinding so that they could be more freely creative.

As I had suspected, they loved reminiscing about the good old days and how simple, slow, and easy things had been. It also drew out their appreciation of the scale of change and of the way they kept meeting challenges that seemed impossible at the time. In effect, this was drawing nutrients up from their subsoil, from their memory, from their subconscious—cycling them into the topsoil, where they could be harnessed.

When I asked the group to picture their future, they were able to voice their fears, exaggerate them, and laugh about them. The ambitious person's vision was: "In 10 years' time, we have only one employee left in Europe. The good news is it's me. The bad news is I work for the computer." By freeing up their tensions and drawing on the nutrients of past success, they moved on to a view of the future that was both realistic and optimistic.

Cycles in the Organization

Most organizations are still very far from acknowledging or developing human sustainability; their prevailing culture and practices do not sit easily with natural cycles. Typically, the word *cycle* would only be used to describe the planning or budgeting procedure.

Despite this, a growing number of companies now acknowledge pressures pulling them toward natural systems approaches. These issues include dissatisfaction with work-life balance among many workers at all levels and ages; the reluctance of a rising number of graduates to consider careers in businesses with too much pressure; and the continuing increase in stress-related problems. Recent compensation awards in the courts show that employers are increasingly being held responsible for stress and depletion in their staff. And some trends in the workplace are encouraging—flex time, working at home, and the virtual office all offer potential for working cyclically.

Humanizing Culture

The real motivation to address these issues comes when there is a business benefit as well as a human one. Improving the quality of working life can be acknowledged as desirable, but it won't, of itself, get the issue onto a company's action agenda. To align its culture with natural cycles, an organization or team should start with the business's needs and results. If the culture can promote the idea that full and balanced cycles are good for the business, then cycles are likely to take root. If using both sides of the brain, slowing down to harvest, taking time for rest and review, and rotating high output with renewal tasks are endorsed as helpful

123

to the profits as well as the people, this will create the ground conditions from which appropriate skills and processes can develop.

Examples do exist of businesses that have improved performance by humanizing their culture; some of these are described in *The Dance of Change*. The Japanese business culture particularly endorses cyclical approaches. *The Art of Japanese Management* by Richard Pascale and Anthony Athos compares Japanese and American large businesses. The authors comment that in a Japanese office, sitting at your desk and staring meditatively into space would be regarded as acceptable and, in fact, productive behavior. In an American business, you'd probably be bawled out within a minute or two.

Promoting Process

Cyclical work processes can include such approaches as job enrichment, where members of a team learn additional skills so that each person performs a range of tasks. There is also job rotation, where individuals move between jobs more frequently. In Japan this is called the spiral staircase model of career progression. Instead of climbing vertically up the hierarchy within one department, people move more slowly, diagonally upward, through a series of different job functions. This philosophy is coming into favor in Western businesses, following the trend to flatter organizational structures.

Processes can also be used to encourage the full four-seasons cycle and the balance of left- and right-brain thinking. Established methods often focus on one or two seasons of the cycle and on one way of thinking—usually the active, analytical approach. The story of David Marsing at Intel, quoted in Chapter 4, is a good example of using a meeting cycle to create a balanced approach by encouraging receptive peripheral vision.

A further example from *The Dance of Change* of using a process to create cyclicality involves Lotte Bailyn, of M.I.T.'s Sloan School of Management:

Sometimes a different way of structuring time can make a difference. We conducted a time experiment with one product development team who worked excessively long hours. We originally proposed closing the doors at 6 p.m. and making everybody leave, but they wouldn't hear of it. They knew that this wouldn't get to the core of their problem. Individuals couldn't finish their work because they were constantly interrupted by meetings, schedule checks, and management reviews.

We worked with them to restructure the workday into "quiet times" and "interactive times." The results were astounding: the team launched the product on time and received quality rewards. Moreover, they now felt a greater sense of control, which eased some of their personal stress. The managers learned that engineers perform better without continuous surveillance. The VP even gave up his weekly ops [operations] reviews.

Career Management

Both culture and processes are important in helping organizations and their people manage the competence cycle to best effect. Better processes, such as succession planning and human development reviews, are one way to manage this cycle better. However, the speed of change makes such anticipation difficult.

An alternative is the approach a telecommunications equipment manufacturer uses for its professional engineers. The company recognized that most people no longer expect a job for life and are skeptical about an employer's ability to plan their careers for them. It ran career-management workshops for its engineers. By giving them the skills to clarify their personal goals, handle career uncertainties, and assert what they want from the company, it has empowered each individual to manage his or her competence cycle. This organization believes that if the individuals are motivated and in appropriate positions, this will achieve the best productive results for the business.

Cycles in Daily Practice

As you start to change your habits and seek a counterbalance to some of the pressures on you, formal methods can be useful. Scheduling quiet time will help you keep your commitment to balancing the cycle, as it did in Lotte Bailyn's work with the product development team mentioned above.

In the early stages of the transition, reviewing your ways of working every week or month will ensure that you regularly check which parts of the cycle are neglected and where you need to balance your approach. Over time, you should find that you start to balance your activities and operate with cycles instinctively and habitually.

chapter 6

RESILIENCE THROUGH DIVERSITY

IF YOU CLEAR A PIECE OF LAND AND LEAVE IT, over many years its ecosystem will become increasingly sophisticated and sustainable. Initially, it will be a crude or pioneer ecosystem with a small number of species and little diversity. The pioneer species, many of them weeds, consume fertility and grow fast but produce low-quality outputs. Over time more diverse, slow-growing species will take over. This process culminates in what are called climax ecosystems, of which rain forests are a classic example. These are highly diverse and self-sustaining, and they produce an abundance of crops and fruits that are useful to humans and other creatures.

If you look at the overall human use of environmental resources, what kind of ecosystem does it equate to? Despite recent progress, it's more like a pioneer ecosystem than a climax system. The same is true of human energy resources at work—the potential for improvement is great. Diversity plays an important role in contributing to this evolution, and organic farms and gardens offer particularly useful examples relevant to the work environment. They make constructive use of biodiversity but also embody customer and enterprise diversity. Whether you work full-time for one organization or freelance for many, you can increase the diversity in your ways of working.

Diversifying for Survival

Out of the blue, I received a phone call from Alison Martin, the hospital manager whose story is featured in Chapters 1 and 2. She was distraught. "Alan, they've let me go. I'm at my wit's end, honestly. Can I meet you to talk about it?"

A few days later, we converged on Magdalen Farm. It was a blustery March afternoon when showers and sunny spells alternated rapidly. Alison glared at me when we met.

"You seem angry," I began.

"Angry!" She burst out. "I'm furious, if you really want to know."

"At?" I asked.

Alison scowled, but her hunched shoulders straightened up as she described her feelings. "At you. At me. At them. Everything I depended on has let me down. I mean, I really trusted you."

"But I couldn't save you from this, could I?" I asked gently.

Alison shook her head and moved from anger to tears. "It was going so well. I was actually enjoying the job for the first time in years and then. . . . It's like being thrown out of a plane without a parachute."

Taking Stock

Later, after a cup of tea, we strolled through the fields. "So where do I go from here?" Alison asked.

I looked at her. "Well, let's take stock for a minute. How is your ground condition?"

She blew her nose. "A bit waterlogged right now, but basically pretty good. I feel I manage my energy pretty well most of the time." Alison grinned at me. "And you don't have to remind me about composting all this anger and fear. I will do it, you know."

"So if we stay with the farming analogy," I said, "what is this dismissal like?"

There was a long pause as we walked on across the fields. At last she said, "It's like a crop failure, on a giant scale. It feels as if my entire farm has been wiped out by one freak event."

"Go on. Where in farming do you see that kind of problem?"

There was another long pause. "Ah yes!" she suddenly exclaimed. "It's like those resistant strains that Peter talks about. On conventional farms you get superpests evolving that are immune to the chemicals, the pesticides."

I smiled to myself. This was starting to get somewhere. "But how," I asked innocently, "would one pest wipe out an entire farm?"

"It's obvious," she said. "It's that monoculture thing you talk about. Very common with intensive farms, right? The whole farm put down to one crop. The more years you go on with that one crop, the more vulnerable you are, and the more dependent. . . ." Her voice tailed off as the penny dropped. She laughed and punched me on the arm. "OK, smart aleck, I get the message! You walked me neatly into that one. And you're right. Even though the hospital has changed like crazy, I kept my job largely the same. For the last 12 years I've been a medical records manager."

"So you thought if you were indispensable, you were safe?" I asked.

Alison nodded, "Exactly. I'd gone stale in the job, but it was my way of limiting change to what I thought I could cope with. Anyhow, I get the point. You can impose monoculture for so long, then the problems burst out, megastyle. What do I do about it?"

I smiled. "Sounds like it's time to go and ask."

You can impose monoculture for so long, then the problems burst out, megastyle.

Change Is Good

We found Peter Norman in the polytunnel, or hoop house, a form of greenhouse made of polyethythene sheeting arched over metal frames.

Alison looked around. "What kind of things have you planted here?"

"A lot of different varieties," Peter answered. "Let's see . . . tomatoes, three kinds. Lettuces, five kinds. Bok choy, salad herbs, three types of cucumber. . . ."

"It sounds horribly complicated," Alison exclaimed. "Can't you make it simpler for yourselves?"

Peter laughed. "We'd rather not—not yet anyway. We've planted a lot of different things to see what likes it here."

Alison snorted. "That's ridiculous! Surely you can look that stuff up in a book?"

He looked surprised. "Not really. Every piece of land is unique: the soil type, pests, predators, diseases, history—it's all a unique combination. By planting five kinds of lettuce, I've a good chance of finding a couple of winners. If I planted one or two, I might get an OK one and I might have complete failure."

"But once you've got a winner, you'll stick with it?" Alison persisted.

Peter frowned. "Not so simple. The longer I repeat the same crop in the same place, the more I risk problems. After three years, I'd either change the crop or move the whole polytunnel to a fresh piece of soil."

Alison looked around the polytunnel dubiously. "I still don't get it, Peter. In my mother's greenhouse she's always spraying like crazy to keep the pests down. I mean, what you're doing here is fairly repetitious, isn't it?"

Peter gave one of his vague smiles. "Yes, it is a bit intensive, and I don't know why it works, really. It's basically a matter of trusting the system."

Alison growled. "How the hell am I supposed to learn from an answer like that?"

"What I mean," Peter answered, "is that if the general system is right, you don't have to take specific actions to prevent pests. The field margins are pretty crucial, but I couldn't say exactly how."

"What do you mean, field margins?"

"Most organic growers leave an uncultivated margin around the edge of their fields," Peter explained. "That provides a space for wildflowers, wild grasses, and weeds. The field margins provide a habitat for birds and insects, like the hedges do. It means that whatever pests we have, we've usually got the predators around, too. So most of the time, nature keeps things in balance for us."

"Don't you ever get major disasters?" Alison asked. "You know, a whole crop wiped out at a stroke, so it brings you to your knees?"

Peter shook his head. "Very rarely. Sometimes we get crops and livestock below the target yield, or running late, but I'll still earn something on it. And anyway, it's only one string on my guitar."

"Can you explain the guitar?" I asked.

Peter smiled. "I say that a monoculture farm is like a guitar with one string. It's horribly boring for everyone, and if your one string breaks, you really are screwed. Magdalen Farm is like an eight-string guitar. If one of them breaks, I can work around it for a while. All the strings resonate and enrich the music. That way, you get this synergy that Alan's always talking about."

Biodiversity: Nature's Rivets

We know biodiversity is important, but why? What does it do for us? How much of it do we need? Think of biodiversity as rivets on nature's airplane. You can lose a number of rivets and the plane will still fly, the planet's ecosystem will still function. But if you keep losing more rivets, as we are losing biodiversity, at some point the plane will crash.

In considering why biodiversity is important, a specific example may help: human food. It is estimated that 90 percent of all human food consumption now depends on 20 plant species; rice, wheat, and potatoes are the most important of these. Within these 20 species, the rapid growth of intensive farming worldwide means that much of this production depends on a very small number of specific plant strains, which have been specially bred for high yields under intensive conditions. This has already produced several major crises. For example, in 1993, 80 percent of the North American corn crop was threatened by a single disease. The risk was only averted because the corn strain was enhanced by crossing it with a much older strain found in Mexico.

Because of the extremely high use of a single strain of species such as wheat, these strains have to be replaced or enhanced every 10 to 15 years. The source of the improvement is usually an obscure, traditional strain. If we turn to the analogy with the workplace, how many species of working style and culture account for those in most large organizations? As with intensive farming, the pressures for immediate output have led to a steep increase in conformity.

The rise of intensive farming is a significant cause of lost biodiversity. The dramatic increase in pesticide use since the 1950s has killed off numerous insect species. Many of these insects brought benefits as well as problems—for example, providing food for the birds, which kept slug levels in check. The push to maximize production led many intensive farms to eliminate hedgerows and other habitats that had supported a large variety of plants and wildlife.

Biodiversity on the Farm

Any farm is less biodiverse than nature in the wild, but the organic farmer or gardener actively fosters diversity. As Peter's polytunnel illustrates, this is achieved by cultivating a wider range of crops and livestock, often choosing plant species and animal breeds that are more traditional and less common. The seed mix for an organic pasture will typically contain 10 to 15 varieties of grass, clover, and

Resilience is essential when you know you can't control change.

herbs, while a conventional mix might simply be one strain of grass. In fact, organic standards specifically require growers to maintain the genetic diversity of the agricultural system, including protecting plant and wildlife habitats in the surroundings.

Biodiversity is also helped by maintaining hedgerows, field margins, and other habitats, such as small ponds, thickets, and areas of scrub. Organic growers do this partly because it's the right thing; it's good stewardship of natural resources. They also do it because greater biodiversity adds resilience, although these benefits often can't be quantified or anticipated. Resilience is essential when you know you can't control change, since it creates the means to respond to change actively and harness it to advantage. The equivalent in human health is to develop a robust immune system, and reduce your susceptibility to the viruses and bugs to which we are all constantly exposed. The analogy to the intensive farming approach would be trying to sanitize your environment, to suppress and eliminate all the threats. This is exhausting and unsustainable.

Other Kinds of Diversity

Enterprise diversity is another aspect of the organic farm's resilience. Even a smallish holding is likely to have several business enterprises. This may mean losing some economies of scale, but it creates both internal and external resilience; if one enterprise suffers production problems, others can sustain the income flow. The enterprises will be chosen for their symbiotic benefits: The combination will be more resilient and productive than any one or two activities on their own. For example, manure from the livestock feeds the plants, and plant waste in turn is used to feed the animals. Internal resilience also rises because more diversity means more change, more rotation, and hence, less risk of pests and other problems. External resilience is improved because the farm is less dependent on any one market. If demand or prices suddenly drop in one sector, this will not threaten the financial viability of the whole operation.

Enterprise diversity also makes experimentation, learning, and innovation easier. Many organic farms have stumbled on a profitable market niche by accident. An intensive farm is unlikely to embark on such experiments—because labor is minimized and specialized capital equipment is used, small-scale diversification is difficult.

Livestock diversity is a feature of many organic operations. The three main types of livestock—pigs, sheep, and cows—complement each other in the benefits they bring to ground condition: churning, conditioning, and cycling. The earth benefits from periodically being deeply churned over by pigs that grub up persistent, deep-rooted weeds such as docks. Sheep are often said to have golden hooves: Their feet will aerate and condition soil that's been recently sown or is

The pressures for immediate output have lead to a steep increase in conformity.

damp, soil that would be compacted by heavier animals. Cows, as we have seen, create an excellent nutrient cycle to sustain fertility. Livestock diversity also helps to reduce pests. For example, the main sheep and cattle parasites have different life cycles, so rotating these animals in a clean grazing system prevents both sets of parasites from building up.

Personal diversity, the variety of tasks and expertise needed by organic growers and their teams, is remarkable; every organic farm is certainly a learning organization. *Staff diversity* is also common. Organic methods are more labor intensive; the number of hands needed has wide seasonal swings, which are met from a variety of sources, including volunteers, interns, and customers.

Most organic growers also have an instinctive drive toward *customer diversity*. Although big customers, such as supermarkets, are important to many growers, they generally seek to develop a range of customers, including some direct local links. Diversification into new products is frequently motivated by the desire to extend the customer base. This is explored further in Chapter 7.

As you consider the implications of all this for the workplace, you may conclude that an organic farm is a network of cottage industries, while an intensive farm is typical of any large-scale industrial production process, whether it's a factory or an office. The truth is less simple. The largest organic farms are similar in size to big factory farms, 1,000 to 2,000 acres. Nevertheless, large organic farms still embody diversity and provide a model of economic, human, and environmental sustainability that a large factory farm cannot. At this size, an organic farm will use specialized mechan-ical equipment and will tailor its processes to achieve economies of scale. However, it will rarely do this as a monoculture; the aim is to achieve economies of scale, but in diverse enterprises that provide mutual synergy.

Creating Diversity

If, like Alison Martin, you have a stretch-ing, full-time job in a large organization, the prospects of bringing diversity into your work may look poor. The pressures toward standardization and conformity can be high. However, there are other trends that may help you, such as flatter organizations, shifting responsibilities from service staff to line managers, matrix organization structures, and the use of project teams. These trends typically in-crease the variety and variability of indi-vidual roles and offer more scope to harness the organization's needs to create diversity in your work content.

I have worked with many middle man-agers who were in part-time M.B.A. pro-grams and who doubted if they could diversify their job within their current or-ganization. Most were in jobs that fulfilled only a fraction of their talents, and this had been a motive for doing an M.B.A. As their new learning showed them areas they wanted to explore in their work, their uncertainty increased. Often the limitation was in the narrow views of a boss, or a boss's boss, not in the organiza-tion as a whole. I encouraged these man-agers to use their project and research work on the M.B.A. to broaden their con-tacts and to discover which people and what priorities in their organization aligned with their diversification goals. In many cases a fit did exist, and they were able to expand or change jobs without having to change employers.

Rethinking Work

A useful method of exploring diversity in your work is Charles Handy's portfolio con-cept, described in his book *The Age of Unreason*. He likens the benefits of in-vesting in a diverse portfolio of financial as-sets to those of investing our working energy in a range of activities. This does not necessarily mean giving up the full-time day job. As Handy says, "We will do well to broaden our definition of what work is. Instead of seeing it as paid employment, why not see it as any activity with a pro-ductive purpose?" He outlines five dif-ferent types of work, as follows:

- *Wage work*: money paid for time worked
- *Fee work*: money paid for results delivered
- *Home work*: activity involved with your home and family, including cleaning, shopping, and child care

- *Gift work*: voluntary work outside the home, including work for charity or the local community
- *Study work*: developing your own knowledge and skills

Even in a demanding full-time job, you may have room to develop two or three strands in your portfolio. Recognizing and valuing what you receive and how you can develop through work outside your main job are also important. It took me years to realize that cooking a meal for my family could be renewing.

Encouraging Interests

Diverse interests are sometimes best kept separate from the main job, although sometimes they can interweave to create synergy. I recall a successful sales manager for a large computer firm who still wished he had become a professional saxophone player. With a family and mortgage to support, this was not a realistic option. He realized that his best way through was to soundproof the garage and play around on the sax just for fun. As he said, "I don't want to make a second career of this. I have to be so disciplined and accurate in my main work, I need expressive messing around outside of it."

By contrast, Glenda had worked in the call center of a large bank for several years. She was getting bored with it, to the point where her health and vitality were suffering. Outside the job she had developed a deep interest in tai chi, but this no longer offset the monotony and stress of her main work. In a personal development workshop I was leading, she

2-MINUTE *CHECKUP*

THE WILD MARGINS

We know that the fringe areas of land that ring organic farms and gardens support a profusion of plant, insect, bird, and animal species. The equivalent to this in human terms are your "fringe" interests that aren't part of your main, paid work. The lesson here is to value and encourage the wild margins of your nature because they can help support sustainability.

Take a moment now to identify any "wild margin" activities of your own, along with the benefits they bring you now and how they could possibly help in the future.

We have seen how in mainstream farming it's often the obscure varieties or wild plants whose qualities are needed when an overused monoculture strain of plant has problems. In the same way, imagine that your eccentric side could hold the key when you or your organization run into problems and need a creative solution.

described how bored some of her colleagues also were. One of them had jokingly said she should start a lunch-hour tai chi class. Glenda told us this story as if it had been a silly idea, but in telling it, she realized its potential. Although she was nervous about leading a group, especially for colleagues, it worked. Glenda became a kind of seed bank for this group, adapting complementary methods for stress management.

Client Diversity

Customer or client diversity is another application of the principle. This applies as much to the employed as the self-employed. If you develop your links with a range of senior contacts within an organization, you gain resilience. You and your abilities are more widely known and you gain access to a wider range of opportunities. A surprising number of people remain overly reliant on the relationship with their direct manager. This can be like monoculture: Without a diverse customer base, if the manager moves on or has a falling out with you, you're vulnerable.

Task Diversity

Task and skill diversity will also increase your resilience to change and help you renew your resources. Make this a criterion for the way you develop both your main work and other activities. Aim to use a wide variety of skills and develop more diverse new ones. The Working Rhythms Checklist on page 119 is one way to identify gaps. Remember that monoculture—in this case, excess repetition of one task or skill—is likely to deplete you and sap your resilience.

An example of this principle is my own career. For many years I poured most of my work energy into one job at a time. As a result, I would typically exhaust my potential in each role within three or four years and would leave to join another company. Since 1990, I have developed four strands to my work. They are diverse but mutually reinforcing. All are renewing for me and are sustainable over the long term. Within my main business, Working Vision, I offer consulting and facilitating for a variety of organizational clients. I also lead personal development workshops for individuals, which have quite a different character and enable me to experiment. My gift work since 1990 has been the establishment of the Wessex Foundation and Magdalen Farm. My main wild-margin activity has been a 70-acre woods I own near my home. I have indulged my love of nature, my secret desire to be an architect, and my interest in woodworking by establishing Hazel Hill as a retreat center and helping to design and construct a range of wooden buildings for this purpose. Overall, this portfolio gives me enterprise diversity and also customer and livestock diversity.

Diversity in Organizations

In her book *The Change Masters*, Rosabeth Moss Kanter explores the differences between large organizations that change successfully and those that fail. She comments that in giant groups that learn to move, the crucial expertise often comes from a subsidiary on the margins of the group. This may be seen as a maverick or rebel outfit—successful, but uncomfortably different. These wild-margin divisions might have been threatened with sell-off or cultural clampdowns in the past. However,

(continued on page 139)

Exercise: Diversity by Design

This exercise is designed to help you assess and cultivate diversity in your work, both at the overall, structural level and in daily practice. The first part asks you to apply the portfolio concept. Remember that one job position can include several roles. For example, as a department manager, your role portfolio could include: 1) the people and task responsibilities of your main work; 2) a secondary role as mentor to several graduate trainees; 3) membership on a creative product development team. The work activities you list may not all be paid and may include hobbies and leisure pursuits.

STRUCTURAL DIVERSITY

See if you can identify a portfolio of four to eight main work activities. Number them, and use these numbers for the assessment in part 2. Check off which of the four work categories each fits into.

Main work activities/roles	Wage/Fee work	Home work	Gift work	Study work
1.				
2.				
3.				
4.				
5.				
6.				
7.				
8.				

If all your activities fit within one or two of these categories, ask yourself if you're defining work widely enough—it can include any activity with a productive purpose. A spread of work between at least three of these categories is desirable. If you want to increase the diversity of your work categories and activities, use the space below to identify three steps you can take to achieve this.

1. _____

2. _____

3. _____

CLIENT DIVERSITY

Who is/are the main client(s) for each of the four to eight work activities you have identified above?

Client	1	2	3	4	5	6	7	8

Take a moment to consider how diverse or varied your client list is. For example, do most of your work activities serve only one or two people or organizations (low diversity), or do they serve several? Do you have a diverse mix of such criteria as client type (individuals, corporations, other organizations), client needs, and client backgrounds (for example, size and industry sector for organizations, age and personality for individuals). Now rate the diversity of your clients/customers, using a scale from 0 (very low) to 10 (very high). If this diversity needs to be improved, identify three steps you can take to achieve this. For example, you may simply aim to increase the number of clients/customers or to vary the type of clients and possibly the types of skills and services you provide for them.

1. _____

2. _____

3. _____

Diversity by Design—*Continued*

SKILL/TASK DIVERSITY

For each of your four to eight work activities, identify one or two main skills or tasks that they involve. For example, if one activity is membership on a new product team, the main skills/tasks could be teamwork and creative development of ideas. Note on the matrix to what extent the same skills or tasks recur in several of your activities, indicating a lower level of overall diversity.

Skills/Tasks	1	2	3	4	5	6	7	8

If you want to do this analysis in more detail, listing more skills/tasks for each activity, create your own matrix on a larger sheet of paper.

Looking at this matrix, how do you rate the diversity of the skills/tasks in your work as a whole? Use a scale from 0 for very low, to 10 for very high. If this diversity needs to be improved, highlight three skills or tasks that would significantly increase the diversity level:

1. _____

2. _____

3. _____

when the monoculture problems of the main group reach crisis level, the exiles become the new kings.

The Wild Margin

Few businesses can compete without a fair degree of focus and efficiency. The art is knowing when to draw the line, how to encourage the wild margin within the organization. A successful example of this is 3M; it requires its development engineers to spend 15 percent of their time on projects they have personally initiated, as distinct from priorities set for them by senior management. Through this wild-margin time, major new products such as Post-it notes have originated. 3M also has a suggestion scheme whereby any employee can request time and resources to investigate an idea for a new product or operational improvement.

Community Initiatives

Another successful approach is taken by the British nonprofit organization Business in the Community, which creates opportunities for staff from large businesses to work on local social- and environmental-improvement projects. Typically, staff will do this during paid work time. Employers involved in the scheme report paybacks for their businesses through increased capabilities and motivation of the people involved.

Just as organic growers foster biodiversity partly as a good thing in its own right, many organizations support community initiatives and other voluntary work among their staff for equally broad motives. There may be potential benefits from staff contri-

butions to the company, or from customer attitudes, but these are too diffuse to specify. Often, the main benefit is in building resilience to change; when the company hits an unexpected problem, there are skills and support to meet it in a way that could never have been preplanned.

The Resilient Patchwork

As we have seen, the diverse patchwork of crops and livestock on organic farms creates more resilience than is present in monocultures. In the same way, some leading businesses have recognized the need to increase diversity among their people. This is not specifically intended to address issues of equal opportunities and recruitment of minorities. The aim is to increase diversity along a range of criteria: thinking and learning styles, temperament, gender, age, educational level, regional background, and ethnic background. For example, Ann Lamont, human resources director of a BP subsidiary, comments, "To stay as successful as we have been, we know that we have to keep reinventing ourselves, thinking outside the box. We are deliberately cultivating diversity in our intake of people, to ensure that we raise the level of internal challenge, constructive conflict, so that we can change even faster than our competitive environment."

Volunteer work builds resilience to change.

Diversity is not the same as diversification. Business diversity can be achieved in several ways. It may mean leveraging core competence through a range of different products or markets. For example, the original expertise of the Honda Corporation was in motors, but it has achieved strength through diversity by applying this expertise to a variety of markets, including cars, motorcycles, outboard motors, lawn mowers, and generators. In other cases, diversity may be achieved through a portfolio of enterprises that are basically different but provide synergy or counterbalances.

Diversity in Daily Practice

Cycles and diversity are closely linked: They require and enable each other. If your day-to-day working style is cyclical, this will help to make it diverse. *Structural* diversity probably needs to be your main concern. If you can set up variety in your work enterprises and customer base, and if you give time to your wild margins, diversity in daily practice should flow from this.

Create new patterns, rhythms, and habits to help you achieve diversity in your daily work. I counter my workaholic tendency by taking regular breaks and challenging myself to do something recreational before I go back to the main task. Use the Diversity by Design exercise on page 136 to show you where you want to increase the diversity in your work and start to weave new skills, activities, or contacts into your daily work. Think of this like adding new instruments to your orchestra: It can add richness, quality, and pleasure to the peformance. And . . . remember to indulge your wild margins!

chapter 7
REAL
QUALITY

THIS CHAPTER BRINGS US TO REAL QUALITY, the last of the seven principles of the Natural Advantage. It completes our journey through the sustainable production cycle, which started with ground condition and finishes with the quality of outputs. As you would expect, this last stage in the cycle feeds back into the first. If your outputs have real quality and emotional value, this naturally helps you renew your ground condition.

I use the term *real quality* to cover products and production processes that create value, including organic marketing, a range of innovative approaches to build dialogue, adaptability, and cocreativity with customers.

If you go into a supermarket and compare the prices of organic and regular produce, the premiums may surprise you. Many organic products cost 25 percent more, and some are up to double the price. Why are such a fast-growing number of people paying so much more for produce that seems similar on the shelf? The answer to this question can teach us a lot about the true meaning of quality. It is found not just in the products but in the way they are produced, in their certification, and in the supplier-customer rela-

tionship. Because so many organic producers cultivate direct contact with their customers, organic consumers have some sense of the people and processes involved in producing the food they are buying, and this personal link is part of the quality in their purchase.

The best test of real quality is the satisfaction of all parties involved in a transaction. It's a feeling as much as a fact. To explore this, look at yourself as a product. Who are your customers? How do your transactions create value for them and for you? Often the emotional value of the exchange counts as much as the tangible benefits.

The Value of Real Quality

Imagine it's your birthday and you're going out to dinner with a friend. How would you choose where to go? Would you pay more for this meal than for an average night out? If so, what exactly are you paying the premium for? In our personal lives, we easily recognize and value real quality. We don't pay a premium to get a larger quantity of food in a fancy restaurant—quite the reverse. The value could be called semitangible; the value lies in the taste of the food, the service, the ambience, and the sense of occasion.

Product Quality

Numerous consumer studies have been conducted on the motives for buying organic food. Nutrition/health benefits and better taste are generally the main motiva-

tions. Product research shows that crops grown organically contain more protein, vitamin C, and valuable trace nutrients. They are typically slower-growing and more mature when harvested. The faster-grown, less-mature, intensively farmed produce is more watery. There is also a difference in durability; organic produce has been shown to stay fresher longer.

With all these advantages, it may seem surprising that organic products have difficulty meeting supermarkets' quality standards. The reason is that the supermarkets focus more on superficial or nominal standards. They believe their sales depend on consistency of shape, size, and a lack of surface blemishes, all of which are easier to achieve with the chemical inputs and suppressants of intensive farming. However, the growth in sales of organic produce shows that more consumers now understand the difference between real quality—taste, nutrition, and satisfaction—and nominal quality. Organic food sales make up the fastest-growing segment of the grocery business in the United States, tripling in the past decade to become a $6 billion industry that provides an endless variety of products to farmers' markets, neighborhood stores, and mainstream supermarkets.

In our personal lives, we easily recognize and value real quality.

All the features of real quality in organic production apply in the workplace. In both cases, true quality includes the how and the what of production, the tangibles and intangibles, the emotional and rational benefits. And quality is enhanced by a sense of dialogue and rapport between producer and customer.

Process Quality

It is clear that many people now consider the ethics and sustainability of the production process in their purchase decisions. As an example, take the growth in demand for Café-direct coffee and other fair-trade products. Wholesome production is becoming part of the wholesome product, often governed by a certification scheme that ensures credibility.

In organic growing, the certification standards are strict and explicit about the methods of production. They include environmental sustainability, animal welfare, wildlife protection, and the health and well-being of the people involved.

The production methods in conventional farming can hardly be called high quality in the true sense. Battery chickens, or factory-farmed chickens, are just one example of how many animals are kept in painful, cramped, unnatural conditions. This is not malice; it's what happens when minimum production cost overrides all other considerations.

Conventional farms are pretty unhappy places for people, too. Farmers have one of the highest suicide rates in America, taking their own lives three times as often as the general populace. The level of occupational health problems and work injuries among farm workers is also high. Imagine working in a highly mechanized dairy parlor, milking 400 cows on your own in two hours. Workers on intensive farms complain of isolation and stress, in much the same language as the workers in a large, automated industrial process.

Although organic growers and their teams work hard, they mostly seem happy in their work, and their mental and physical health is better than those in conventional farming. Organic methods are more labor intensive, which contributes to job satisfaction and output quality. More of the work is paced by humans, not machines, and more of it involves working with other people. When production processes are naturally aligned and there is real quality of output, you would expect the people involved to feel satisfied and sustainable in their work.

Emotional Exchange

When I introduced the idea of real quality to Salim Hussain at Virosoft, he was both intrigued and perplexed. "You have to remember, I'm an engineer," he said wistfully. "For years I've been told that if you can't measure it, it's not real. To me, quality is something you can certify."

I grinned at him mischievously. "OK, but remember our discussion with Aziz? What did he say he most valued about you?"

Salim had his head in his hands, looking even more baffled. "Ahhh . . . He said he sleeps better at night; he feels reassured by my abilities."

I nodded. "So it's quality assurance, but not as we know it. Think of him as your customer, and you as a supplier. There's a positive emotional exchange between you."

Salim stared at me blankly. "Emotional exchange? What do I get back?"

"Remember we talked about your need for recognition, to have your standing acknowledged?"

"Yes. And sometimes I get that from Aziz."

"Do you ever tell him you want it?"

He looked shocked. "Well, no, I'd be . . . embarrassed to say it."

"So how's he supposed to know it's important to you?" Salim was at a loss. I went on, "It's a bit like asking your supplier to guess what your quality spec is."

He looked at me keenly. "Ah, but you said I was the supplier, and he's the customer."

I nodded. "Yes, but real quality is a two-way process. Each party in a sense is both supplier and customer. I mean, Aziz pays you for the services you provide, but I'd say the emotional income you get is more important than the money."

There was a long pause as Salim pondered this. Then he looked up and smiled at me. "Hmm, it's true—the recognition in my work is most valuable to me. And you're right, I'm more likely to get what I want if I specify it. Even if it's qualitative."

"Now what about the people who work for you? Do you tell one another about your quality needs?"

Salim was clearly agitated by this one. He got up, paced around the room, called for a coffee, and at last sat down nervously and looked at me. "This is horrible," he said. "I've been treating them like diodes."

"Diodes? What do you mean?"

"A diode passes current in one direction and not the other. My department is my circuit board. I design the links, I plug the people in, and I just expect them to work. I just couldn't stand to see them as people...."

"Do you know why?" I asked gently.

There was a thoughtful pause. Then he said slowly, "I was afraid if I really listened to their needs, it would overwhelm me. My god, I have people with boyfriends leaving, parents dying. Can I cure these problems?"

"Do they expect you to? Have you asked them?"

He sighed. "No. And maybe recognition is enough."

I went on. "With the people I manage, I keep finding that what I need is the same as what they need. If there's something you want, Salim, ask for it and give it to others; model it."

The concepts of emotional content and exchange gave Salim a kind of engineering

You are most likely to get what you want if you specify it.

framework for human relations in his department. His approach to his people had been much like intensive farming: He applied plentiful inputs of pay, briefs, and deadlines, and he expected the output to happen. Now he could see that the personal details his staff had tried to share with him, and which he had found irrelevant and uncomfortable, were part of the transaction. As he explained to me, "I used to be afraid that if I met them as people, we'd never get any work done. The whole department would be a chat room and then I'd be jumped on from above. In fact, it's the reverse. The productivity has gone up. We're all working better because they can talk to me."

Emotional Quality

Whether it's vegetables, cereals, or livestock, most of the produce from a farm has a 70 percent water content. Figuratively, the same could be true for your work outputs: Remember that the water element equates to emotional energy. For real quality, the emotional content is essential. In *Blur*, Davis and Meyer are eloquent on this point, in the business context:

Figure out which parts and what proportion of your offer are intangible. . . . Figure out how to grow the intangibles faster. . . . When listing your intangibles, include all services . . . other forms of information . . . and all emotions (which include brand loyalty, customer relationships, employee commitment, and the like). . . . Remember: every sale is an economic, informational, and emotional exchange. . . . When you make a sale, be sure you also know what information you want to collect during the exchange and are able to do so. Do the same for emotions. Identify the ones you are selling and the ones you are buying. . . . Put emotions into every offer and every exchange.

It was from Peter Jansen that I really learned about the emotional aspect of quality and how to cultivate it. Early on at the board meetings he chaired, I would sit there perplexed. How did he generate such involvement, such clarity, from everyone? How did he draw out the key issues, and the truth about them, with such ease? The answer had nothing to do with simplistic approaches, such as asking, "How are we all feeling today?" It had a lot to do with high emotional intelligence, as described by Daniel Goleman in *Emotional Intelligence*. This means being articulate and skilled in communicating, sensing, and handling feelings—your own and those of others.

If you apply organic principles, you can develop emotional intelligence and emotional quality. Many of the stories in this book show how openness about feelings develops real quality in working relationships. This links with another lesson from organic farming: The quality of the output grows from the quality of the process. If your ways of working are sustainable, it enriches the end result for you and your customer.

Servicing the Customer

Outpost Natural Foods is a venture that shows how the organic food sector can achieve real quality in all aspects of the customer relationship, and how organic marketing produces some astute innovations. The benefit to individuals and organizations should be apparent.

Outpost Natural Foods is a cooperative that was established back in 1970. While the word cooperative may suggest a few earnest hippies selling stuff from a shack, the reality of Outpost is nothing like that. The company operates two large stores in Milwaukee—very professionally, but very distinctively.

Pam Mehnert, Outpost's general manager, is clear that an organic approach is central to their successful differentiation. She says, "Most of the products we sell are organic, but our strategy is to offer far more than just the produce. We offer information, entertainment, innovative services, and a sense of partnership between Outpost and the people who shop here."

The staff training at Outpost emphasizes customer rapport, customer problem solving, and product knowledge in the widest sense, including nutrition and organic production methods. Pam comments, "We want our customers to feel they can ask any staff member anything, from health issues to cooking queries."

The consumer who buys at Outpost gets a sense of the whole organic production process standing behind the products in store. Outpost has direct trading links with many of the farmers who supply their produce; these farmers come into the stores regularly for sessions where consumers can meet them and learn how their food is grown. Both staff and customers are also offered trips to visit the

2-MINUTE *CHECKUP*

FEELING THE QUALITY

This is a quick, simple method for moving toward real quality in your transactions with customers and suppliers. With practice, you can use this in real time during a transaction.

Focus on the transaction between yourself and a supplier or customer. You can do this during an actual meeting, or visualize the scene. Use a piece of paper and draw two circles to represent yourself and the other party. Put yourself in the third point, the witness position, where you can look at yourself and at your customer/supplier. Look beneath the words, below the apparent transaction, and sense the feeling and spirit of the engagement. Is it right? Does it need changing?

Now look more closely at the other person, at your customer/supplier. Do you believe they are getting the emotional value they need from the transaction? If not, how can you understand what they need, and then provide it?

Now look at yourself. Are you getting the emotional value you need? Have you helped the other party understand your needs and how they can meet them? What else do you need to do to achieve this?

farms themselves. This direct rapport is a source of new product ideas both for Outpost and their suppliers.

Over time, the organic approach has led Outpost to some creative promotional approaches and new services. Increasing concern about diet and nutrition is one of the consumer needs they have cultivated. Outpost now has a dietary technician on their staff, and a Health Notes computer in each store for customers to use. They also offer free lectures at their stores on such topics as natural approaches to weight loss and the healing power of food.

Real quality arises when you accept and apply organic principles completely; it won't work as an add-on. An example is the way Outpost set up their second store. Lyn Falk of Retailworks is a specialist in holistic, sustainable design. She helped Outpost develop the new store using sustainable design practices and earth-friendly finishes. This is not just doing right by the planet—it enhances the total product. Falk says, "I didn't want to just design pretty spaces; I wanted them to affect the bottom line."

Partnership and community are important concepts in real quality, and Outpost achieves these in many ways. Whereas many cooperatives are owned by their workers, Outpost encourages ownership by its customers. For $25 a year, a consumer can become a co-owner of Outpost. The benefits include social events that build a sense of community, as well as savings on special offers. Outpost also gives a small percentage of their revenue to local non-profit organizations.

Outpost publishes a monthly magazine that is a great example of organic synergy: It combines Outpost product promotion with education about organic food and healthy living, plus it provides service to the local community. *Exchange*, Wisconsin's food and wellness magazine, is published monthly by Outpost, free of charge. The magazine carries a range of articles, listings, and advertisements for the food and health sectors, as well as a specific section with news about Outpost. A nice feature is the Values page, where an Outpost customer or staff member writes why an organic diet is important to him or her.

Real Quality in Organizations

If we could monitor the language of companies, the use of the word *quality* would surely have increased a great deal in recent years. Movements such as total quality management have increased employees' involvement in the production process and have led to some impressive advances. While they have improved some aspects of real quality, such as product reliability and delivery, they have overlooked others. Organizations are only slowly realizing that the intangibles of real quality can be measured and managed.

Smart, Sincere Business

How can a no-frills, low-cost airline get outstanding ratings for customer service? Answer: by embodying all seven principles of the Natural Advantage. Real quality grows out of the other six and feeds into them. Southwest Airlines is proof that a big business with a human culture and empowered people can also deliver on hard measures such as safety, profit, and punctuality. The story below is typical of many at Southwest, but it's also unusual because it shows the smart natural systems that create real quality.

From the San Francisco *Examiner*:

A random act of creativity was the last thing John Voyles had in mind to "commit" as he looked at me—a coffee-crazed customer standing in the ticket line.

Voyles, Southwest's Oakland station leader, saw in me all the classic signs of a stressed-out traveler: frantic glances at my watch, then to the seemingly endless ticket line, and an "I'll never get out of here on time" expression, prompting Voyles to take action.

An innocent "May I help you?" elicited my tale of woe: This commuter had spent his last two dollars on a Starbucks double latte, leaving no money to tip the Skycap. The closest ATM was miles away, all of which meant waiting in a too-long line to check my bag.

Voyles reached into his wallet and gave me $2 to tip the Skycap. Problem solved. "Have a great flight," Voyles said, wishing me well and moving on. Voyles offered a stunning response to a totally ambiguous opportunity for memorable customer service. Yet Voyles was simply responding to the culture at Southwest, where the unexpected request, the unusual problem, and the bizarre are commonplace.

Voyles rescued this flier by employing three qualities that are essential to dealing effectively with "customers in motion," especially those in unfamiliar territory:

You're always on: A finely tuned intuitive antenna picks up real needs and concerns within the blur and din of a highly charged environment like an airport. Nonverbal cues can make powerful statements, but only if you are switched on and ready to act to solve those human needs.

Be committed to respond to the opportunity before asking the question: You may not like the response you get to "May I be of service?"—especially if you follow up the client's response with a real probe to get at the truth of the matter. You are then engaged and obliged to act decisively.

Fix the problem, not the blame: You didn't create the problem, but don't make it worse. Your creative response coupled with genuine concern could provide a most memorable moment in that customer's experience with our company.

Christopher Springmann
San Francisco *Examiner*,
23 January 2000

Southwest has grown rapidly from a maverick Texas start-up to one of America's 10 largest airlines. How do they deliver real quality through a large, dispersed workforce under conditions of constant change? The answer, as in most natural systems, is both simple and subtle and lies in using turbulence instead of suppressing it.

Real quality at Southwest grows from the great ground condition they cultivate in their people. They create a culture of nurturance, community, and fun for their own staff, so naturally, they serve customers in the same way. Despite the low-cost profile, Southwest spends generously on selecting, training, and supporting their people. One way this saves money is their low rate of staff turnover.

Staff are selected for their fit with the company's real-quality culture. Elizabeth Sartain, vice president of People for Southwest, explained: "If you join us and don't fit in to our culture, you really do stick out like a sore thumb, so we spend a lot of time and effort assessing the culture fit." Rita Bailey, director of Southwest's University for People, told me how their training builds on this. "Our recruits don't become hires until they pass the induction training. This includes role-plays of actual customer situations, to raise skills in listening, handling conflict, and assertiveness."

Real quality is the way Southwest cultivates the natural talent and character of their people; they don't impose a synthetic, dictated standard for good service. Diversity and eccentricity are welcomed and woven into the operation. As Rita Bailey put it to me, "People know when service is sincere. We hire that; we tell our staff, you can be yourself here."

Fun and celebration are two of the natural energy sources Southwest uses to renew their own ground condition and to

Real quality includes taste, trust, and rapport.

give emotional value to their customers. As a passenger, you may be treated to comedy turns in the flight announcements or to seeing staff dressed up on Halloween. And Southwest is proud to share their culture and their achievements with their customers, so the process really is part of the product.

Cultivating the Opportunity

The ingredients for a shift to real quality standards are already present in many individuals and organizations. These include quality measurement and feedback systems, the concept of internal customers, and large-scale communications and data-processing technology. All that's missing is a radical change in attitude. The pressure on most organizations for quantified results is acute, so it takes courage to give attention to the intangibles. Yet the business case from organic growing is clear: Over time you can build sustained price premiums by delivering real quality benefits such as taste, trust, and rapport.

Many organizations, and the people in them, will need to operate a dual voltage system for quite some time. Where supply chains demand tight nominal quality standards, these have to be met alongside intangible values. A mistake some companies make is to create quality for customers without creating it for their own people and processes. As this book explains, real quality arises from ground condition and from the methods of production; it has to apply *within* the organization as well as to customers.

Another lesson from organic farming's success is the need for trustworthy production standards—independently verified, and balancing the needs of the producers, the consumers, and the environment. Creating this takes medium-term vision and unselfishness from the big businesses that shape most production standards. We still largely lack intermediary bodies that can provide independence in quality standards: organizations with wide consumer membership, willing to engage with producers in developing realistic and trusted quality standards.

Real Quality Marketing

Organic growers have evolved a range of distribution methods that are impressive in their quality and ingenuity, and all the more so because this is homegrown marketing—it hasn't come from M.B.A.'s or management consultants. In marketing, as in other areas of organics, the key seems to be the combination of organic principles with a co-creativity that evolves naturally on the job. Although the forms of distribution described here are tailored to food, the implications have a much wider relevance.

One of the basic principles in organic-food marketing is to grow value per unit of output, rather than quantity of output. Farmers achieve this in a number of ways:

- Progressively moving into higher-value crops
- Adding value by providing extras such as salad packs, ready meals, or bread, and not just raw ingredients
- Creating distribution methods that increase the producer's share of total transaction value
- Building trust, dialogue, and other intangibles as part of the product value
- Obtaining value from the whole output so there's no waste

Another fundamental element of organic marketing is *dialogue distribution*: creating channels that enable close, two-way communication between producer and consumer. This dialogue creates resilience, loyalty, and value. A supermarket customer who's looking for a product that's out of stock may feel angry and go elsewhere. If an organic grower's production is disrupted, dialogue channels enable the farmer to explain the problem and devise a stopgap solution with customers. The dialogue is often an exchange of action as well as words. Farm visits are common and can include a progress review and discussion of production plans, live education about lambing, helping to pack vegetables, or celebration with a harvest supper.

Here are four more of the principles in organic marketing:

Locality. Locality is what organic growers call local food links. It makes both marketing and environmental sense to trade with the consumers who are nearest to the source of production. The idea of food miles is steadily gaining consumer awareness; the extraordinary distances a typical piece of food travels between producer, processor, distribution warehouse, store, and consumer averages 1,300 miles in the United States.

Economy. Most organic growers are undercapitalized, and the blessing in the problem is that they have to develop low-cost approaches.

Partnership. Partnership is vital, both with other producers and with consumers.

Humanization. Organic marketing actually prefers to add labor content, increase personal contact, and integrate the business and personal aspects of life.

Some examples of these principles in action are outlined below.

Joint Ventures

This is a major form of organic distribution in the United States, with more than 600 active programs. The approach is also well established in Japan, where it originated. Community-supported agriculture is in effect a joint venture between the producer and the consumer. A group of customers agree to a production plan with an organic grower, and they contract to purchase this produce. The customers pay in advance, thus financing the operation, sharing in its risks and rewards. If the harvest is below expectations, they receive less food, but they will know why. If the crop is abundant, they share the benefit: more produce, or a share of the income from external sales. The arrangement stimulates interaction between a grower and the customers. It is common for such consumers to provide labor for the operation. Some will deal with packing and distributing produce in return for lower prices, while some will come as volunteers at busy times just for the fun of it.

Cooperatives

Producer cooperatives have enabled many organic growers to find the economies of scale for larger marketing or processing initiatives. Pioneering organizations have been formed by vegetable producers who recognized that their local markets were not big enough to support them. They decided to supply supermarkets and created a dedicated packing and distribution operation.

One of the problems some co-ops have had to overcome is outgrades: usable produce that supermarkets would not accept because of their tight nominal quality demands. These co-ops processed the rejected produce into ready-made salad packs, turning a potential waste product into one with added value that helped develop local sales. Co-ops have found ways to harness the diversity of their members. By tightly coordinating production schedules, they have been able to provide better supply continuity to the supermarkets.

First-Hand Feedback

Farmers' markets have been well established for some time in the United States and are now spreading rapidly abroad. Like many good innovations, in hindsight the idea seems obvious. Local farmers and growers bring their produce regularly to a downtown venue where consumers can meet them and buy direct. It is a great example of shopping as entertainment and of dialogue distribution. Producers can try out new products and get first-hand feedback on customer needs.

Branded Products

A number of kitchen-table attempts to create added-value organic products have grown over the years to become successful brands with national distribution. Celestial Seasonings, which has become a major brand of teas, is a good example. Back in 1969, a 19-year-old named Mo Sigel started making tea from wild herbs he found in the Rocky Mountain canyons and forests around his home in Aspen, Colorado. Soon he and a friend, Wyck Hay, picked a bunch of the wild herbs, blended them, and started selling bags of herbal teas in a local health food store.

A few years later they expanded their market to the East Coast and started buying loads of herbs rather than picking them all themselves. The company soon revolutionized the industry, providing flavorful, healthy teas made from such things as hibiscus flowers, which are bought from herb growers as far away as Asia. In a world where customers are growing more and more health-conscious, the giant Kraft Inc.

bought Celestial Seasonings in 1984, turned it into a national brand, and eventually sold it back to the managers who started the company.

Customer Ownership

These are various arrangements in which the customer is the owner and equity investor in a farming enterprise. Such customer ownership schemes may involve trade buyers or consumers. In Britain it is common for wholesalers to supply livestock for rearing, with the organic producers receiving a fee and having no financial risk.

There are also some creative examples of consumer ownership schemes, such as one fund-needy farmer's invitation to potential consumers to "buy a calf" by purchasing the livestock that he would then raise for them.

Real Quality in Organizations

How do the innovative real-quality marketing and distribution methods of organic farming apply to your work? There are three main principles in these approaches: personal links with customers, dialogue, and cooperation.

The creation of local links and dialogue with customers may seem impractical for large organizations seeking economies of scale. In practice, a great deal can be achieved by combining a genuine service orientation with technology.

Information technology enables businesses to accumulate and apply informa-

tion on the detailed preferences of every customer. Recent innovations in production technology, in a whole range of sectors, make multiple product variations and customization for individuals readily achievable. New approaches to dialogue distribution can harness this scope for customization, ensuring that the producer learns from the customer and that they adapt to changes together.

We can see in organic production a striking range of joint ventures, some among producers, some between producer and consumer. The message is to move beyond the cult of the competitive, heroic individual. In recent years, even the largest and proudest multinationals have formed webs of cooperative ventures to achieve such benefits as resilience, synergy, and cocreativity. Each of us can achieve these benefits by increasing collaboration with colleagues and customers.

Real Quality in Daily Practice

Whether you are employed or independent, it helps to see yourself as a product. You need to know who your customers are, how you add value, and how to market yourself. The concepts of real quality and organic marketing can help you achieve this. Imagine yourself as a farm, cultivating a diversity of enterprises, interlinked and mutually supportive.

Cultivate dialogue with your customers and suppliers. Know what real quality means for them. As much as possible, be explicit with them about what you offer and what you need. The more your customers know about how your production processes work, the more loyalty and resilience grow in the relationship. If you work best by going swimming in the afternoons and staying up late, tell them. If you'd like more appreciation to energize you, say so.

Applying this principle begins simply. All you need to do is review the nature of your transactions with your customers and suppliers. Are these transactions fully satisfactory for all of you? Do they contain emotional value? Do you have dialogue and rapport with your supply chain so that you can handle change cocreatively?

The answers to such questions may be less simple. They may deeply challenge your current way of working. That's why, back in the introduction on page 15, I suggested that you read all seven principles before starting the change process. Use the Real Quality Queries on the following pages to explore these questions.

Exercise: Real Quality Queries

Use the Real Quality Queries (below) to develop your vision of the outcome you want. If your way of working is to be truly sustainable, it must deliver real quality—not only for you, but for those with whom you interact. Develop your sense of the qualities you want in your work, without trying to define what form or style of work will deliver them. Then use this overall vision to guide your application of all seven principles, starting with ground condition.

1 Do you know who your clients are and do you have a direct relationship with them?

   (Apply this question to several of your work roles or activities and take time to explore who your key clients or customers are. For example, if you work in a telephone call center, your key clients may be your supervisor, his or her boss, and the training and quality managers.)

2 Do you know what "real quality" means for your key clients? What gives them satisfaction, nutrition from your work? What emotional value do you deliver in your output?

3 Do your key clients know what "real quality" means for you? Have you told them what gives you satisfaction and emotional value in your transactions with them?

4 Do the processes by which you personally produce your output embody "real quality"? In other words, are your ways of working, as well as your outputs, satisfying and wholesome?

5 Do you have a "dialogue relationship" with your clients: a dynamic, two-way relationship that enables both of you to adjust to changes in either party's needs or circumstances?

6 If your answers to questions 1–5 highlight a case for change, list below three steps you can take to begin this.

a.

b.

c.

chapter 8

GOING ORGANIC

THE TERM USED TO DESCRIBE the shift from conventional to organic production methods is *conversion*. In farming or gardening it takes several years of natural cycles and organic cultivation before the ground condition fully recovers its fertility and resilience, and the first two or three years of the conversion period are typically a tough transition. Crop yields, which have depended on artificial fertilizer inputs, usually drop. Because natural predators and the soil's resilience to problems have been suppressed, weeds and pests often get worse before they get better. The main issues in a farm's conversion from an input-based management system to an organic sustainable system all have parallels in a human shift to sustainability at work.

This chapter focuses on the practicalities of moving toward sustainability. It offers guidelines condensed from my personal experience, from Magdalen Farm, and from clients with whom I have worked.

Conversion on the Farm

Francis Blake comments in his book *Organic Farming and Growing:*

The first step in the conversion of a farm is the conversion of the farmer. There are two requisites. The first is a change in your attitude and your thinking. . . . You will need to get away from the conventional approach to any problem . . . that of seeking to dominate it by using outside inputs—and instead cultivate the ability to look at it in the context of the rest of the farm, to see behind the problem to what is causing its undue development. . . . Look at the farm as a whole, for each part has an influence on everything else.

The second requisite is a belief in your own mind that the organic approach is the right one. In order to feel confident and positive about this new direction, so that you can carry it through even in the difficult times and against the barracking of your neighbors, then you have to put your faith in it. . . . Without that whole-hearted belief, there is no room for the development of either the pioneering spirit or the understanding that organic farming requires for its successful operation.

Every word of this applies as much to the workplace as to the farm.

Generally, it is easier to convert a farm if you have operated it conventionally for a year or more before moving to organic methods. That way you already know the farm's characteristics: the typical weed and pest threats, which crops grow best, and how it reacts to different weather conditions. In contrast, on Magdalen, we started conversion as soon as we bought the farm; the result was two years of continual surprises. The analogy for your work is to know yourself well before you embark on a change of this scale. In the same way, in my consulting with Alibi Publishing and Virosoft, I sought to build trust and understanding in each team before we considered sustainability.

When conversion gets underway, restoring ground condition and raising fertility are the fundamental issues. You have to create the conditions for growth. Most farms and gardens start the conversion phase from a state of depletion. At first, the emphasis is on less demanding, less valuable, renewing crops, such as grass or clover.

It is also common to import some extra fertility to restimulate the soil and speed up the process of renewal. Under organic standards, some manure, seaweed, and other natural minerals can be brought in when necessary.

Building Fertility

In the first year of organic production, output volumes are likely to be below previous levels. After years of neglect, it takes time for the soil to come back to life as an organism and produce its own fertility. Weed problems also tend to be bad at the start, before the natural system's checks and balances come into play. These early weeds are like the turbulence we find in many transitions: Along with our desire to change, there may be some fear and resistance within us and in those around us.

Although the volume of production may drop, the value per unit should rise. It usually takes three years of conversion before a farm and its produce qualify as organic, but during this period, they qualify for "transitional" status. The high demand for organic produce means that even the conversion-grade produce sells for more than conventional farm goods. So don't panic if the volume of your output drops during the transition; value the quality, and seek customers who will do likewise.

Easing the Stress

An organic grower knows that the conversion period is likely to be stressful. Production and income are at risk. There is a huge amount to learn, and many of the issues can't be anticipated: They will have to be met in the moment. Every farm is unique to some degree, and at best, you can embark on this voyage with only a rather generalized map.

There are many ways to mitigate this stress in your own conversion process. One is simple awareness: Make sure that you, your colleagues, customers, family, and friends know the scale of the change and are ready to support it. Another is to set up some sort of financial cushion so you can take off the pressure to maintain your output.

A further way to reduce the stress of conversion is by planning. The pioneers of organic farming had to proceed by trial and error; nowadays, the conversion process is well researched and there are specialist consultants who can help you apply this experience to your situation. Of course, conversion cannot be fully planned; some issues can be forecast and quantified, but many can't. Producing a conversion plan is certainly helpful, but it needs to be reviewed frequently and there has to be willingness to change it substantially as the process unfolds. The same is true of the transition to human sustainability, whether it is on the personal, team, or organizational level.

Value organic quality, and seek customers who will do likewise.

The Organic Journey

What have I learned about sustainability from ten years' involvement with Magdalen Farm? The grand answer is that sustainability is more a journey than a destination. The humble answer is that we're not there yet! Magdalen completed its initial conversion to organic methods in 1992, and the farm has met organic production standards since then. However, the farm has faced several changes that have led to some of the conversion challenges coming around again, much like repetitions of the competence cycle described in Chapter 5.

When I look back at the original conversion that Dirk Hoostra and I managed, I feel we did pretty well. It was often tough and surprising, but we had a good framework. The professional support was excellent, producing a conversion plan that provided a sound overall action plan and budget. Having a well-established organic farmer as a friend and local role model was also invaluable. The toughest part of the whole process was to get two hard-driving bulls, Dirk and me, to learn cocreativity. We both wasted a lot of time and emotion before we learned to work with the problems instead of trying to wrestle them to the floor.

When Dirk and Marika left in 1994, bringing in new farmers was a bit like starting over. Peter Norman was our first fully qualified, experienced farm manager, and he showed us that significant changes were required to make Magdalen sustainable in the full sense.

Market conditions had changed greatly since we'd started, and our 20-cow dairy herd was no longer economical. We also knew that the size of the farm, 130 acres, was small for a commercially viable enterprise. We set up a joint venture agreement that enabled Peter to invest some personal capital to start new enterprises and expand

2-MINUTE *CHECKUP*

CREATING YOUR FARM

This exercise helps you use the farm analogy to develop the future direction of your work. Choose a quiet, comfortable place to do this, and have some plain paper and colored pens.

Picture you and your work roles as if you were a farm. What kind of farm would you like to become? Imagine that you are a landscape, a range of fields, facilities, and enterprises—a network of fruitful flows and cycles, earning the income you need, and enhancing your underlying resources as you do so.

You can use this analogy literally or figuratively. Picture your work as actual farm enterprises: cereals, vegetables, cows, and so on, and then see what they symbolize for you. Or explore how your work roles could evolve so that they're productive, synergistic, diverse, and sustainable, like an organic farm.

Either way, remember that the future of a farm is shaped by its past and present. What are your soil type and ground condition? What crops have you grown well; which customers already value you? And what history of weeds and pests do you have to learn from?

Spend some time daydreaming about these questions, feeling receptive to new images. As they arise, start drawing them, creating a picture of the farm you would like to be.

the farm by renting 50 acres of organic land nearby. As a result, Magdalen now has more enterprises—and ones where our scale of production should be competitive. Peter and his partner, Christina, have also addressed a major deficiency by bringing in organic marketing methods. We now have a good local customer base, with dialogue and diversity. Previously most of the produce had been sold to one or two large national customers, and no personal relationship had existed.

Looking to the Future

I recently asked Peter if he regarded Magdalen Farm as sustainable yet. He replied, "It's pretty good and improving, but there's a way to go in several areas. The environmental sustainability is fair, but we're not yet humanly sustainable. The farm team is working longer hours and feels more stretched than I'd like. But we're only in the second year with a lot of the new enterprises, and each annual cycle should get a lot easier. We're not financially sustainable yet either. We're still in the start-up phase. We expected losses last year, and we lost more than I thought we would. Some of the learning was quite expensive. This year's a lot better. I should be able to pay myself this year, and next year should show a decent profit."

I hope that this account of the Magdalen experience underlines the point that sustainability is not some nirvana of stability, a never-never land where nothing needs to change any more. In fact, it's more like the concept of bounded uncertainty from chaos theory: turbulent, but in a constructive way. What I can also see by reviewing 10 years of organic growth at Magdalen is how applying sustainable principles increases resilience and the capacity for change. As Peter says, "The two farmers before me helped to renew ground condition and establish an organic foundation I could build on. Starting three major enterprises in the same year was seriously ambitious, and I've depended on the resources in the land to support me."

Preparing to Go Organic

You will learn and embody the principles of sustainability by using them repeatedly. As you manage your energy and your work in cycles, you move through the conversion process to the stage where applying organic principles becomes habitual and intuitive, and renewal is a natural process.

So how do you make the switch? This section offers you two kinds of answers. The first is 16 pointers for your transition phase, drawn from my own experience and from others with whom I have worked. The second is specific suggestions on how to develop a conversion plan, drawing on the analogy with organic growing.

Making the Transition

If you're ready to convert to sustainable principles, should you expect two years of turmoil? Probably not. Human beings are capable of much greater and quicker adaptation than farms. Your productive output may not drop at all, but it's wise to be prepared for it to do so. Accept that going organic is not a plug-and-play move; it's a cyclical process.

You don't have to wait. You don't need the world or your employer to reach a crisis before you make your move. Even if you work in a culture that tends to deplete people, you can operate on dual voltage and do a great deal to sustain yourself.

You don't have to do it alone. Remember how organic farmers collaborate. There are organizations and individuals who can support you with this change and from whose experience you can learn.

It is better to act on feeling than on fact. By the time the problem is categorically proven, it may be too late to resolve it. If you sense that your work is depleting you, even if you don't know it for sure, act on the feeling.

When in doubt, intensify the problem. Exaggerate your feelings, caricature the situation, and use humor to open it up. Apply the composting principle. Delve more deeply into the creative tension that exists. Keep believing that the gift is in the problem.

Work with the profit motive, not against it. You may feel angry that the economic system exploits you, but don't start from there. Finding synergy with the organization's needs will get you further. As

an individual, you're not big enough to confront the system, but by aligning your nature with its needs, you can reshape it.

Start with principles—and stick with them. You're initiating a major change, and the form of the outcome is hard to guess. Use the principles from this book, or shape your own. Either way, the principles of sustainability are your compass and your fudge detector.

You don't have to jump off a cliff. You can't plan every detail of a change like this, but you can plan for it, just as a farm does. Learn from others' experiences before you start. Recognize your needs and risks—emotional and practical. Line up the resources and support you may need. And keep your plan cocreative; review and replan as you progress.

Anchor the ends of the cycle, and the middle will follow. Focus your attention on your ground condition and on the full, real quality of your outputs, for yourself and your customers. Getting these right should naturally move you into the whole cycle of sustainability.

Find allies. Look out for the individuals and groups, within your work and outside it, who can develop sustainability with you. If you can avoid getting evangelical, you may find your colleagues surprisingly receptive. Often when I have helped a team explore this issue, the comment afterward has been: "I never knew so many of us shared these values."

Be a trailblazer. A change like this has to involve risk. You can reduce it and cushion it, but you can't eliminate it. The whole area of human sustainability at work is a pioneering one; by exploring it, you serve not only yourself but others who can learn from you.

Create standards. The conversion period is usually messy. The pressure and clarity of immediate profit and performance goals can feel hard to counterbalance. Develop a standard, a way to measure your progress, for each of your sustainable principles. Don't worry if your standards are homegrown. And if they're qualitative, so much the better!

Pack lunch. Gather your resources before you start the journey. Give time to cultivating your ground condition, building up your resources and resilience, before you start the conversion process.

Transform your energy productivity. The catchphrase "work smarter, not harder" has been around for years. Organic principles offer the way to do this substantially and sustainably. As you combine your brain power with natural cycles, and as you consciously manage your energy levels, you create the potential for dramatic rises in the value created per unit of your energy. Carry a vision of doing more with less, and look for the synergy to achieve it.

Find your market. Believe that there are customers who will value real quality as you develop it, and persist until you find them. They may even be your current clientele.

Celebrate. When most people lived and worked on the land, celebrating the seasons and cycles was widespread. Marking and enjoying your progress through your cycles will help to sustain you. Probably, the seasons you find the hardest are the ones you most need to celebrate!

Remember to renew. Both the mechanistic mind-set and the culture of the hero-achiever may make you think that the only way to get progress is to push. In fact, most heroes, from Odysseus to Batman, are highly cocreative: They know when to push, but also when to retreat, rest, review, and receive. You will need persistence to make this change, but that means knowing when to stop as well as when to keep going. And if you become depleted or frustrated, don't be tough on yourself—go back to the principles to see how to renew your resources.

Making a Conversion Plan

If you want to work sustainably, planning the transition phase is worth the effort. It's a good way to consolidate and apply your understanding of all seven principles as a whole. The idea of a plan may sound rather fixed and formal; treat it as a framework for co-creativity, a way of clarifying your intent before you plunge into the flow of events. The Diamond Process, described on page 94, is a good way to develop your plan so that your intuition and analytical talents are both involved. Treat the topics and questions that are explained below as suggestions for possible inclusion in your plan. Tailor your own format and contents to your taste and your circumstances.

Ground condition survey. What is the state of your underlying resources? How fertile or depleted are you currently? Are your four energy elements each at a good level and in balance as a whole? If your ground condition is poor, explore how to renew it systematically; in other words, address the root causes. Rebuild structure and fertility in a way that moves you toward a sustainable balance of energy inputs and outputs.

Energy sources. Use the Personal Energy Audit on page 61 to identify current and potential energy inputs to your work. Consider sources within you and around you. Notice any imbalances and deficiencies, and plan how you can address them. The level of energy inputs you can access will directly influence your level of productive potential. If you are physically fit, bathed in support from colleagues, mentally alert, and inspired by the corporate vision, it will make a difference. Remember that waste is a potential major energy source.

Soil type and potential. Look back at the section on soil types in Chapter 1, and, if possible, identify your type: for example, sand, clay, or loam. By considering this soil type alongside your data on ground condition and energy sources, you can explore your productive potential. What kind of crops will suit you best? What mix of enterprises will be renewing and resilient for you?

For example, if you're a chalky soil type, with low reserves and limited energy sources, you need to consider relatively simple, undemanding crops, or you will deplete yourself. On the other hand, if you are a loam type, with good energy sources (including waste), you can aim for higher-value, more demanding crops, but you should still alternate these with renewal crops and ensure that energy flows are balanced.

Market review. Having considered the production side of the equation, it's now time to look at sales. By now you may know what you can produce—but what can you sell, and what do you *want* to sell? Apply the principles of Chapter 7. Consider both current and potential products and present and potential customers. Where is the best prospect of achieving real quality and an ongoing relationship, both for you and your customers?

At this stage, it may be useful to explore different options and create some scenarios. For example, one option could be a low-output plan—if your sustainable production level seems low, can you adjust to lower financial income but earn it through crops that are satisfying in other ways? Alternatively, if you want to continue in a high-output, demanding occupation, can you invest some of your earnings to increase your energy inputs and support to sustainable levels?

Work-life balance. Trade-offs between the areas of work and life are worth considering explicitly. For example, you may choose to stay in a depleting job and meet the deficit by drawing support from your family. You may opt for this because it provides enough income to support your family in the lifestyle you all want. Often we make such decisions alone, heroically. The most resilient way to make such a choice is through open discussion with those involved, so they can agree and support the work–life balance you decide on. Here, too, it may be worth considering different scenarios.

Vision. This should be a good stage to turn to intuition and inspiration to show you the best choice among various priorities and options. If some of your goals seem incompatible with one another, remember to use this creative tension, to look for the synergy between them. "Creating Your Farm," the exercise on page 160, offers you one method to explore this further.

Evaluation and action plan. When you have a vision that feels right, you can evaluate it against the practical issues you have already identified. Can you produce this vision sustainably? Will it bring in the money and satisfaction you want from your work? Is it resilient to change? Does it balance your work and personal life? If your overview is positive, you can check it out in detail by preparing an action plan, including the points explained below.

Energy budget. An organic farm will budget the flows of a key nutrient, such as nitrogen, to ensure that fertility is not depleted. Although the key human energy flows are intangible, you can guesstimate inflows and outflows using a format such as the Personal Energy Audit on page 61. This is a good sanity check on your vision, to assess if your available energy inputs will meet the demands renewably.

Maintenance. Compare a Grand Prix car with a family sedan. The racing car delivers extraordinary performance but must have large, frequent inputs of labor and materials to keep it on the road. Err on the side of conservatism in assessing the maintenance and support you need for your work. The risks from overproviding are relatively low. Be clear about what you need, and negotiate with those around you to get it. If you need to play pool with your pals three nights a week to handle a difficult job, ask your partner if he or she is willing to accept the equation. Much of your support may come from yourself, friends, family, and colleagues, but look seriously at the idea of paying for professional support, too.

Financial budget. A budget is essential to a farm conversion plan. There will be new items to spend money on, as well as savings, different income sources, and more uncertainty. One of the reasons for budgeting is to quantify the financial risks in the conversion phase and provide contingency funds to cover them. If you can do the same for your own transition, it can reduce the stress of the change for you and those close to you.

Measurement and review. How will you know if your plan is succeeding; when and how will you review your progress? One of your motives for this change is presumably to improve your well-being, so find some benchmarks, however qualitative they are. More tangible measures are also useful, such as hours worked, and regular Personal Energy Audits.

I strongly advise setting up a regular review cycle, perhaps weekly or monthly, as a way of steering and sustaining your change. During the Magdalen Farm conversion, we had quarterly reviews with our professional adviser. A periodic review of your plan with a friend, counselor, or mentor can give you an objective view and the benefit of wider experience.

Going, Going, Gone

Alison Martin, whose story was described earlier, has been persistent in bringing sustainable principles to her work, and her experience is illuminating (some of the tools she mentions are included in Chapter 9).

"It's been two years since I took part in my first workshop about the Natural Advantage. I was in a pretty bad way then: Successful at work, but half-crazy with stress, and it was knocking hell out of my health and my personal life. I didn't know much about sustainability, but I had some idea that it might help me.

"As soon as I did the Personal Energy Audit, the whole thing was obvious. I could see that my way of working was burning me out, and I was getting by with a load of quick fixes that only made it worse. That conversation with Peter Norman about sending in the pigs was such an eye-opener. Ever since, I use the image of myself as a farm, a piece of land, as a way of seeing what I need.

"I came away from that workshop at Magdalen Farm determined to change things, but I jumped in too fast, which is what I often do. I know Alan spoke about planning the conversion phase, but I didn't. I was in a panic about my health, and I just wanted to get going.

"In the conversion stage, I expected things would get really messy before they got straightened out, and that was true. When I started facing the feelings I'd been stuffing down, I had a lot of turmoil for several months. I got weekly counseling sessions, and they were great. The connected breathing and composting helped when I felt swamped with emotions at work. In the first few weeks, that happened almost every day. Usually I'd just excuse myself and go for a quick walk around the block, and that was enough time to clear it.

"I did speak to my boss, and she was pretty understanding. I didn't go into details, but I told her I needed to change my way of working because my health was suffering. For the first couple of months, we set up a weekly review. She'd tell me what she needed from me that week, and I'd warn her if I was having a really bumpy time.

"One of the things that helped me a lot with the conversion phase was the idea of real quality. I liked the way that organic farmers have more of a personal relationship with their customers, so there's a kind of mutual adjustment to change. A lot of my work was easy to do impersonally, and that's how I'd preferred it. I was damned efficient, but you wouldn't have wanted to know me. I was burning myself out in the effort to avoid any risk of criticism. After the Magdalen session, I let myself develop a bit of a personal relationship with my main work contacts. If I was feeling exhausted, I'd actually tell them so and negotiate deadlines instead of saying yes to everything.

"I guess Peter Norman's way of working gave me a role model, and this idea of cocreativity is really neat. It kind of fits with the chaos of real work; these days I see the mess as a productive flux. It helps that I soon got a lot of appreciation from the folks at work about the way I'd changed. Even when I was in a bitchy mood, we all learned how to handle it. The main part of my conversion period was around six months. After that, things were on a fairly even keel at work, and my personal life felt sustainable, too.

Going organic is about adapting to far more change and less security.

"A few months after that, I had a very good annual appraisal from my boss—and then I was let go a couple of months later. So it came as a hell of a shock; it felt like a real kick in the teeth when I felt I'd just learned how to do the job well without exhausting myself. It showed me I still had a lot more to learn. Not just about diversity, but also about adapting to far more change and less security. I must admit, even with what I'd learned from the Natural Advantage, I was quite depressed and angry for a few months after the dismissal. Then I went back to basics and worked on my ground condition.

"This time, I did plan things better. I used the Diamond Process to figure out the work I wanted, what kind of farm I'd like to be. For a start, I could see that I need both security and variety, so I had to find the synergy between them.

"My main work now is managing the membership department of a large mail-order business. It uses my previous experience, and the great thing is I'm doing it three days a week. It's a very commercial business, much faster moving than my old job, but I can manage it fine on this part-time basis. One thing I realized I've always missed in my work is physical activity and contact with nature. These days I do volunteer work one day a week with a non-profit group called Therapeutic Gardens. We create and maintain gardens for people who are partially sighted or mentally handicapped. It's about the best renewal crop I could imagine for myself."

Conversion in Organizations

How does an organization become humanly sustainable? It's difficult to find a company that fully embodies all these principles, but I can offer both ideas and the results of some pilot work. Working organically is not an easy proposition for most organizations. Although it offers the prospect of higher-value output and improved performance, results are less controllable. This is a hard risk for any manager to take when the pressure for constant results is so strong.

The way that other innovations start and spread may offer a model for this one; often the early experiments are likely to be in smaller, privately owned companies and in a handful of larger, progressive groups, probably in one of their wild-margin subsidiaries. As a body of experience gathers, conversion processes evolve, the benefits to customers and employees become apparent, and demand grows.

Most of the pointers in this chapter about individual conversion are also relevant to organizations and teams. There is the same risk of trying to do the right thing, but trying too soon and in the wrong way. The first step is ground condition—roots, not fruits. A group needs to develop its skills and culture, as well as understanding and motivation, before moving into the maximum growth phase.

Go for It

Our work with Alibi Publishing proved sustainable and survived the appointment of a new chief executive. I asked Steve Raleigh,

Alibi's human resources director, to give his account of the conversion process:

"That first workshop we did with Alan was quite remarkable. I've been to a lot of workshops, and I'm pretty skeptical, but this one really had a lasting effect. All the principles and skills presented were related to our needs, both personal needs and the business situation. They bought into the fact that Phil, our chief executive, would be moving on so we were really hungry for a solution. What we realized from that first workshop was that no one could prescribe the answer; we had to make the solution ourselves, but they gave us the tools to do it.

"The few weeks after that first workshop were strange, and quite funny really. Mostly we were doing it differently and seeing that it worked. Every now and then one of us, usually Phil, would fall back into old habits. He'd start answering the question as soon as he'd posed it, and the rest of us would just stare at him. Usually he stopped in mid-sentence and ground his teeth while the rest of us got messy and cocreative and eventually found an answer. At least he admitted that our answer was sometimes better than his.

"Having the second workshop without Phil was brilliant. What still amazes me about that session is the honesty. There are quite a lot of power struggles within our team, and I would never have guessed that we could talk openly about them in the whole group. But we did. It certainly proved the composting concept. After that, we realized that being open about our conflicts is tremendously energizing. And we'd learned enough of the skills to start doing it with our subordinates.

> **The first step is ground condition— roots, not fruits.**

"At that second workshop, we knew that Phil's move was imminent, and we had a gutsy, straight-out talk about how we were going to manage the business as a group of peers. We also wanted to do it without having Working Vision or anyone else holding our hand all the time. The question of how to do this sustainably was a good point of reference. Simon, our quality director, and I are accepted as neutral parties in the power struggles, so we acted as mediators when people couldn't solve their own disputes. When Phil was promoted, we had several months without a boss and managed remarkably well. His successor is an engineer. He spent time figuring out why we'd worked so well, and he bought into the approach.

"I know that Alan has developed his ideas further since they worked with us, and I don't think we're applying all of his model here. The stuff about ground condition, composting, and cocreativity has helped us a lot. We still have to deal with the output pressure from our parent company, but we have enough freedom over here to work out our own ways of doing it.

"My advice to a company considering the Natural Advantage model would be this: go for it, but make it your own before you start. Adapt it and tailor it to your situation, your culture. Spend time exploring it and building up ground condition before you really launch it. Otherwise it'll be what we call a Chinese-dinner initiative—the whole bright idea will be through the system and out the other end before you've had time to digest it. The other thing I'd say is that you don't have to go deep into the farming analogy to use this process. We just called it working naturally."

Natworking

With many innovations, widespread uptake is preceded by a wilderness phase when a few people see the need and the solution, but general opinion is still blinkered. Organic farming was in this wilderness place until the mid-1990s. The concept of human sustainability is in the same posi-

tion now, but I'm optimistic that this will change over the next few years. A scenario of how it may change is given in "Epilogue: A Healing Crisis," on page 203.

I coined the term *natworking* to describe ways of working that embody natural principles and that are productive and humanly sustainable. If you choose to develop a natworking approach in your work, you will be helping to create the ground condition for this idea to grow into the mainstream. And as these ideas take root with more individuals and organizations, the process of conversion becomes easier.

Conversion in Daily Practice

Follow the ideas above: Explore them, adapt them for yourself, and gradually develop your ground condition before you take it further. The best way to do this is cyclically: Reread the book and see how the principles support one another as you consider how to apply them to your situation.

I have found that for myself and many others, the principles of the Natural Advantage make intuitive sense, so they take root easily. I have been applying this approach in my work and personal life for the past four years. It has been a time of difficult change as well as high productivity, and I know that my reserves and resilience are much higher now than when I

started. Over the years I've learned that working sustainably can be turbulent and sometimes chaotic. My habitual need for control is greatly reduced; most of the time I can handle uncertainty and use it productively. I still get tired and stressed in my work quite often, but I move through it fast and usually find the learning in the problem quickly.

If I were to offer three keys to conversion, they would be these.

- Look after your ground condition.
- When it gets sticky, get cocreative.
- Keep aiming for real quality—satisfaction for you and your customers.

chapter 9
THE ORGANIC GROWTH TOOL KIT

THIS CHAPTER OFFERS YOU SOME TECHNIQUES to supplement the exercises that you'll find throughout the rest of the book. These further tools are especially relevant for cultivating organic synergy, cocreativity, and composting, but since these are central to the whole approach of the Natural Advantage, they will help you as you learn how to apply all seven principles.

The Natural Advantage principles are interdependent. If you've started to nourish your ground condition, harness natural energy, and compost your energy waste, you're already well on your way to enhancing your cocreative abilities. And as you develop your cocreativity even further, this will move you toward embodying all the other principles.

The Witness Triangle

This is a plan for exploring two positions or drives that are in tension and then moving to a third point. The process uses physical movement and visualization to help you stay with tension and find the synergy in it.

Preparation

Begin by clarifying your intent, the outcome you want from this process. Then review the various issues and factors involved in the situation. Focus on the main tension or uncertainty that's holding you back from making a clear, easy decision. If possible, identify the primary pull, the underlying tension or conflict you need to resolve. Often this is between a "yes" and a "but": desire for action and resistance to it. The process here is written for this kind of conflict, but it can be adapted for others.

One way to use the Witness Triangle is to ask someone to read the following guidelines for you, stopping when you give a signal, to ensure that you go at your own pace. If this is not possible, ask someone to record it on tape for you or do this yourself. Alternatively, read the instructions through several times and take yourself through them from memory.

Process

Sit comfortably, and take some long, deep, slow breaths, relaxing into any tension you're feeling. Place your hands in a comfortable position, apart from each other with the palms facing upward, with your fingers relaxed and in an open position.

Now, focus your attention on your right hand, and in relation to the question you're exploring, feel the "yes" side of the equation. Sense the desire, the drive in you toward this outcome. Imagine that you've already achieved this outcome—let yourself feel how this is for you. Savor the satisfaction fully. Sense the energy of all this, and let it focus and gather in your right hand.

Now, move your attention to your left hand. As you continue to picture the "yes" side fully, let your awareness of the "but" side emerge. What are your fears, doubts, and uncertainties about this move? Let them express themselves fully; give them an attentive hearing. If you feel tension rising as you do this, breathe deeply, and keep relaxing into it. Believe that you'll soon find the synergy between these sides of the question. Let yourself feel the force of your resistance, and focus this in your left hand. If your attention starts to wander, bring yourself back to the sensations in your hands and the rest of your body.

Now, move your attention to a third point, the witness position. Focus your attention on the "third eye" point in the center of your forehead. From this place, witness the power and the energy in both your right and left hands. Feel the tension vividly, but know that you are bigger than this conflict: You encompass it, and you can witness it and find the purpose in it. Start slowly moving your hands together. Keep your breathing deep, and embrace this tension as a creative and positive force. Continue bringing your hands together and breathing into the tension. Stay with this until you get a sense of an answer emerging.

The Aikido Approach

Cocreativity and synergy may seem like abstract concepts. It can be useful to have a visual map, like the Diamond, or a physical embodiment, which is what aikido offers. The word *aikido* literally means "the way of blending energy." It is a Japanese martial art based on the principle of using conflicting forces constructively. I first met aikido through a workshop led by Thomas Crum in 1990, and it was here that I was introduced to the concept of cocreativity. Tom's all-American win-or-die attitude to competitive sport had been demolished when he was floored by an aikido expert far smaller and older than he. He has written a book, *The Magic of Conflict*, on applying aikido principles in life and work.

Imagine that someone is attacking you, trying to punch you in the chest. An aikido response would be to turn through 90 degrees and step slightly to the side, so that the attacker's fist is traveling past you, not into your chest, and then to move with the energy and direction of the attack. As you move with it, you can use your energy, strength, and intention to steer the attack away from you and in a different direction, in effect, finding the third way that is crucial in any cocreative process.

It takes training and discipline to respond to conflict in this way. The principles by which aikido engenders this ability are well described in Thomas Crum's book. The main ones are summarized below.

Staying Aware

Imagine the attack scene again. To handle it successfully, you need your full powers of attention and observation on what is actually happening; your response must arise from them. If you get into worries, fears, or theories, you'll be on the floor. With practice and as you become more centered, you can discover a remarkable sense of spaciousness, of time slowing down, and the ability to see fully, even in a situation where the other person is moving quickly, with an aggressive emotional charge.

Conflict Is Not Competition

Many people, especially men, are conditioned to see conflict as a win-or-lose situation—they must either prevail or be humiliated. Phil Morris, profiled in Chapter 1, is an example of this. The more you can see conflict as an interesting, instructive opportunity, and the less you prejudge it on your fears and beliefs, the better.

Stay Centered

In aikido, as in tai chi and many Eastern disciplines, you need to be centered at all levels: physically, emotionally, mentally, and spiritually. Physically, this means keeping your awareness focused on the *hara*, your physical center of gravity, in the abdomen, below the navel. When I tried this in Tom's workshop, I discovered that this makes it hard for anyone to push you off balance. Another aspect of staying centered is the ability to embody "fluid power": to be strong yet fluid like a fire hose, not tense and brittle like a stick. This is the principle of relaxing into tension while maintaining active awareness.

Flow to Outcome

This is what Tom calls the key cocreative stage. In all the conflict resolution training I've led, letting go of attachment to the form of the outcome is a crucial learning point. It is appropriate to have a vision of a desired result but to carry it lightly; envision the qualities and the essence of an outcome, and don't hold on to them. Let go and be fully present in the flow of the process. Doing so creates the scope for the right-brain leap, the synergistic solution.

2-MINUTE *CHECKUP*

CONNECTED BREATHING

Try the following to increase relaxation and alertness and to help in composting.

1. Take four short breaths and then one long breath. The short breaths emphasize the connecting and merging of the inhale and the exhale into unbroken circles. Let the long breath fill your lungs as full as you comfortably can.

Pull the breaths in and out through your nose.

2. Do four sets of five breaths—that is, four sets of four short breaths followed by one long breath, without stopping—for a total of 20 breaths. On the inhale, consciously draw the breath in with a relaxed manner. Let go completely on the exhale, while continuing to keep the inhale and exhale the same length. Since most of us have developed bad breathing habits, you may initially experience some physical sensations, such as light-headedness or tingling sensations in your hands or elsewhere.

Merge the inhale with the exhale so that each breath is connected without any pauses. All 20 breaths are connected in this manner, so you have one series of 20 connected breaths with no pauses.

3. At all other times, breathe at a speed that feels natural for you. It is important that the breathing be free and rhythmic rather than forced or controlled.

Negative Energy Recycling

This exercise is adapted from one developed by the Hoffman Institute, with permission.

Identify

Most of us have a lot of negative energy trapped in repeating patterns of feelings, beliefs, and behavior. Begin this process by identifying a pattern you want to transform.

For example, after yet another disagreement with my boss, I realized that I have a repeating pattern of responding to conflict by withdrawal. I become cold and aloof; this freezes out any possibility of finding a constructive solution, and it leaves me feeling angry and tense inside. I realize that this pattern occurs in many of my relationships.

Relive the Pattern

Relive a recent problem situation in which you demonstrated this negative pattern. How are you behaving? Get in touch with what it's doing to you. How do you feel? Where do you feel the pattern in your body? Place your hand there.

Transform

Visualize the negative pattern of behavior as having a tangible form and shape. Imagine removing it from your body and holding it in your hands. Start to work with the negative behavior pattern as you've visualized it, physically moving your hands as if you were handling a ball of clay. While you do so, picture transforming this negative pattern into pure energy. Sometimes this transformation will happen quickly, and sometimes you may have to persist for a while to reach this point.

Keep your hands apart from each other, visualizing the negative trait between them. Increasing the speed of movement of your hands can help. Now rub your hands together rapidly, and picture this pure energy expanding into a ball of shining light energy. Let your hands move slightly apart, still feeling the power of the energy between them.

Look inside this ball and see a message written just for you. Typically it will be a message about how to redefine and recycle the negative pattern. For example, if I'm processing my withdrawal pattern, the message might be, "stay present and say how you feel."

Now hold the ball containing your message above your head, and let it descend slowly as it enters your body. Allow yourself to feel and experience the sensation being created in you by this energy. Feel this new sensation fill your body.

Experience

With this sensation inside you, go back to the original problem. This time, as you relive the situation, get in touch with what you're thinking, how you're feeling and how you're responding. Let this new feeling be the feeling that replaces the old one and relates to new, positive types of behavior.

Creative Conflict Resolution

This is a process I've developed, partly based on Edward de Bono's book *Conflicts*. It is designed so that you can learn and apply it in real time, without having to keep reading the instructions. This process is an effective way of bringing mental heat and light to emotional situations, as relevant for conflicts within you as for conflicts with others.

In most cases, conflict is made more bitter by two factors: the emotional content and our beliefs about conflict. Our sense of face, our sense of our own identity and self-worth, often feels as if it's fundamentally challenged by a conflict. This is where the intense emotions of anger, fear, and pain arise, and we can easily see ourselves in a fight for our survival because the emotional level has taken over. Often the current issue carries old emotions from past issues. It is important to understand repeating patterns. For example, if I was let down when I was younger, I'm likely to have repeated experiences of betrayal and letdown throughout my life, and they will bring up feelings of intense anger that are out of proportion to the immediate provocation. At least, they'll do so until I recognize the repeating pattern and start to choose to react otherwise.

Until we understand the pattern of carrier emotions, we risk getting sucked into escalating every conflict. We risk believing that all of our emotions are about the immediate issue. We also risk believing that all the emotion expressed by the other party in the conflict is aroused by and directed at us personally, instead of making allowances

for their carrier emotions. The other factor hampering us is our beliefs about conflict. We often see conflict as a fight, a battle to be won or lost. We believe that our personal self-worth is at stake if we "lose."

Creative conflict resolution is a three-step process to defuse a situation, develop understanding, and find constructive solutions. The three stages are cooling, clarifying, and constructing.

Cooling

There are three needs to be met during this stage.

Accept the emotions involved. In the early stages of a conflict, when the tension and heat are rising rapidly, each party typically feels that he or she is not heard by the other. This may be literally true, in that people are denying that there's a conflict and are avoiding facing it; or it may be true in the sense that each party is so preoccupied with his or her own feelings that he or she doesn't truly hear anyone else.

Without structure, this heat is often intolerable for one or both parties. Intense emotions are like boiling water or steam: dangerous, powerful, and hard to handle. The heat needs to be managed to use the tension and bring the temperature in the conflict to a level where progress is possible. Although I've called this stage *cooling*, it's a composting process, and therefore, the heat may need to rise before it falls.

There are occasions when it's best not to confront a potential conflict. However, if the relationship is important to you, then it's probably best to do so—the question is when and how? If you confront the other person too soon or in the wrong way, you risk escalating the conflict, being hurt by the reaction, or provoking them to leave the situation. The first rule about confrontation is to do it when you are feeling reasonably calm and clear. If you feel this is unlikely ever to be the case, then almost certainly you need a third party to mediate the conflict. The second principle is to confront after the cooling phase if at all possible.

What is important at this stage is for each party to recognize that the other party feels strong emotions about the issue, that he or she accepts these emotions as valid and is aware of them. Assertive methods are good coolers. Reflective comments such as "I can see that you feel very angry about this" help greatly. What neither party should do at this stage is to argue back, defend, or justify a position, start an apparently logical debate on the issue, or throw new arguments and counterarguments into the ring.

Slow down the process. Remember the points above about win-or-lose situations: One or both parties in the conflict probably feels an intense need to end it soon, either by fighting to a conclusion or by withdrawing from the situation. The steps described above should help slow down the conflict. In particular, if each party can hear the other's emotions without reacting or arguing back, this usually reduces the sense of pressure to get the conflict resolved one way or another. However, one or both parties may feel so emotional that he or she wants to bring the situation to an end, and such expression of emotions may include threats to attack the other party in some way or to get out of the situation.

Feelings such as the following would be quite typical at this stage:

- If you don't climb down and accept my demands immediately, I'll make you regret it.
- I've wasted enough time talking to you—I'm going to take this into my own hands now.
- There's no point talking to you any further. I resign.

These kind of statements typically come from a person who feels a weak bargaining position. He or she, for example, a subordinate who's talking to a boss, or a supplier whose customer has many alternatives, may truly have little power. Or he or she may simply feel less skill in expressing himself or herself and handling the feelings and may be scared to be "talked into" a resolution that won't meet their needs. Such statements may also be an attempt to bounce you, to push you into revealing your hand, to bring a difficult situation to a conclusion.

It is helpful if you believe that you don't have to respond to the ultimatum in the way it's put. What is more important is that you acknowledge the feelings behind the other person's statement, and if possible, that you ask open questions, which give the other person the chance to keep talking about how he or she feels. For example: "Look, I'm really sorry you feel like that. It would help me a lot if you could explain to me why you feel that way. Can you just bear with me for a few minutes and explain this to me, please?"

Help save face. Being heard, and having your feelings reflected back by the other person, helps both parties feel that his or her "face" is not under threat. Once the intense emotional heat begins to reduce, aim to move to a stage where both parties can affirm the importance of their relationship with each other and can talk of things they appreciate in each other. This sense of being valued as a person is a vital ingredient in enabling each party to feel that the conflict is about base issues and is not a personal attack, even though there might have been some personal put-downs earlier in the conflict.

If you can take the initiative to tell the other person how you value the relationship and what you appreciate in him or her, you're likely to find him or her starting to follow suit. It may well feel hard to take the first step, especially if you feel that the other person "started it." Try to be as specific as you can; it will help you to feel the warmth of the relationship between you. For example, recall particular times when the other person helped you out, remember early times when you were getting to know each other, and appreciate specific good points from your own experience of each other.

Clarifying

This stage can begin when both parties' emotional heat has reduced to a level where mental skills can take the lead, where they can both talk about how to proceed from here and can brief each other about the issues and the needs they have. Don't be concerned if the conflict shuttles back and forth a few times between the clarifying and cooling stages.

The clarifying stage has four aims:

- To deal with any power and safety issues that could prevent true negotiation
- To form an initial, provisional agreement on the aims, norms, and process to resolve the conflict
- To get all the needs and issues out on the table and understood by both parties
- To develop an atmosphere of trust, safety, and collaboration as a basis for the third stage

Power and safety issues. It is common for one party to feel less powerful, as described earlier. The sense of inferior power makes this party more emotionally volatile; he or she will feel less safe and less able to negotiate freely. It is up to the party with more power to take the initiative to create a sense of safety.

Ideally, part of the clarifying stage is to have each party say what he or she needs in order to feel safe. Remember that some of the power imbalances may be perceived imbalances or emotional ones. For example, one person may feel that he or she can't express himself or herself as well as the other because of a difference in formal education level. Using a third-party facilitator is one of the best ways to deal with these types of imbalance, but simply expressing the feeling helps to diffuse it, and standards can be agreed to that mitigate these problems.

Draft objectives. Seeking agreement on the outcome that both parties would like from the conflict is hopefully the start of collaboration, an opportunity for both parties to affirm the value they see in an ongoing relationship and to appreciate the benefits it could give them. Mutually agreed-upon norms will contribute to keeping the emotional heat down for the rest of the process. Here are some examples.

- We agree that we'll only discuss this face to face and with the mediator present; we will not "negotiate" by making remarks to other people or by trying to catch the other party informally in other settings.
- We agree to keep all of our discussions totally confidential throughout the process.
- If either party starts to feel emotionally threatened, he or she can call for a time-out and suspend the discussions for up to 48 hours.
- We agree that neither party will take any action that may jeopardize the future relationship.

It is also good at this stage to seek a provisional agreement on the process for resolving the conflict. This agreement could include an overall time period, when and how often to meet, who should be involved, who should be informed, whether to use a third-party mediator, and so on.

Needs and issues. This is the central part of the clarifying stage. It should be given abundant time—several sessions, if necessary. The primary aim is to know and understand all the needs and issues of both parties, not to resolve them. It is best not to insist on too much structure at this stage; the priority is to get everything on the table, including emotional needs and issues as well as cerebral ones.

As part of this stage, it can be useful to talk about how the conflict arose and why it became so emotionally heated. This enables each party to concede that he or she played a part in bringing the conflict about, while allowing them to get away from the adversarial or quasi-legal view that one party is guilty and "started it," and the other is an innocent victim. Ideally, by this stage, both parties are able to recognize the emotional "hot buttons" and the repeating patterns that were triggered by the latest events.

The term *issues* is used here simply to mean any points of conflict between the parties. Here is one way in which the issues can be sorted into categories:

Factual issues. Many conflicts arise or are aggravated because there is a misunderstanding or only a partial knowledge of the facts. For example, a bus driver doesn't report for duty after his car breaks down, but because of a history of absenteeism, management regards this as the last straw and takes disciplinary action without exploring all the facts.

Interest issues. These represent the benefits or outcomes that each party wants from the negotiation.

Power issues. These involve a power imbalance between the parties—a sense that one has an unfair degree of power or that each party's rights need to be renegotiated.

Value issues. Such issues are conflicts about whether something is right or wrong, good or bad, based on differing beliefs and values.

Face issues. Some emotionally charged issues can affect each person's sense of self-esteem.

These categories are listed in increasing order of their difficulty to resolve. Putting the issues into categories like this gives a mediator—or the parties themselves—some guidelines on the order in which to tackle them, as discussed below.

Building collaboration. The experiences of having one's needs and issues heard, explored, and understood, and working together on common tasks such as agreeing on objectives, should build trust and collaboration to offset any emotional wounds left over from earlier in the conflict. Although resolving the issues is the work of the third stage, it's wise to aim for a few easy "early goals" in this second stage. For example, you could clear up some of the factual issues and create a sense of give and take in negotiating about the norms and the process.

Constructing

The aim in this stage is for the parties to work together to construct a satisfactory solution. It can begin once all the aims of the clarifying phase have been fulfilled. It is worth having a distinct change in style or a break between sessions, since the goal in this third stage is to work creatively and collaboratively toward the final outcome of the whole process.

Anchor on the vision. If possible, harness inspirational energy, and do so explicitly, during the construction process. At the least, seek mutual agreement that both parties are working toward the highest good for the situation as a whole, and clarify what this means in specific terms. If negotiations look as if they're going to stall on a conflict between the interests of the two parties, invoke the question of what will serve the overall vision, the shared view of the outcome, as a way of gaining perspective.

Design future solutions. It is more fruitful to get both parties working as a team to create a new approach that meets future needs than to push along in linear, logical fashion, seeking a solution to each historical problem.

Focus on interest and power issues. Jointly designing solutions to meet future interest and power needs for both parties often enables a constructive and collaborative approach to success and produces a viable outcome to the overall conflict. This may mean leaving the apparently central problem—the "hot" issue that sparked the whole conflict in the first place—parked to one side. The apparent issue is often emotional, but a good process and an outcome that meets the main interest and power needs for both parties can diffuse the emotional issues altogether.

Mapping the situation. Focusing only on needs and problem issues can narrow the picture too much. Mapping the whole situation, not just the apparent problem, can help; for example, try getting each party to highlight areas of mutual agreement, disagreement, and irrelevance to the current topic. The process of mapping the whole situation can bring in other parties' views and needs in a useful way.

Role reversal. A powerful way to stimulate creative thinking is to get each party to role-play the other's position. At the extreme, and as a game, get each party to negotiate from the other's viewpoint. If people can suspend their attachments to their usual roles and original agendas, this can unblock the process.

Try-ons. This is another way to get outside the limitations of logic and find creative solutions. A try-on means suspending or varying one apparently fixed constraint in the situation. In a wage negotiation, for example, some possible try-ons might be:

- The existing job description doesn't exist.
- There are instant, infinite development resources, free of charge.

- Managers don't have to justify their actions to shareholders.

The suspension rule. As much as is possible, conduct the construction phase with a mutual agreement that all preconditions are suspended and there are no fixed blocks, taboos, or assumptions to be considered.

This description offers a process to deal with a major conflict, starting from scratch. The same basic stages, in abbreviated form, are relevant in minor conflicts. For organizations it's also worth considering the creation of a conflict procedure by training some management and other staff in conflict resolution processes and setting up a way to call for their help.

Your Own Tool Kit

Organic growers don't expect to anticipate every problem. They rely on the natural resilience of their soil and their systems—composting, cycles, diversity, and so on—to act as an immune system that can withstand a variety of pests and diseases without conscious, active intervention. In the same way, as you develop your own ground condition and organic ways of working, you should find that your ability to deal with problems and stress grows substantially. You may find that many issues resolve themselves in the flow, without the need to figure out a conscious methodology.

You are also likely to find that appropriate methods or tools shape themselves and emerge in the heat of the moment, as they did with Dirk Hoostra in the examples in Chapter 4. Many of the tools in this book developed this way, as real-time responses that came to me in the heat of a workshop session.

If you develop new tools for organic growth, you're welcome to share them on the bulletin board at the Web site for the Natural Advantage, www.thenaturaladvantage.com. If you'd like more sourcebooks for tools, please see "Resources," starting on page 211.

chapter 10

THE NATURAL SYSTEM

WORDS CANNOT FULLY CAPTURE the beauty and dynamism of a natural system, whether it's a farm, a garden, or a human being. The best I can do is explain how such a system works and the vital ways in which the seven principles of organic growth combine with and reinforce one another. This chapter offers you three views of natural systems in action: on the farm, in my personal experience, and at a successful large business. May it teach by example how to apply the Natural Advantage to your lifestyle and in your workplace.

Seeing Is Believing

You can learn a lot about how natural systems operate from reading a book or attending a workshop or lecture. But the most powerful way to understand the organic farm/garden model is to experience its workings for yourself. It was by leading programs at Magdalen Farm that I developed the ideas in this book. At the start of each program, before even mentioning the seven natural principles, I take people on a guided walk around the farm.

Let me make an admission here: Most organic farms are a tad messy, and Magdalen Farm is worse than average. This farm walk is nothing like a nature trail in a state park, with helpful signs at every turn to tell you what you are seeing. No, this farm walk is a head-on meeting with nature in the raw. After the farm walk, I ask the group to call on their powers of observation to describe how the farm works as a natural system. Here is how one group saw things.

INPUTS

Labor	Compost
Energy	The earth
Natural products	Supplies
Inspiration	Money
Passion	Knowledge and learning
Sunlight, air, and water	Time
Attention	Attention to consequences

OUTPUTS

Crops	Relationship
Work	Interconnectedness
Learning	Wildlife habitat
Community	Weeds and pests
Compost	Money
Beauty	Employment
Respect of nature	Accommodation

PROCESSES

System of cultivation
Management processes
Rotation
Goals
Rhythm
Monitoring
Observation
Digestion
Standards
Planning
Not forcing
Accepting
Steering
Responsibility

Facilitate
Creative manipulation
Acceptance of failure
Experimentation
Listening
Cooperation
Networking
Flexibility
Communication
Inventiveness
Relationship
Focus on sustainable
   foundations (soil)
Long-term approach/belief

QUALITIES

Long-term outlook
Respectful
Delayed gratification
Morality
Courage
Satisfaction with stages
   of progress
Holistic
Elegant
Getting what you want
   subtly and gently
Flowing
Integration

Natural
Creating
Cultivating naturalness
Harmonious
Nutritious
Enjoyment
Closed cycle
Celebration
Historic
Constant process of discovery
Trust
Security

If you look closely, you can see the richness of organic natural systems and the way they combine simplicity and subtlety. For the sake of commercial production, some conscious choice and human intervention is required, like the decision of what crops to plant. Still, the productive *power* of the natural system comes from millions of natural processes, most of which don't need to be actively managed or even thoroughly understood. Examples include the action of microorganisms in the soil and the subtle web of checks and balances between pests and predators. Ultimately, what you get is a far better system than you could ever create through human awareness and action alone.

Living the System

In this section, I want to share with you my own experience of living and working the natural systems way. For me, it has been a time of high output: Not only have I written written and launched this book, but I have also experienced a lot of growth and yield with other major projects. I have also faced some major challenges, including dealing with my kids leaving home for college along with the end of a 27-year marriage, and having to relocate my home and office twice. These changes have distressed me, but each time I have stayed with the tension and found the gift in the problem. I don't feel I am carrying stress or scars from these upheavals. Rather, I've maintained my good health and energy, and I owe this to the natural systems way.

Over the years, I have tried quite a number of self-development books and workshops. Many have struck me as prescriptive, exclusive, and mechanical. A common message is that if you rigidly follow these rules, these methods, and ignore everything else, you will do well. This is very different from my experience of the natural systems approach, in which my inner sense of myself as a natural organism produces an intuitive response in many situations. Even the seven natural principles that I identify in this book are just one way to describe a natural system. Someone else could describe the organic growth system through a different set of principles, which could still be valid and effective.

I have described my experience of the natural systems approach below in order to give you one specific, tangible account of how an individual can apply it. The best way for you could be very different. It depends on your circumstances, your ground condition, and your soil type or temperament. For example, Alison Martin is a clay-soil type, and her ground condition risk is of getting waterlogged—emotionally swamped and lethargic. For her, taking up squash as a hobby was a great catalyst. It got her energy moving and helped her enjoy some competition in her life. Alison had always preferred to avoid competition, and she could see that she needed to change this to grow.

Time to Grow

If you feel you don't have the time or resources to adopt some of the ideas I describe below, I suggest you question this belief before you dismiss them. Most people need more maintenance than they allow themselves in order to maximize their productive potential. You risk falling short of your highest potential if you think you don't have time to renew your resources.

What I describe below are some of the habits, rhythms, and intuitions through which I live the organic way. One of the ways I reinforce my inner sense of natural systems is by spending time out in natural environments. Each month I spend some time at the two land-based projects I have created: the organic farm and the woodland retreat center. I also take my exercise out in the country whenever possible.

The principle of cultivating ground condition needs very little thought or effort for me now. I have an intuitive, gut-level desire for it, much as a healthy plant opens to the sun and extends its roots to find nutrients. If I feel tired or troubled, I pause, and a sense comes over me that an element in my ground condition needs attention. I have also evolved personal habits and rhythms that help me maintain good ground condition.

To sustain physical energy, I have several routines that require no effort or willpower: I simply feel unhealthy and unhappy if I don't do them. These include 20 minutes of yoga and stretching every morning, aerobic exercise, cycling or walking, at least four times a week, and hot baths and massage for relaxation. Emotional maintenance is less routine because the stress is less predictable. But I often use a weekly rhythm I call Wobbly Wednesday: a couple of hours every Wednesday evening to gather and compost any emotional stress that is clogging my system.

> **Most people need more maintenance than they allow themselves in order to maximize their productive potential.**

Ground Condition

Mental maintenance is like keeping a fire burning steadily: Sometimes it needs stirring up and sometimes damping down. My intuition usually tells me when the fire needs tending. In my ground condition, maintaining good inspirational energy is a continual priority because my tendency is to tense up, to squeeze the air out, and to lose touch with the vision that motivates me. I have several ways to manage this tendency. One is to meditate for 20 minutes each morning. Another is to notice my breathing frequently throughout the day. When I notice it, I pause in what I am doing, breathe deeply, and use my breath to connect with my sense of purpose. I also have an intuitive sense of when I need to take more time for spiritual renewal. This usually occurs in nature, often at Hazel Hill Wood.

Natural Energy

My habits for natural energy inputs are not so well developed as for ground condition. The ideal is preventive maintenance: keeping energy inputs flowing at a high level so that the system is always resilient. In practice, my approach is often reactive. It's only when I notice I'm tired or distressed that I realize I need a refill.

Appreciation is a great tonic: I have learned simply to ask when I need it, from colleagues and friends. When I remember that my soil type is sandy, I stop beating myself up for feeling the need. Another important source of natural energy for me is to work in a congenial setting whenever possible. I take care about lighting, seating, and room colors. Some of my clients have also seen that an ambience that sustains all four energy elements delivers better outputs.

Composting

Composting is something I now do often and easily. My attitude toward waste is this: I step up to it as a useful source of energy and nutrients. I have evolved a wide array of composting methods ranging from the quick breathing process to inner dialogues, cocounseling with friends, and various professional therapies. These processes may take some time and energy, but I know I will quickly bounce back to a state of high productivity instead of carrying problems that could drag me down.

Organic Synergy

Looking for organic synergy has become natural and intuitive for me. Like much of the natural systems approach, this has its roots in my body. When I experience conflict or uncertainty and I notice I am starting to tense up, a new set of physical responses comes into play. I become aware of my posture and my physical response to the stress, like my breath getting shallow and my stomach feeling disturbed. As I notice these reactions, a kind of automatic response kicks in without the need for me to think about it or make it happen. I start to breathe into the tense areas and relax them. I become more aware of my physical center, what the Japanese call the *hara,* and I imagine myself like a dancer or martial artist moving with awareness amid the turmoil. The tension can still be upsetting or tiring, but I have had so many experiences of using tension creatively that I now have faith in the process.

Riding the Cycles

My use of cycles is often intuitive. One of my favorites is the renewal cycle, and I have evolved a habit I call "taking a sandwich to work." My working days often include a pile of demanding tasks, but I no longer put my head down and drive through the pile of tasks until I am exhausted. I sandwich the

tough jobs by putting in thin slices of renewal. Even 15 minutes of shooting the breeze, sitting in the sun, or calling a friend has terrific power of renewal. The four-seasons cycle is also vital to sustainability: I still have to review my work schedules periodically to ensure enough time for the fall and winter seasons.

Resilience through Diversity

The importance of diversity is something I learned the hard way: by working like a monoculture and getting ill. Most of the time now I sustain good diversity intuitively, without conscious planning. However, a six-month review using the Diversity by Design checklist on page 136 helps highlight the structural issues.

Real Quality

The same is true of real quality. What has made a big change to the level of real quality I now enjoy is that I express my need for emotional value and satisfaction to my clients. I used to believe that suppliers should be satisfied just with getting paid; I have taken a great step beyond this. Knowing how much the process adds to the end result for all of us is a great reminder to stop getting hung up on outcome alone.

As I commented in Chapter 1, the move to sustainability is not one giant leap but more a matter of progressing cyclically. I've learned a lot about human sustainability, but I haven't yet reached my goal and maybe never will. The challenge always is to produce more output, new outputs, and handle yet more change, which calls for yet more learning and creativity.

The Natural Corporation

As mentioned in Chapter 7, Southwest Airlines is a great example of a successful organization that embodies all seven principles of the Natural Advantage. Southwest's track record of success is indisputable: It includes profit, customer satisfaction, safety, and a happy workforce evidenced by turnover rates way below the industry norm. One of the fascinating features of the airline is that the employees deliver a highly predictable quality service through a naturally turbulent culture.

The corporate ground condition at Southwest has all the features of healthy organic soil. The organization has vitality, resilience, and excellent structure, meaning strength combined with openness. This owes a good deal to one of the company's challenging core values: *We don't put the customer first, we put our own people first.* It also owes a lot to their distinctive culture. I see many corporations who don't like or understand the concept of culture. At Southwest, in an organization of few committees, one of the key ones is—guess what?—the Culture Committee.

Aspects of Southwest's culture contribute to all seven principles we are exploring. Among those that support good ground condition, one key is the way the company nurtures its people and in turn the people nurture one another. Words like *community*, *love*, and *family atmosphere* may be hijacked by some companies, but here they are genuine concerns. These qualities are evident in the way Southwest service personnel step out of narrow roles to pitch in and get the job done. At busy times it is quite common to see pilots helping load baggage, and check-in staff cleaning planes. And if an employee faces big hospital bills for a sick child, they may well find colleagues raising money to help them, or a surprise check from the company.

Ground Condition

This superb ground condition doesn't just happen by chance, nor can you force it by rules and mechanistic systems. So how do they do it? The answers are many and subtle: I recommend that you read a book called *Nuts!* by Kevin and Jackie Freiberg if you want a fuller picture. Part of the answer comes from the values, personality, and behavior of the company's founders, people such as Herb Kelleher, Southwest's chairman, and Colleen Barrett. Colleen started out as Herb's personal assistant, and her current title of VP Administration hardly describes the way she embodies the spirit and culture of the business. Another answer is in the terrific care that Southwest puts into recruiting and training its people. Rita Bailey, head of Southwest's University for People, explained to me that the first week of their induction training is focused on self-development and values. This leads into the second week, which focuses on interaction: teaching the skills and modeling the desired ways of supporting colleagues and serving customers.

One aspect of Southwest that has both surprised and impressed me is that they don't use formal measurement or control systems to maintain ground condition and other organic qualities in the organization. I thought an organization with tens of thousands of employees would have to use formal systems like staff and customer-satisfaction surveys, but no. When I asked about these, they made it clear that the system does it naturally. They don't survey their staff to check morale or ground condition. As they explained it, managers are expected to listen, and anyone can write to Herb if they are unhappy. In the same way, the staff and managers' ability to listen and respond means that customer feedback flows easily into the organization. And since a lot of this is positive, it contributes to principles 2 and 3 (see page 12).

Natural Energy

Southwest's approach generates high levels of natural energy. Staff appreciate and affirm one another, and the company excels at celebrating success. Southwest is also energized by a strong sense of vision and mission, which has been sustained throughout their expansion. The culture itself is part of this vision, and they have a clear mission of serving customers better, both through the human quality of the transaction and through lower fares. The third great source of natural energy at Southwest is humor. This is a culture that really encourages people to have fun in their work and to share that sense of fun with the customers.

Composting

Although Southwest would not use the term composting, it is clear that this principle contributes to their success. They are explicit that they delegate high levels of discretion to their staff and truly accept the occasional failure. Their communication-skills training enables their people to handle conflicts and failures constructively, and they know how to use humor to break the tension.

Organic Synergy

The ability to find organic synergy seems to grow naturally from a creative, turbulent natural system like that at Southwest. The strength of the organization's ground condition and the skill training they provide mean that uncertainty and turbulence are accepted and used. A good example of this arose a few years ago, when there was a major dispute between the flight schedulers and baggage handlers. The baggage handlers reacted angrily to new schedules that they felt pushed them too hard. The response from management was to ask staff from each department to swap jobs for a week so that they truly understood the situation. The result was a classic piece of synergy: The dispute resulted in much better mutual understanding and collaboration between the two departments.

A fine example of strategic cocreativity at Southwest is the way they have used competitive pressure. From the start, Southwest faced vicious attacks from larger airlines trying to drive them out of business. Herb Kelleher's response has in effect harnessed this pressure, turning it to advantage. Early on, when Braniff Airlines temporarily undercut Southwest's low fares, the response was a superb ad cam-

The manager's ability to listen means that feedback flows easily into the organization.

paign with the headline "Nobody's going to shoot Southwest Airlines out of the sky for a lousy $13." Southwest astutely used its underdog position in this David-Goliath battle to generate terrific loyalty, to the extent that many customers chose to keep paying the regular $26 fare even though they had the option of paying $13.

Riding the Cycles

The best example of how Southwest uses cycles to sustain success is its cycles of celebration. These include monthly Winning Spirit awards for outstanding service, an annual awards banquet, and the annual Heroes of the Heart award. Heroes of the Heart honors entire departments that have made an outstanding contribution to the company. The group that receives the award has its name painted on a specially dedicated aircraft that carries Southwest Airlines Heroes of the Heart insignia. The energizing power of these awards is amplified through features in the staff magazine *LUV Lines*, in the inflight magazine *Spirit*, and through displays at corporate headquarters.

The company is also a great example of horizontal nutrient cycling: moving positive energy around the organization to where it is most needed. A striking example of this was in 1994, when Southwest faced its

biggest competitive threat: the launch of the United Shuttle. Southwest staff volunteered to work unpaid weekend shifts at the crunch cities where the airline was in direct competition with United.

Resilience through Diversity

You have already seen an impressive example of task diversity in the way the Southwest staff will step into one another's roles to help out at busy times. This doesn't just get the job done, it actually creates personal renewal for the staff and feeds the organization's ground condition. The airline also encourages personality diversity. As Rita Bailey at Southwest told me, "We tell our staff, you can be yourself here." The culture encourages wild margins, which clearly reaps benefits for the business. Individuals with eccentric talents share them to make both customer service and in-house celebrations real and distinctive.

Real Quality

The real quality of Southwest's service is evidenced by the way their own staff sustain high morale as well as by the delight of the customers. It is also clear that their quality embodies emotional value: humanity, rapport, and real consideration, as in the example quoted on page 148 in Chapter 7.

The Natural Step

One of the risks in using the natural system as our teacher is the human tendency to romanticize nature—to equate natural with easy. This section offers you a

more rigorous, science-based description of how the Earth functions as a natural system and of the many aspects of current human activity that disrupt that system.

Understanding the system sheds light on how people and organizations can function as sustainable natural systems.

The scene is Konferenzaal 2 at DuPont Nylon's factory in Oestringen, Germany. I am nervous, proud, and amazed. What am I doing, facilitating a workshop for scientists, about science? I am not just the only nonscientist in the room, I'm the only person there without a Ph.D. At least my worst fears were unfulfilled: None of them had long white beards or talked like Sigmund Freud. Despite my nerves, I stayed with my intuition and began by asking each person to say why the environment mattered to them personally. Suddenly the room was full of *people*, not scientists, talking with feeling, mostly about their horror at the environmental legacy we are leaving our children.

This was my debut workshop for The Natural Step, a new organization whose main aim is to enable businesses to move toward sustainable development. I facilitated two of their ten pilot projects in the United Kingdom: one for DuPont Nylon Europe, the other for Air BP, the aviation refueling division of BP. The Natural Step's approach provides deeper understanding of human as well as environmental sustainability, and I would like to share it with you.

Tremendous progress has been made in recent years toward environmental sustainability by improving physical energy productivity, and by developing clean energy sources. In the same way, sustainability in the workplace will depend upon transforming human energy productivity and energy sources. To explore this, I would like to go further into the basic energy workings of our planet's ecosystem and the scientific principles this embodies. These give us a blueprint for the principles of human energy sustainability.

The Science of Sustainability

In 1989 a Swedish cancer specialist, Karl-Henrik Robert, became concerned by the similarities between society's rapidly growing destruction of natural resources and the impact of cancer cells in the human body. He was appalled that the scientific community was having little effect on this crisis, commenting, "The scientists were like monkeys chattering amid the leaves, squabbling over details. We weren't looking for the root and trunk of the problem."

Side-stepping the debate about detailed environmental solutions, Karl-Henrik turned the process on its head. He simply kept asking: "Can we agree on the basic scientific conditions for sustainability?" He began holding what he calls consensus debates, the first of which involved many of the leading scientists in Sweden and took 24 drafts and two years. They eventually agreed on four science principles and four system conditions for sustainability. These make up the basis of what is called The Natural Step, a set of principles and processes to identify what sustainability really means and how to move toward it. Although The Natural Step is focused on environmental sustainability, it has helped greatly with my understanding of sustainability in other fields.

The Natural Step has been widely used in business, education, and local government in Sweden and is now being applied in Great Britain, the United States, and several other countries. Through its use, many companies have achieved both business and environmental benefits. For example, McDonald's in Sweden moved itself from one of the worst-rated to one of the best-rated companies in Sweden for environmental performance. This improvement both saved costs and added revenue, through initiatives such as more sustainable building design, heating systems, transport, and packaging. It also introduced organically produced food, as well as educational videos explaining its new approach.

Two of the main concepts in The Natural Step are the natural cycle and the four science-based principles.

The Natural Cycle

The natural cycle provides us with a basic blueprint for sustainability. It is essential for human life on Earth and provides us with our food, air, waste disposal, and much more besides.

For nearly the first two billion years, the atmosphere on this planet was a soup of toxic gases, unsuitable for life of any kind. The crucial stage in the development of life was the evolution of green plant cells, with their capacity for photosynthesis. Plants played a central role in the slow cleaning up of the Earth's atmosphere and surface material. Over the next two billion years, increasingly complex forms of plant and animal life evolved, and eventually, so did human life.

To grow, green cells in plants use energy from the sun, combined with water, carbon dioxide from the air, and minerals from the earth. Oxygen is produced as a by-product of this process, so plants provide two of the most essential requirements for animal and human life: oxygen and food. Plant waste returns to the soil and becomes an input to future growth.

People and animals consume oxygen as they breathe. They exhale carbon dioxide, which is recycled by plants. Human and animal waste returns to the earth and provides a further source of fertility for plant growth. Intriguingly, if we drop the concept of waste from this cycle, we can see just how balanced and productive it is—every by-product and residue serves a useful purpose. The output from plants provides the input to humans and animals, and their outputs in turn provide essential inputs to plants.

Threats to the Cycle

At a basic level there are three main threats to this cycle. All of these have to do with waste and composting. Two are problems of the volume and type of waste being generated; the third concerns the diminishing capacity to process waste.

Carbon dioxide. Global emissions of carbon dioxide more than doubled from 1965 to 1990. This emissions level is well above the recycling capacity of the planet, so we have a buildup of carbon dioxide in the atmosphere. The problems this creates include the greenhouse effect—carbon dioxide in the atmosphere prevents some of the sun's heat from dispersing away from the Earth. In many cities it's also causing a reduction in the level of oxygen in the atmosphere, and hence, poorer air quality and an increase in respiratory diseases.

Man-made chemicals. A large number of chemicals and compounds foreign to nature are emitted into the air and water. Even in small quantities, many can have serious effects on the natural cycle. Many synthetic chemicals break down slowly, or not at all. They disrupt nature's recycling capacity and threaten the health of humans and all other life on the planet. For example, a chemical analysis of breast milk from healthy mothers in the United States showed traces of numerous synthetic chemicals that are toxic and would never be allowed in food manufacture.

Natural recycling. Both the amount of land that's covered by forests and plants and the diversity of species are decreasing sharply. This cuts the amount of human and animal waste that can be recycled and lowers the natural cycle's resilience to climate changes and new forms of waste.

4 Science Principles

The four principles in The Natural Step's basic science are summarized below. The Natural Step was developed around the goal of environmental sustainability, and the applications of its principles to human sustainability are explored in the following section.

Matter and energy cannot be created or destroyed. This is a principle that few scientists would dispute; yet it's quite different from the common belief that we spend or use energy, as if it disappears. In fact, energy never disappears, and we don't use it up; we consume it in one form, and it continues in another.

For example, gasoline is an exceptionally concentrated, useful form of energy. When we burn it to power a car, all the energy continues, but mostly in forms that are no longer useful, such as heat emitted to the atmosphere. From this point of view, we can see that so-called waste is energy and matter in forms that we can't use. It also underlines the fact that waste will never actually disappear—it can only disperse or transform.

Matter and energy tend to disperse spontaneously. This is the second law of thermodynamics, which explains the ways in which many of our waste and pollution problems arise. If the residual energy from using gasoline in a car or fertilizer on a field remained in concentrated form, it could easily be identified and reused.

This principle highlights two essential features for a sustainable energy system:

- The need for an ongoing energy refill to the system, compensating for dispersal losses: We depend on the sun for this.
- The need for a process to harness this refill, which is provided by green cells, discussed below.

Quality can be expressed as the concentration and structure of matter. Both quality and value are created by using energy to bring some kind of matter to a higher level of concentration, purity, and structure. To visualize this, compare the value of polluted and purified water, crude oil and refined petroleum, earth and vegetables, raw financial data and audited accounts. This principle offers a different way of looking at waste, as matter or energy whose concentration and structure are low in quality and value.

Green cells are essentially the only net producers of concentration and structure. The green cell and its process of photosynthesis are our means of harnessing the input from the sun. Photosynthesis is essential for all human and animal life. It produces concentration and structure in both plant matter and air. This plant growth is our basic power source; it provides the energy in our food, either directly, as fruits and vegetables, or indirectly, as animal feed. Green cells also provide most of our other energy, as fossil fuel. Plant growth also provides such life-sustaining natural services as clean air and water.

Principles of Human Sustainability

Although the four science principles describe the physical environment, they can also be applied to people. The human being is a living organism, a natural system, so it seems reasonable that our energy and sustainability will follow the same principles as the natural systems of which we are a part and on which we depend. Let's explore what the principles of the Natural Step can teach us about human sustainability.

Matter and energy cannot be created or destroyed. Does human energy come from nowhere, get used, and then disappear? It seems unlikely. Whether we consider physical, emotional, mental, or inspirational energy, it's part of a cycle. Human energy has a source: We use it,

change its form, and create an output, and all the energy continues in some way.

Suppose my boss gets angry with me because I forgot to give a customer some information I had promised. My reaction is resentment. She didn't ask why I forgot, and I was overloaded with priorities. She treated me like a machine, not a person. Still angry, I phone the customer and brusquely give them the information. The task has been done, but the atmosphere between the three of us is polluted; the negative energy has not disappeared.

This principle illuminates the concept of natural energy for the human system. It tells us that unless we use clean sources and processes, waste will accumulate.

Matter and energy tend to disperse spontaneously. The first lesson from this principle is that human energy does not sit passively in reserve, like water in a tap. Our reserves will dissipate over time. To have energy available when we need it, we have to maintain our energy flows. We need means of reconcentrating energy as well as clean sources of refill energy. Composting can play an important role in this.

This principle also warns us that our energy residues will spread. In other words, unless it is collected and composted, human energy waste will disperse and accumulate in your body and energy system, just as environmental waste becomes pollution in earth, water, and air.

Quality can be expressed as the concentration and structure of matter. This is a powerful and different way of considering people and their work. Quality can be seen as a measure of people's well-being and productive potential, not just of their productive output. A human being is an organism whose innate quality is extraordinarily high; we represent a remarkably sophisticated concentration and structure of matter. By contrast, the quality of an intensive farm is poor; its methods progressively degrade the purity and structure of the soil and the crops. Conventional ways of working create similar quality problems.

This principle offers us a more constructive, less emotive way of viewing our waste at work. We can see it as an abundant raw material whose quality we can improve by natural means, and not as an unsightly obstacle. If you can consider yourself as a natural system and follow the principles of organic growth, you will move toward real quality in your work processes and output.

Green cells are essentially the only net producer of concentration and structure. What is the counterpart of the green cell for human energy? Drawing the analogy is tricky, since human energy is both physical and metaphysical. An emotion or an idea involves physical energy and reactions but is more than that.

I see the whole organism—the person, team, or organization—as the equivalent of the green cell. The organism as a whole, if it operates by natural principles, can combine the four elements of human energy: physical, emotional, mental, and inspirational. Through this combination we can reconcentrate dispersed—and even polluted—energy and harness the external energy inputs we need.

So what is the human equivalent of sunlight, the external energy that augments our natural system? You may ask yourself, what is the sunshine in *your* life? Where do you get a sense of natural vitality as an input? For me this comes from several sources: from my sense of purpose and service, from the love of family and friends, from job satisfaction, and from nature. The more you live out the principles of natural growth, the more clearly you'll see if your energy sources are clean and sustaining or not.

Adopting the Natural System

This chapter has given you several different views of what the natural systems way means for individuals and organizations, plus a deeper view of the system principles. We have a global financial system that currently pressures most corporations toward a mechanistic, depleting way of working. There is a growing minority of businesses that buck this trend: Southwest Airlines and Interface are two examples. But, you may ask, can I reproduce the organic qualities of Southwest Airlines in my organization? My answer is yes, but there are some enabling factors to highlight.

The fact that Southwest's leaders deeply believe and fully live the values of the airline is crucial. So, too, is the way that money aligns with values. I doubt if Southwest Airlines would be so successful, or if values like family and community would ring true, without a payment system that is congruent. All Southwest employees are in a profit-sharing plan, and a generous 15 percent of profits before tax goes to fund this; 25 percent of an employee's profit share goes into stock purchase.

The result is a terrific convergence between individual and corporate goals over a long time period. Both the annual profit share and the value of shareholdings are very substantial for Southwest Airlines staff. When you read the history of the airline, it is clear that the company really has grown like a natural system: unpre-

dictably, organically, and with setbacks leading to positive surprises. Southwest managers have achieved their success without consciously using the natural systems model in this book. However, if you want to emulate their success and their culture, the principles and processes of the Natural Advantage give you a great way to do so.

Learning the natural systems way is like learning a new dance, but it's the dance of life itself. Learning this dance amid the pressures of our time demands vision and courage, but as you connect more deeply with natural principles in your own human nature, in your team, and in our beautiful planet, you can do it without thinking—it just comes naturally.

Alan Heeks in the courtyard at Magdalen Farm, which was built by Lord Portman in 1890 and transformed into a residential teaching center in the early 1990s.

Participants in one of Alan's Natural Advantage training workshops at Magdalen Farm experience the vitality of organic soil firsthand.

Alan and members of a Natural Advantage workshop make friends with one of the farm's resident pigs. The pig herd improves fertility organically by churning up packed soil so that air, warmth, and water can penetrate deeply.

A small group meets in the communal area inside Magdalen Farm Center. This room was converted from the cow milking parlor into a modern work space.

Farm walks are central to the fieldwork conducted at a Natural Advantage workshop. Businesspeople use all their senses to experience the synergy operating in a sustainable natural system.

The down-and-dirty nature of so many organic processes, such as composting negative energy and draining emotional swamps, is illustrated by these muddy boots. Also on display here is a tolerance for creative disorder and diversity, which is vital to the organic success of any organization.

Participants in a Natural Advantage workshop check out Real Quality for themselves. As one said, "The look and feel of these tomatoes . . . you can tell the difference."

One of the organic growth principles people learn about at Magdalen Farm Center is the importance of natural cycles such as the four seasons. Spring is a crucial time of seeding, feeding, and weeding; these seedlings need close attention and the proper balance of nutrients to establish strong roots for the next stage of growth.

EPILOGUE: A HEALING CRISIS

MAJOR CHANGE OFTEN COMES ABOUT BECAUSE OF A CRISIS. You can find many individual examples in this book, including Salim Hussain, Alison Martin, and Dirk Hoostra. My experience with organic growth has led me to the concept of the healing crisis: intensifying a problem in order to resolve it. The principle of a healing crisis is that the solution grows from the problem, the gold is in the muck—in other words, the issue needs to get worse before it gets better.

This is not to suggest that all organic change happens by crisis. But I do want to challenge the common notion that "naturally" means easily. The natural world is full of conflict and upheaval, as well as grace and harmony. And part of the organic way is learning to cultivate and use conflict and crisis.

One example of a healing crisis comes from the conversion period on a new organic farm: the transition from conventional methods to sustainability. A good example of a large-scale healing crisis has been the consumer revolt against genetically modified foods and the way this has reversed the views of big business and governments. If you look at the growth of awareness and controls on environmental sustainability, you see another clear example of the healing crisis principle. Appalling disasters such as Bhopal, Love Canal, and the Valdez have yielded a gift from the problem: major initiatives that have moved us forward.

I have built on such examples to offer a personal view of how three worldwide crises of sustainability will intensify and resolve. This future vision offers pointers on how you can contribute to resolving these crises on the large scale, as well as in your own work and in your organization.

The Three Crises of Sustainability

We have a global crisis of sustainability. The first field where this has become evident and acute is in the environment, but I expect this to be followed by crises of human and business sustainability. These are really three phases of addressing the one basic issue: our depleting and polluting ways of using natural resources. The same principles can resolve all three.

Accepting the need to move toward sustainability to deal with the environmental crunch will sow the seeds for the crisis of human sustainability: establishing how to work in ways that are at the same time renewing, fulfilling, and productive. As individuals make this change and demand that organizations support them, we are likely to see a much wider crisis of business sustainability. We will confront the basic questions of whether business serves the general good or just its shareholders, and whether its fruits should only be weighed in current profits. The questions of real quality, intangible benefits, and longer-term contribution will all come to the fore.

I have led many future-visioning processes for businesses and individuals. One of the most powerful tools in such work is to picture the future and then envision how to get there. So open your imagination and travel forward in time with me to the year A.D. 2020. I'd like to offer you my personal vision of how these three crises will develop and heal.

2020 Vision

Under the hype about the millennium, many people in 2000 were deeply worried about the way the world was going—and with good reason. Problems such as climate, health, and the quality of our air and water have become far worse since then. Yet now in 2020, most people feel hopeful about the state of the world and its future. What has changed is that the principles of sustainability are being widely applied and the benefits are emerging. Pollution problems often take decades to build to crisis levels, and the solutions also take decades to work through. Many indicators of environmental quality are at worse levels than in 2000, and some are still rising, but we know that steps have been taken that will improve them.

People have been talking about the world environmental crisis since the 1980s, and much had been done even before the millennium. However, in the year 2000 no one could claim that our overall ways of living and working were anywhere near environmentally sustainable. Many of the crucial technologies and policy tools existed in 2000, but the will to act on them was not present. Most businesses, governments, and public opinion were still shrinking from the scale of change required.

The climate crisis in developed countries tipped the balance: Disasters from drought, floods, and hurricanes increased sharply from the late 1990s on. It was also clear that widespread problems were emerging for human, animal, and plant health as a result of environmental pollution. Intense public concern moved rapidly from being a minority to a majority sentiment. This change was catalyzed by several influences: the press, lobbying groups such as Friends of the Earth and the World Wide Fund for Nature, and a few major businesses that stuck their necks out and proved that a solution was possible. Eventually, public concern reached such a pitch that political leaders were obliged to act.

Genetically Modified Food

The crisis over genetically modified foods around the turn of the century proved to be a blueprint for the wider crisis that followed. Back in 1998 a handful of retailers and food producers had been the trailblazers. The crucial move came from companies like Ben & Jerry's, the Vermont-based ice cream company that refused to use milk from cows that had been given biotech hormones to increase their milk production. Ben & Jerry's ice creams were so popular that their position had credibility. You could say the company represented the wild margin within the mainstream of the food industry. This was at a time when the major food manufacturers and retailers were all chorusing Monsanto's line that genetically modified foods were unavoidable, that they were mixed up in everything already, so we had no option but to accept them.

But the explosive sales of natural, organically produced food was a clear enough signal to the rest of the food industry. Consumers were changing their buying behavior, not just their opinions. The following months saw an avalanche of change, as the foremost manufacturers like Unilever, plus leading supermarkets, dropped genetically modified products. Once big business had altered the stance, government policy followed.

The Energy Revolution

When the environmental crisis reached its peak, two main changes were central to resolving it. Each depended on the governments of the leading economies worldwide introducing them together. The first of these was an ecotax system: The burden of taxation was shifted from labor to resource use. Governments agreed to impose steep tax rises on all uses of fossil fuels and on all raw materials that were nonrenewable and polluting. Manufacturers were also taxed on the disposal costs of their products. The shift to ecotaxes was phased in over 10 years, but they had a significant effect from the start. This had been forecast by Paul Hawken back in 1993 in his book *The Ecology of Commerce*.

The second crucial move was the introduction of a credible international standard for sustainability: GEN, the Global Eco Norm. This grew from pioneering work in several countries and industries, for example the German ecostandard, Der Grune Punkt, and the British Forestry Stewardship Certification scheme. GEN integrated the views of producers and consumers and provided clarity amid a welter of sham ecoclaims.

These two moves engendered the shift toward worldwide environmental sustainability. The form this took was essentially a revolution in energy and resource productivity. This, too, had been forecast in the 1990s, in books such as *Factor Four* by von Weizsacker and Lovins and *Natural Capitalism* by Hawken and Lovins. The technologies to quadruple the wealth created per unit of natural resource were available by the millennium, but before ecotaxes, business lacked the motive to commercialize them.

One significant example of this was motor vehicles. By 2010 most cars sold in the developed world were hybrid electrics that were powered by electric motors, charged by an onboard generator and battery. Major car manufacturers had been developing hybrid electric designs before the millennium, and by 2005 they were stampeding to climb on the bandwagon and launch them into mass production. By 2010 most had gone further and introduced hypercars, which combined hybrid electric drive with ultra-light materials and low-resistance tires, offering gas mileage of 200 miles to the gallon. Some models had already eliminated fossil fuels by using hydrogen fuel cells, and in 2020 these have become widespread.

The Demand for Organic

By the late 1990s the organic sector was growing fast in many countries but still represented a small percentage of the market. After the millennium, this growth increased dramatically. The catalyst was the big business establishment. The early sales successes with organic foods came from the smaller players. By 2000 the big supermarkets had noticed this and were vying with one another to expand their organic ranges. Belatedly, the multinational branded food producers joined the party. One result was the "ecofudge" scandal. Some of the larger and more cynical food giants combined to create what they called a "Natural Way" standard, with extravagant claims of ecofriendliness. Press exposés showed that this standard was merely a flimsy cover for intensive methods.

Consumer demand for certified organic produce kept rising. As branded products like Kellogg's organic cornflakes and Heinz organic beans appeared, the pressure from food manufacturers to increase the supply of organic produce became desperate. This led to the supernatural movement in farming and elsewhere. Supernatural methods sought dramatic productivity rises by augmenting natural systems, not overriding them. The research teams of big food manufacturers allied with mainstream seed and farm equipment producers to work with organic farmers. As a result, plant and livestock breeds and cultivation methods evolved that gave high productivity to organic systems.

When ecotaxes steeply raised the costs of conventional farming, the profit advantage of organics became overwhelming. By 2010 a majority of farmers in developed countries had gone organic. Many others used the ecofudge standards that still lurked at the bottom of the market.

> **When ecotaxes steeply raised the costs of conventional farming, the profit advantage of organics became overwhelming.**

Human Sustainability

By the late 1990s, writers like Peter Senge and Arie de Geus were proposing ecology and biology as better models for the workplace than mechanics. Early in the new century, the environmental crisis took center stage; as a result, the principles and language of sustainability spread into most areas of life and work. The term *natworking* emerged to describe ways of working that aligned with human nature and were renewing and humanly sustainable.

As with previous healing crises, the issue moved from a murmur at the margins to become a mainstream debate. Several factors acted as catalysts. One was a growing number of liability lawsuits awarding hefty damages against employers for stressful and depleting work methods. Another was the pioneering companies that developed natworking approaches and proved that they had profit benefits.

Another factor fueling the debate was the emergence of an informal international coalition called Friends of the Humans, which brought a range of interest groups together to lobby for a shift to natworking principles. These included networks of progressive companies, such as Business for Social Responsibility in the United States and Tomorrow's Company in Great Britain. It also drew in nonprofit bodies engaged with sustainable development, such as The Natural Step, the Rocky Mountain Institute, and Jonathon Porritt's Forum for the Future. Recognizing the impact of this issue on quality of life generally, consumer and special interest groups came in, such as Families Need Fathers. Some trade unions also joined, recognizing that adversarial campaigns for shorter hours were beside the point: The real issue was finding natural means to higher productivity.

Once more, another catalyst for change was consumers' buying behavior. To their consternation, companies found their sales affected by press exposés of their unsustainable work practices. An early example of this had been British Airways. Its harsh treatment of staff during 1997 had led to a widely publicized strike, which dented its reputation as a well-managed company. This loss of standing, coupled with poor staff morale, contributed to painful drops in market share and profits in following years.

As with the environmental crisis, the crucial change was in productivity: this time in the output value per unit of human energy and resources. Once the corporations and consultancies grasped the principles of human sustainability, there was a ferment of innovation. Natworking became the next culture fashion, and a wide range of super-natural processes and packages emerged. Fortunately most were sound. Companies' annual reports started to feature statements on human as well as environmental sustainability, and the demand for benchmarking and objective standards grew.

Expertise in standards for organic growing and the environment was now applied to the workplace. Although it was harder to create a quality standard for human sustainability at work, this had emerged by 2010. The Green Heart symbol took its place alongside the Green Circle for environmental sustainability, both supervised by GEN. While the networking approach was taken up by many organizations of all sizes, others spurned it. A sizable number of business leaders regarded the Green Heart standard as intrusive, a distraction from their basic economic purpose.

Toward the Green Dollar

Around the millennium, the stance of most big businesses on sustainability could be called clearly ambiguous. They knew that others saw it as important, so they made cosmetic moves to address it. Meanwhile, their overwhelming concern was still short-term profit. And who could blame them? This was a time when institutional investors were using their clout and firing chief executives who failed to deliver the numbers.

Views that had been on the fringe in the 1990s now reached the mainstream.

By 2010 the picture had changed. The big-business establishment was by now evenly divided between the bottom-liners and the cultivators. Many still believed that the business of business was business: bottom-line profits. All this human sustainability talk was soft stuff—it was up to employees, not the company, to look after these issues. On the other hand, many firms were by now achieving high profits through organic principles, cultivating their people and their markets, not strip-mining them.

The wider debate about the sustainability of business started in 2010, growing out of the crisis over human sustainability at work. Views that had been on the fringe in the 1990s now reached the mainstream. Wasn't business really serving its own narrow aims and forcing consumers and governments to dance to its tune? How could the capitalist system balance the profit motive with quality of life? And if sustainable principles could apply to companies' relations with the environment and their people, surely they could apply to relations with suppliers, customers, and the wider community?

The debate was fueled by the fact that many companies, large and small, were already making good money from the sustainable approach. The bottom-liners came under fierce scrutiny. Their basic response was: We're only doing what our shareholders demand. Suddenly the focus swung round to financial institutions, and this was where the crisis erupted.

The year 2012 saw competitive turmoil in the product offerings of the pension, investment, and life assurance funds. The subject of ethical, sustainable investment took center stage. Since the 1980s there had been rapid growth in ethical funds, which screened their holdings on such criteria as no animal testing, no involvement in weapons production, and so on. By the late 1990s there was already evidence that ethical businesses were achieving better profits than many others. In 2012 this grew into the concept of the natfund: one investing only in businesses that embodied all aspects of sustainability. Most financial institutions raced to join the trend.

Before long, many bottom-line businesses were ready to change to the new agenda but were still bewildered as to what it all meant. The Green Dollar code was developed by a coalition of business and consumer groups to answer this need. While there are still many businesses around the world fudging on standards and operating unsustainably, most of us in 2020 believe that our basic optimism is solidly grounded. We have independent proof that most firms work sustainably in most respects, and as customers, we can experience this for ourselves.

Back to You

It is often said that all you can be confident of changing is yourself. I strongly believe that change in organizations or society grows from change in individuals. Any steps you take toward adopting the principles of this book will help the wider move toward sustainability. Every such step adds a critical mass that will move us faster toward the resolution of the healing crises that are already here.

We have to face these wider crises, just as we all face extraordinary and increasing levels of personal change. I hope this book gives you the natural advantage to meet those pressures with fulfillment and fruitfulness.

RESOURCES

For information about open workshops on the Natural Advantage with Alan Heeks and colleagues and about corporate programs tailored to your organization, contact Alexandra Ross at (303) 477-4490 (e-mail:camross@earthnet.net) or contact:

Working Vision
P.O. Box 13
Stockbridge SO20 6WR, U.K.
Phone: 44-1794-388707
E-mail: mail@workingvision.com
Web site: www.workingvision.com

The Work Easy Workbook, by Alan Heeks, is available through mail order from Working Vision (see above).

For information about the Wessex Foundation and Magdalen Farm programs and facilities, write to:

Magdalen Farm
Winsham, Chard, Somerset TA20 4PA
U.K.
Phone: 44-1460-30144
E-mail: wessex@magdalencentre.co.uk
Web site: www.magdalencentre.co.uk

Alibi Publishing and several other cases described in this book involved the extensive use of coaching. To find a professional coach in your area, contact the international organization of professional coaches, Coach U, visit their Web site: www.CoachU.com.

For information about the Natural Step, visit www.thenaturalstep.com

If you need professional help composting major problems, I recommend the Hoffman Institute, which operates in the United States, Great Britain, and elsewhere. For details, see their Web site: www.quadrinity.com

Business for Social Responsibility
609 Mission Street, 2nd floor
San Francisco, CA 94105-3106
Phone: (415) 537 0888
E-mail: memberservices@bsr.org
Web site: www.bsr.org

Centre for Tomorrow's Company: www.tomorrowscompany.com

Forum for the Future: www.forum-forthefuture.org.uk

Books

Assertiveness: A Working Guide, by Paddy O'Brien. London: Nicholas Brealey Publishing, 1990.

A good, short introduction to one of the most fundamental ingredients in managing energy and working cocreatively; geared toward applying assertiveness in the work environment.

The Change Masters: Innovation and Entrepreneurism in the American Corporation, by Rosabeth Moss Kanter. New York: Simon & Schuster, 1985.

This book differs from the others listed here because it doesn't include specific tools. I have included it since it is one of my favorite books on the subject of managing change in organizations. If you start developing organic methods within your own work, this book is especially relevant to the issues of how to foster acceptance of this kind of approach in an organization.

Don't Say Yes When You Want to Say No, by Herbert Fensterheim and Jean Baer. New York: Dell, 1975.

A self-development guide to assertiveness, looking at its application in all areas of your life, not just in your work.

The Fifth Discipline Fieldbook, by Peter M. Senge, Art Kleiner, Charlotte Roberts, Rick Ross, and Bryan Smith. New York: Currency/Doubleday, 1994.

An excellent sourcebook for case studies, as well as methodologies, including such topics as systems thinking and team learning.

Gaia: An Atlas of Planet Management, edited by Norman Myers and Nancy J. Myers. New York: Anchor, 1993.

Plenty of good information on biodiversity.

The Learning Company: A Strategy for Sustainable Development, by Mike Pedler, John Burgoyne, and Tom Boydell. New York: McGraw-Hill, 1994.

This guide was developed by three of the pioneers of the learning organization concept. It offers specific methods for developing many of the abilities that *The Natural Advantage* advocates, such as emotional resilience, sensitivity to events, creativity, and analytical problem solving.

Managing People in Changing Times: Coping with the Human Impact of Organizational Change, by Robert Burns. Concord, MA: Paul and Company, 1993.

Burns is an Australian psychologist. This book developed from his experiences leading workshops for professional groups in business and the public sector. Burns includes a good range of self-assessment exercises and practical tools, covering both personal and interpersonal strategies for managing change, including transactional analysis.

The New Drawing on the Right Side of the Brain, by Betty Edwards. New York: Jeremy P. Tarcher/Putnam, 1999.

Provides an accessible overview and the practical applications of some of Roger Sperry's ideas.

The Personal Management Handbook, by John Mulligan. New York: Warner, 1988.

A well-presented overview of a range of methods for managing both yourself and your relationships with others. These include tools for developing your thinking, feelings, and intuition; managing stress; and improving communication and group dynamics.

Further Reading

In addition to my direct experience and personal contacts, I've drawn on two of the standard British textbooks on organic farming. The one I recommend to nonfarmers is Francis Blake's *Organic Farming and Growing* (Wiltshire, U.K.: Crowood Press, 1987), which is relatively accessible to the lay reader. Nicholas Lampkin's *Organic Farming* (Ipswich, U.K.: Farming Press, 1990) is more technically detailed and cites a wide range of research and reference sources.

Collins, James C., and Jerry I. Porras. *Built to Last: Successful Habits of Visionary Companies.* New York: Harperbusiness, 1995.

Covey, Stephen R. *The 7 Habits of Highly Effective People.* New York: Simon and Schuster, 1992.

Crum, Thomas F. *The Magic of Conflict: Turning a Life of Work into a Work of Art.* New York: Touchstone, 1987.

Davis, Stan, and Christopher Meyer. *Blur: The Speed of Change in the Connected Economy.* New York: Warner, 1999.

De Bono, Edward. *Conflicts: A Better Way to Resolve Them.* NewYork: Penguin Books, 1986.

De Geus, Arie. *The Living Company: Habits for Survival in a Turbulent Business Environment.* Boston: Harvard Business School, 1997.

Freiberg, Kevin, and Jackie Freiberg. *Nuts!: Southwest Airlines' Crazy Recipe for Business and Personal Success.* Marietta, GA: Bard Press, 1996.

Gallwey, W. Timothy. *The Inner Game of Tennis.* New York: Random House, 1997.

Gawain, Shakti. *Creative Visualisation: Use the Power of Your Imagination to Get What You Want in Life*. San Rafael, CA: New World Library, 1995.

Goleman, Daniel. *Emotional Intelligence: Why It Can Matter More Than IQ*. New York: Bantam, 1997.

Handy, Charles. *The Age of Unreason*. Boston: Harvard Business School, 1989.

Hawken, Paul. *The Ecology of Commerce: A Declaration of Sustainability*. New York: Harperbusiness, 1994.

Hawken, Paul, Amory Lovins, and L. Hunter Lovins. *Natural Capitalism: Creating the Next Industrial Revolution*. Boston: Little, Brown, 1999.

Hay, Louise L. *You Can Heal Your Life*. Carlsbad, CA: Hay House, 1988.

Kanter, Rosabeth Moss. *The Change Masters: Innovation and Entrepreneurism in the American Corporation*. New York: Simon and Schuster, 1985.

Nattrass, Brian F., and Mary Altomare. *The Natural Step for Business: Wealth, Ecology, and the Evolutionary Corporation*. Gabriola Island, B.C.: New Society Publishers, 1999.

Pascale, Richard, and Anthony Athos. *The Art of Japanese Management*. New York: Simon and Schuster, 1981.

Rosenbluth, Hal F. *The Customer Comes Second*. New York: Quill, 1992.

Senge, Peter M. *The Fifth Discipline: The Art and Practice of the Learning Organization*. New York: Currency/Doubleday, 1994.

Senge, Peter, Art Kleiner, Charlotte Roberts, Richard Ross, George Roth, and Bryan Smith. *The Dance of Change: The Challenges to Sustaining Momentum in Learning Organizations*. New York: Doubleday, 1999.

Stacey, Ralph. *Managing the Unknowable: Strategic Boundaries Between Order and Chaos in Organizations*. San Francisco: Jossey-Bass, 1992.

Von Weizsacker, Ernst, Amory Lovins, and L. Hunter. *Factor Four: Doubling Wealth, Halving Resource Use*. London: Earthscan, 1997.

INDEX

Note: Page numbers in *italic* refer to illustrations or photographs. Those in **boldface** refer to tables.